The
Remittance
Landscape

SPACES OF
MIGRATION
IN RURAL
MEXICO AND
URBAN USA

The
Remittance
Landscape

Sarah Lynn Lopez

UNIVERSITY OF CHICAGO PRESS
Chicago and London

Sarah Lynn Lopez is assistant professor in the School
of Architecture at the University of Texas at Austin.

The University of Chicago Press, Chicago 60637
The University of Chicago Press, Ltd., London
© 2015 by The University of Chicago
All rights reserved. Published 2015.
Printed in the United States of America

24 23 22 21 20 19 18 17 16 15   1 2 3 4 5

ISBN-13: 978-0-226-10513-0 (cloth)
ISBN-13: 978-0-226-20281-5 (paper)
ISBN-13: 978-0-226-20295-2 (e-book)

DOI: 10.7208/chicago/9780226202952.001.0001

Library of Congress Cataloging-in-Publication Data
Lopez, Sarah Lynn, author.
The remittance landscape : spaces of migration in rural
Mexico and urban USA / Sarah Lynn Lopez. — 1 Edition.
pages cm
Includes bibliographical references and index.
ISBN 978-0-226-10513-0 (cloth : alk. paper) —
ISBN 978-0-226-20281-5 (pbk. : alk. paper) —
ISBN 978-0-226-20295-2 (e-book)   1. Emigrant remittances—
Mexico. 2. Mexicans—United States. 3. Mexico—Emigration
and immigration. I. Title
HG3916.L674 2014
332′.042460972—dc23

                                                    2014020844

FOR CHESNEY

Contents

Prologue

This book began in a small café kitchen in Berkeley, California, where I worked as a cook with three migrants from a village near Leon, the capital city of Guanajuato, Mexico. Over time, I learned about their aspirations to build new homes—not in Berkeley but in their hometowns. My coworkers earned meager salaries, lived in cramped apartments in Oakland, and had been in California for over a decade. Why, then, were they investing in new homes in rural Mexico? As a historian of the built environment, I was curious about the homes themselves. What did they look like? Who built them? How did my coworkers (undocumented Mexican migrants who did not travel home) manage the construction process from a distance?[1]

Upon further reflection, this book began long before I ever spoke with my coworkers about their uninhabited dream houses. I am the product of the aspirations, ambitions, and discomfort that come from such spaces of migration. My mother is a Cuban Jew, born and raised in Havana, whose parents had fled Poland and Romania in the early 1930s. My father's family made their pilgrimage in the 1950s from a Chihuahuan mining pueblo in Mexico to strawberry fields in south Texas and ultimately to the mining and refinery town of Trona in the Mojave Desert. I grew up reflecting on how processes of migration, with the necessary adjustment to radically new and different contexts, shape one's experience of everyday life. This project builds on such reflections, investigating what the spaces of migration mean for migrants themselves.

To research the architecture of migration, I interviewed migrants who conceived of, funded, and managed remittance construction. This initially took me, in 2004, to the north-central mountain state of Guanajuato, where I spent a summer with my coworkers from Berkeley, collecting life histories and drawing plans of their houses. Years later, I began research on the central bajío state of Jalisco—the subject of this book. I chose Jalisco for two reasons: One, it is a state that Paul S. Taylor and Manuel Gamio researched in the 1920s and 1930s, during which time they recorded a few important examples of how the built environment of Jalisco was transformed by migration at that time. And two, due to the long history of emigration from Jalisco to California and elsewhere in the United States, Jaliscienses have been sending remittances to finance homes for almost a century, and they are well organized in migrant hometown associations (HTAS) that finance public projects. Starting in California, I contacted HTA members associated with the Federation of Jaliscienses, who invited me to their pueblos to see what they had accomplished, acting as town boosters. The president of the Federation of Jaliscienses in 2007, Salvador García, identified eight towns for me to visit that had particularly impressive remittance projects. During my first two months in Jalisco, I visited twenty-three pueblos, of which only two appeared to be unaffected by remittance-financed building projects. Out of the twenty-one pueblos with evident remittance construction, I was drawn to three in the south of the state that had ambitious, distinct, and well-developed projects. The rodeo arena in Lagunillas, the cultural center in San Juan, and the old age home in Los Guajes—all on García's list—were dramatic, typologically distinct interventions in previously homogeneous and traditional building fabrics. These public "architectures," unlike my coworkers' dream houses in Guanajuato, were not only "modern," symbolic of the success of migration, but also spaces consciously intended by their patrons and sponsors to bring about social and economic change in their hometowns.

Throughout the process of researching and writing this book, I have become an interdisciplinary scholar. As an architectural and urban historian, I was always interested in the material history of migration, yet I quickly found that I could not write about remittances (or better yet, remittance landscapes) without understanding contemporary development policy and the sociology and anthropology of migration. While my primary interest still lay in the history of how migration shapes places, when I started this project in 2006, little had been written on the Mexican government's 3×1 program. In order to understand the architectures resulting from this program, I extended my work beyond the world of the built environment to explore the

Mexican government's development policy and how it influenced individual and familial social relations in rural Mexico. Finally, my theory of "remittance space"—explained in the introduction to this book—provokes questions about the mutual constitution of cities and distant rural hinterlands as part of a transborder continuum, many of which remain unanswered. In this book I argue that migration creates remittance landscapes, that migrants live in remittance spaces. The book aims to set the stage for future research on remittance landscapes and spaces across disparate migration streams. Further research is required to understand the history of how remittances have been used throughout the twentieth century, evolving remittance building styles, and the history of Mexican urbanization, modernization, and development in relation to the built environment of small towns and midsized cities.

Exploring the processes that shape places, architectures, and people required me to interact with how development discourses, economic policy, and the form and meaning of ordinary architecture in rural Mexico interface with one another. After hundreds of interviews and informal discussions with Mexican migrants and their families in Mexico, I am convinced that the experts on remittances, development, and Mexican building construction are migrants themselves, from whom I am continually learning and to whom I'm deeply indebted.

Acknowledgments

This project would not have happened without the assistance of several coworkers and friends—Mexican migrants from Guanajuato, Michoacán, and Jalisco—who opened their homes to me and shared their life stories with me. Individuals in Jalisco and members of hometown associations from Jalisco and Michoacán in both Chicago and Los Angeles have been extremely generous with their time and patient with my questions.

My interest in migrant spaces and landscapes has also benefited from institutional support and an interdisciplinary group of mentors and colleagues. At UC Berkeley in the College of Environment Design, where I began the project, I would like to especially thank Paul Groth—who introduced me to cultural landscapes as a topic of study—along with Ananya Roy and William Taylor, for their continuous support and critical feedback. Additionally, Nezar AlSayyad, Greig Crysler, Christine Trost, Deborah Lustig, David Minkus, Sandra Nichols, Dell Upton, and the late Allan Pred have all shaped this project in large and small ways.

At the University of Chicago, Mauricio Tenorio and Emilio Kourí helped push my ideas. At the University of Texas at Austin, Dean Frederick Steiner's support was critical to my finishing this project in a timely fashion. Other friends and scholars—Marta Gutman, Peri Fletcher, Roger Waldginer, Michael Peter Smith, Adam Goodman, C. J. Alvarez, Genevieve Negron-Gonzales, and Sylvia Nam have provided salient feedback and support along the way. José de la Torre Curiel at the Universidad de Guadalajara and his wife, Rosa, opened their home to me during my stay in Guadalajara. Their historical knowledge of rural Jalisco and their kindness could not have been a better introduction to my year in the field.

The editors at the University of Chicago Press, Susan Bielstein and

Anthony Burton, have been a pleasure to work with. Susan recognized the importance of remittance landscapes and helped me move the project forward at an ambitious pace. I would also like to thank my anonymous peer reviewers for their timely feedback.

Support from the University of Chicago's Provost Career Enhancement Postdoctoral Fellowship, UC Berkeley's Center for the Study of Social Change, the UC-Mexus Research Grant, the Bancroft Library Study Award, and the Center for Race and Gender allowed me to live in Mexico for the better part of a year and travel between Mexico, Los Angeles, and Chicago for several more.

As with any work that is almost a decade in the making, my family and closest friends have been indispensable. Ruben Martin Lopez-lopez and Felicia Perchuk Lopez, you have given me the gift of curiosity that makes my intellectual work possible. Sigi Nacson and Nina Kuna have employed their many talents to making this project stronger. Finally, there is no doubt in my mind that this book would not be what it is without Chesney Floyd. Our ongoing conversations about remittances, space, and the built environment, his insights during several trips to Mexico, and his close readings of and feedback on drafts at various stages along the way have made this work stronger. Dearest friend, thank you so very much.

Introduction: Remittance Space

BUILDINGS AS EVIDENCE OF SOCIAL CHANGE

I had the Statue of Liberty made with the face of my mother. The book she is hold-ing has my birth date on it. I was in New York, eating a hotdog, looking at the Statue of Liberty, and I couldn't believe how lucky I was—how good the United States has been to me.

ANTONIO RODRÍGUEZ, California, 2008

Migrants are financing and mobilizing physical transformations of Mexico's landscape with money earned in the United States. The re-mittance landscape—distinct elements of the built environment con-structed and altered with migrant dollars—can be found at multiple scales: from the new ornamentation on the facades of houses to the cultural centers, potable water systems, and roads of small towns. Three images—representations of built elements and spatial prac-tices in specific physical locations—collected from disparate places and at various scales begin to illuminate the spaces of this emergent landscape. These remittance spaces span international boundaries and are produced by migrants' grassroots practice of sending cash to hometowns, as well as the government structures and policies that shape migration and the economy today.

Remittance space is often about mediating between *norteños* (a colloquial term used in Central Mexico to describe individuals who travel north) and their hometowns.[1] This space is highly represen-tational and symbolic, and remittance buildings can act as stand-ins for norteños themselves. Antonio Rodríguez, a norteño who has been in the United States for thirty years, commissioned a sculpture of the Statue of Liberty, proudly displayed in the courtyard of his remit-tance house in Pegueros, Jalisco, which was also funded by dollars (fig. 0.01).[2] In the central courtyard of his Mexican home, Rodríguez has appropriated one of the primary images of freedom and democracy in

FIGURE 0.01. Replica of the Statue of Liberty in the courtyard of Antonio Rodrí-guez's remittance house in Pegueros, Jalisco. Photograph by author.

the United States as a symbol of his personal transformation. Differences between the statue Rodríguez commissioned and the original construct a migration narrative: here the sculptor has replaced Lady Liberty's likeness with that of Rodriguez's mother, and the date of the Declaration of Independence on her tablet has been swapped with Rodríguez's birth date. The broken chains at her ankles in the new version remain intact. According to "Tony," the statue is intended to give thanks to his familial origins and recognize his self-determination, while at the same time representing his townspeople in Pegueros as trapped, ensnared, or chained in the past, in "backwardness."

Remittance space also represents collective aspirations for accelerated change in the built environment. Migrants in the United States have formed hometown associations (known as HTAS or "clubs") where they meet and pool their money for projects. In a small town in southern Jalisco's sugarcane valley, remittances have partially funded what is intended to be a state-of-the-art sports facility comprising multiple basketball courts, tennis courts, a concrete stadium for soccer, and an arena for volleyball (fig. 0.02). During construction of the basketball courts, a local entrepreneur (who works with migrants in California) discovered underground water. "We will build a natural pool and spa. An infinity pool, like in the Olympics."[3] Since 2006, the project has remained almost completed but unfinished, unused, and unmaintained.

Performances in both Mexico and the United States also reveal how remittance spaces are meticulously constructed. A migrant visionary from Guerrero has worked for years to produce a *jaripeo* (bull-riding contest) in Chicago during the icy winter months. This important cultural sport is typically performed in the open air throughout rural Mexican towns. To achieve this goal, Pedro Salazar built a "Mexican-style" ranch in the south of Wisconsin where he trains over a dozen first-rate bulls; he has coordinated a binational group of rodeo riders and experts to reproduce the jaripeo in the Midwest; and he re-created the ground that riders and bulls are familiar with by hauling several tons of dirt to Chicago's UIC Pavilion. For his first indoor event, Salazar hired Banda Chilacachapa, an indigenous group from Guerrero who traveled over 2,200 miles to Chicago by bus. In figure 0.03, migrants (and some Mexican Americans) photograph the group as they parade around the "dirt" floor. According to Salazar, due to difficulties with

FIGURE 0.02. One of ten basketball courts with an adjustable fiberglass backboard in the "state-of-the-art" sports arena in Vista Hermosa. The hillside town is surrounded by productive sugarcane fields. Photograph by author.

FIGURE 0.03. The Banda Chilacachapa performs at Pedro Salazar's winter "super jaripeo" in Chicago. Their performance is both a major draw for the migrant audience in Chicago and a critical (and mobile) component of reconstructing an authentic *jaripeo* ritual. Photograph by author.

procuring visas for large indigenous bands, this was the first time that Banda Chilacachapa has performed in the United States. In sum, he described it as a "historic event" for the migrant community.

These three images reflect the complexities of remittance space for migrants, many of whom work tirelessly in the shadows of American society. Migrants represent migration experiences with potent symbols, build visionary projects to transform their *pueblos* (towns), and perform cultural practices common in their hometowns in US cities that build binational cultural infrastructures. These migrant practices produce a field of relations across national boundaries, which are reformulating the social and spatial boundaries of place.

The Remittance Boom

Despite the fact that rural Mexico's *hijos ausentes*, absent sons and daughters, fuel an ongoing remittance boom that has its roots in the early part of the twentieth century, remittances have only recently received the attention of formal institutions, scholars, and certain government agencies. Remittances—defined by the World Bank as the portions of international migrant workers' earnings that are sent back to family members in their countries of origin—are at the center of emerging global discourses and practices. According to the World Bank, worldwide remittance flows, predominantly to "Third World" countries, increased from $72.3 billion in 2001 to an estimated $483 billion in 2011.[4] Researchers at institutions such as the World Bank and the Multilateral Investment Fund (established in 1993) of the Inter-American Development Bank have been investigating the effect of remittances on development.[5] Their research generally focuses on the geographic spread of remittances, the ability of remittances to target the poor directly, and the incorporation of impoverished people into global financial markets as evidence of the positive impact of remittance development.[6] Most important, research funded by government and finance institutions and nongovernmental organizations (NGOs) on the size of remittance flows and how these monies are sent and spent represents a paradigm shift in how we talk about migration. Migration is no longer viewed only as a major social, political, and economic problem; it is also understood to be a powerful economic engine.

Mexico is at the center of debates about the transformative potential of remittance capital for the world's poor. While Mexico is the fourth-largest remittance-receiving country after China, India, and the Philippines, the US-Mexico migration corridor is the largest migrant flow between two nations in the world.[7] Over eleven million Mexican-born migrants live in the United States. In 2012, Mexico received over an estimated $22 billion in remittances. Thus, as a director of the Pew Hispanic Center put it, "migration is not only an escape valve—it is now also a fuel pump," surpassing oil exports and other sources of foreign direct investment.[8]

In specific Mexican states, and especially in rural communities, remittances are ubiquitous. The state of Jalisco is one of four Mexican states—alongside Michoacán, Guanajuato, and Estado de México— with the highest rates of remittances. Almost two billion dollars of formal transactions were recorded in Jalisco in 2012.[9] However, all thirty-one Mexican states receive remittances. In 2007 remittances were a source of family subsistence for 1.6 million Mexican households; in 2012 over six million individuals reported receiving remittances, which allegedly slowed down the growth of poverty and social marginalization.[10] Estimates show that at least half of all Latino migrants who have been in the United States for a decade or less remit, and even some of those who have been in the United States for twenty or thirty years continue to send money.[11] Just under half of these migrants are undocumented, and the majority are "men with low incomes and low education levels."[12] On the receiving end, 60 percent of remittance receivers are female. On average, remitters send from one hundred to three hundred dollars a month to families (their parents and siblings, their wife or husband and children, or both).

While this massive transfer of wealth is primarily understood as a financial flow, it occurs within a specific cultural and environmental context that is transformed through the process of migration. Remittances influence how families are organized, where they live, and how they make decisions. Anthropologists and sociologists have been researching the social and cultural implications of remittances on family life for decades. Such scholars theorize the wide-reaching influence that remittances have on daily life, even arguing that there is a "culture of migration" that can be best understood through ethnographic work. The political implications of continuous remitting have also been closely examined and linked to the rise of "transnational civil societies"—commonly used to refer to migrant groups that implement social change in the public spheres of their hometowns via activism in host locations. Academically, these works reinvigorate immigration scholarship, once wedded to assimilation theories predicated on assumptions about migrants' integration into their host society. Today's transnational theories view remitting as a structural link between migrants and their hometowns.[13]

Remittances have influenced so many aspects of social and political life that the Mexican government has aggressively engaged the spaces of migration. So-called remittance development, cast as a strategy to alleviate poverty, has captured the attention of global financial institutions, NGOs, and state departments. They view the number of collective projects realized by migrant hometown associations, and the persistence of remitting over time, as evidence that remittances will play a role in rural and urban development in the future. The Mexican state has inserted itself into migrants' grassroots practices through a myriad of programs and centers, most notably Tres por Uno (also referred to as Three for One or "3×1"), a government program that quadruples migrant dollars with municipal, state, and federal funds. All of this money is channeled toward development of some kind.

In 2001 President Vicente Fox publicly referred to migrants as the country's heroes. Shortly thereafter, the Fox administration formalized the 3×1 program. From 2002 to 2009, the federal government increased its spending on the program from approximately $15 million to $50 million.[14] While the government has increased its spending, this is a tiny fraction of the amount of informal remittances sent by migrants yearly. Still, the program has become a model for other remittance-receiving countries that are interested in new forms of development that incorporate the poor or others that have traditionally been formally excluded from top-down development.

The remittance development discourse (maturing with the blossoming of the remittance landscape itself) is part of a larger ideological shift occurring in NGOs, governmental agencies, and the financial sector that have come to view the poor as an asset.[15] From Washington, DC, to Mexico City, social workers, policy makers, bankers, and politicians are strategizing new ways to capture poor people's "surplus" capital. The poor represent the new frontier ("banking the unbanked"); their financial inclusion is viewed as the democratization of development itself.

Current research on the social, political, and developmental dimensions of transnational migration contribute to an ethnographic and often multisited approach to the study of migration. Remitting is often incorporated into these studies as one part of a constellation of migration processes (gender, generation, social norms) that take center stage. Yet remitting is a salient structural force shaping migration itself. Remittances are much more than a social, political, demographic, or economic dimension of migration. Remittances are financial transactions with spatial implications, financing construction booms in rural Mexico that affect daily life for migrants and nonmigrants alike. The built environment, greatly altered by dollars, shapes the social spaces of migration. Moreover, remittances are changing the cultural and material landscapes in the United States.

Place, space, and the material world must be brought into the discourse on migration because building is a product of migration that in turn produces more migration. Building projects funded by remittances structure human movement and are powerful evidence of the aims, desires, and fears that drive social change. This book conceives of the remittance landscape as the amalgam of migrants' life stories and the macro political, social, economic, and historical forces that shape migration. Analyzing the built environment in rural Mexico is critical for understanding contemporary migration at large.[16]

By addressing the history of the built environment (space and time), I argue that migration is not only geographical (captured by terms such as *bilocalism, translocal,* and *transregional*) but also spatial and material. By addressing what people operating in the social space of "transnational" migration are building, I bring the better life migrants are building in their hometowns into tension with their spatial practices in the United States. I also trace the ways in which migrants' relations to families and communities change as they establish new forms of agency and identity through their activities in migrant clubs. This analysis of migrant building projects reveals how migrants' lives, their personal and collective aspirations, are shaped by government policies, but also how migrants' choices give shape to the state.

Through an analysis of the remittance landscape, I make several arguments about both migration and the ordinary built environment.

First, and most important, we need more multisited, historically situated studies of the material culture of transnational migration because landscapes and artifacts provide primary evidence of the effects of persistent, endemic migration and remitting on emigrant communities. Such studies are able to provide deep insight into the social and cognitive structures that both give rise to and in turn are transformed by the migration process. Rather than recording migrant stories, my methodological approach documents migrants as motivators of environmental, and then social, transformation at both points of departure and points of arrival. The frame "remittance landscape" brings analytic clarity to transnational discourses, offering historical and material evidence of migrants' shifting attachments, building knowledge about both qualitative change and historical continuity.[17]

The second argument addresses a debate occurring within migration scholarship: Is migration today qualitatively different from migration fifty or one hundred years ago? And if so, how and why? Scholars of transnationalism in anthropology, sociology, and political science focus on contemporary migration streams to convincingly show how, by moving back and forth between two or more places, migrants build alliances "there" through "here," essentially expanding the scope of "home" to include both "there" and "here."[18] They point to the role of modern technology in facilitating connections and the increasing popularity of long-distance political engagements. However, transnational migration and the remittance spaces it produces are not new.

At the turn of the twentieth century, when the majority of immigrants to the United States were from Europe, many returned home and most maintained ties to homelands. An estimated 50 percent of Italian migrants returned to their homeland. Many of these migrants sent remittances (in 1906 an estimated $11,092,446 was sent to Italy in postal money orders alone), and some of this money was used to build private homes as well as public or institutional buildings such as orphanages.[19] These early migrants even facilitated the migration of American materials such as toilets to their native countries.[20] The Italians were not alone. Chinese immigrants financed the construction of homes, roads, businesses, and public institutions through remittances in the nineteenth and early twentieth centuries.[21] However, restrictions on Chinese immigration and the US Immigration Act of

1924, which greatly diminished the number of incoming southern and eastern Europeans, undoubtedly weakened the long-distance migrant networks that were in the making. No comprehensive study has been conducted on the remittance landscapes of the nineteenth and early twentieth centuries.[22] Thus it remains unknown how immigration policy and immigration flows specifically influenced the building of, and people's experiences of, remittance landscapes in Italy, Poland, or China at that time. In contrast to European groups, Mexican migrants at the turn of the century were fewer (only 500,000 migrants compared to over a million Polish, Irish, and Canadian respectively), but they returned to Mexico at higher rates (an estimated 80–90% of the time). Mexican migrants, networks, and remittance flows have followed a trajectory different from those of other migrant groups. Two guest worker programs between Mexico and the United States, one from 1917–21 and the Bracero Program from 1942–64, aided by the nations' geographic proximity and intertwined economies, institutionalized a back-and-forth or "circular migration." While Mexican migration to the United States did not begin its rapid ascent until the 1960s and 1970s, Mexicans have continuously moved between homelands and hostlands throughout the twentieth century.

Migration today is qualitatively different from these precedents. What is new is the way that the accretion of remittance building projects over time shapes the social spaces of migration here (one point on the migration trajectory) and there (the second point on such trajectory), which in turn produces social spheres increasingly structured by the logic of remittance. In this new migratory space, distance is normalized, incorporated into a way of life—that is, *remitting is a way of life*—that manages separation, dispersion, fragmentation, and ambivalence on a daily basis. My work shows how the long-distance financing of building projects with dollars is a process that has gained momentum over time. In high-emigration regions in rural Mexico, building with remittances has become pervasive. In such locations migration, remitting, and the myriad processes, rituals, and events that support them now play dominant roles in defining the social space of the pueblo.

The third argument is that the transformative power of remittance-driven development is being co-opted by the Mexican state unevenly, appropriated by officials at all levels of government and business owners for political purposes, and clouding the relationships between rural Mexican towns and institutions. As the agendas of migrant activists and governmental leaders (and NGOs and financiers) become blurred, their roles and responsibilities, as well as the meaning of completing projects, also slip out of focus.

This book, rather than analyze the success or failure of programs like 3×1, looks to the remittance landscape to understand how so-called remittance development is experienced by those who initiate it and those who live with specific projects.[23] Involvement with long-distance building projects shapes how migrants think about themselves, their communities, and their nation-states. Conversely, those for whom the buildings are intended, who live full time in villages in rural Mexico, are also affected greatly by remittance projects. Remittance development as a subset of the remittance landscape has much to tell us about qualitative change in emigrant societies.

Finally, as a built environment historian, I argue that we cannot understand the American city without addressing the places migrants come from and the ways they too are altered by migration to the United States. The study of migration challenges basic assumptions that built environment scholars use to understand places. Such scholars often use landscapes and buildings as primary evidence to support descriptions of urban and social processes in a geographically circumscribed "place." Buildings crystallize historic moments like no other artifact—technologies are required, desire is enacted, capital is expended, all to create objects that shape future life-worlds. Buildings are thus both practical and symbolic. But the continuous migration of persons back and forth across borders requires scholars of the built environment to rethink the relationship between people, buildings, and their surroundings. Urban historians must look beyond the horizon of the "city" to distant locations that actually constitute important dimensions of the "urban" both as a formal condition and as a lived experience. In other words, to understand the American city, we must expand the definition of the city to include geographically distant places, processes, and people.

It is difficult to research how migrants shape the built environment when many of them do not have the necessary means to build in American cities. While some studies have addressed migrant place-making by analyzing how migrants with social and economic capital spearhead development projects, too few built environment historians have studied how those without extensive resources, theorized by sociologists as "transnational migrants from below," shape places.[24] This may result in part from the fact that migrants do not necessarily invest in the places in which they live. But it is also because migrant influences on the built environment are more ephemeral, temporary, or discrete.[25] We need to address both sides of the border, ephemeral spatial practices as well as permanent structures, to grasp the influence of migrants and migration on cities and towns.

These arguments are contextual and methodological, reframing the way we think about migration and place, requiring innovations that pair methods from one discipline with questions from another. With regard to remittance building, I study what is envisioned, how the construction process influences social relations and local political economies, and subsequently how the built environment affects daily life for those who build it and those who live with it. In other words, I conduct *building ethnographies* on the envisioning, execution, and subsequent use of paradigmatic remittance landscapes funded both outside of and through the 3×1 program.

The terms *remittance landscape* and *remittance space* introduce an analytic specificity to transnational and global studies. Sociologists Roger Waldinger and David Fitzgerald have launched critiques of the terms *transnational* and *transnational civil society* for their invocation of "the nation" when migrants' long-distance engagements across national boundaries are actually strengthening "highly particularistic attachments" to specific places.[26] Anthropologist Lynn Stephens uses the term *transborder* to denote multiple borders beyond the nation, such as ethnic, cultural, and regional borders, that people are crossing.[27] Historians Dirk Hoerder and Nora Faires term the study of migration "transcultural society studies" to bring multiple scales of analysis from the local, regional, national, and transnational into the debate. While I occasionally use the term *transnational* or *transborder* to identify larger societal transformations occurring due to remitting as a way of life, I analyze remittance space to add specificity to globalization and transnational theories by describing what migrants build, why, and the extent to which such artifacts affect people and place.

Throughout this book I refer to individuals as *migrants* to signify that for such persons migration and remitting is a way of life. They are persons who self-identify as *migrantes*, sometimes even after they have been in the United States for over thirty years. Of course, many individuals who leave homes do not identify as migrants. Such individuals might not have ties to hometowns and do not view the experience of migration as fundamentally shaping their experience of the world. In light of this, my work, and that of many transnational, transborder, and transcultural scholars, addresses only a very specific subset of the migrating population.[28]

From Neither "Here" nor "There" to Both "Here" and "There"

While it is easy to view remittance space as a result of contemporary globalization and late capitalism—as labor markets are increasingly fragmented, governments break down trade barriers, and technologies aid human mobility—remittances and their attendant spaces have been important to Mexico for the last hundred years.

Migrant desire and ambivalence, key characteristics in the production of remittance space, also have a historical legacy that goes back to at least the early twentieth century, when individuals began making trips between Mexico and the United States.[29] Political events, environmental factors, technological innovations, and economic change all helped to uproot Mexicans from their pueblos and send them north. The Mexican Revolution from 1911 to the early 1920s, the Cristero War (1926-29), drought, and new railroads produced the structural conditions that encouraged long journeys to the United States and its promise of dramatically higher earning power. In the first several decades of the twentieth century, individuals who went to the United States were recorded as earning from between five to thirty-six times what they could earn in Mexican towns. These ratios were dramatically higher for rural workers, who earned far less in Mexico than townspeople did. Academics have argued that the tremendous imbalance created by enormous wage differentials alone would have sufficed to cause heavy emigration.[30]

By the late 1920s, migrant dislocation, distance, and ambivalence had established historically observable changes in villages in Mexico. Two studies conducted in the 1920s and 1930s provide evidence of the social and cultural impact of migration on individuals and communities. Manuel Gamio and Paul S. Taylor were both commissioned by the Social Science Research Council (SSRC) to study the "Mexican problem," or the impact on Mexican society of mass migration from Mexico to American farms.[31] Gamio, a Mexican anthropologist, organized research that included interviews of migrants living in different US cities to understand their social and cultural adaptation and resistance to American ways of life. Researchers questioned migrants about politics, religion, and gender roles. They also visited migrant hometowns in Mexico to photograph the influence of migration on place.[32] Taylor, trained as a political economist, also became interested in Mexican hometown societal transformations due to migration. He went to live in Arandas, Los Altos de Jalisco, for several months to examine how provincial town and farm life clashed with the dynamism of the industrial North.[33] Aside from conducting interviews and questionnaires, Gamio and Taylor examined US and Mexican customs records—showing what migrants carried when returning to Mexico—and tracked remittance transfers to map migration streams and economic change.[34] According to the *New York Times*, in 1928 Mexico received twelve million dollars in remittances, a handsome sum that documents a remittance trend.[35]

In the 1920s and 1930s, migration brought material change to Jalisco in the importation of durable goods and clothing. Taylor notes migrants' penchant for buying wristwatches, overalls, and sewing machines. These objects had different symbolic and actual effects in everyday life. The wristwatch introduced an American idea of time, and timeliness, to rural towns where people worked with the sun and where church bells structured daily routines. Overalls became a ubiquitous form of dress. According to Taylor, it was "obvious that the migrant standard and kind of dress became a factor in setting new standards for nonemigrants who could afford it."[36] The introduction of overalls marked a moment when foreign dress began to redefine local standards.[37] The introduction of the sewing machine created a great divide between women who used them and those who sewed by hand. This did not end sewing by hand in the pueblo; rather, it created new comparisons and relative satisfactions for those who sewed by hand and those who did not (have to). These imports also signified migrants' contributions to the uneven economic development of fami-

FERMIN AVILA,jornalero,originario de Cerritos,San Luis Potosí,casado,24
años de edad,£ 5' 5" de estatura,moreno,ojos cafés,cabello negro.Este
tipo presenta todas las característica del peón mexicano,pero mostrando ya
cierta evolución o mejor dicho "cambio" en la indumentaria,pues se ve que
usar "over_alls" y sombrero de fieltro.En Tampico,en los campos petroleros
son millares los individuos de este tipo.

FIGURE 0.04. A Mexican migrant photographed by Manuel Gamio in his SSRC study. The caption in Gamio's scrapbook reads, "This type presented all of the characteristics of a Mexican peon, but is showing a certain evolution or better said, 'change,' in his style, one can see his use of 'overalls' and felt hat. In Tampico, in the petroleum camps, there are thousands of individuals of this type." Courtesy of the Bancroft Library at the University of California, Berkeley.

FIGURE 0.05. Gamio's map of remittances received in Mexico in 1926. Courtesy of the Bancroft Library at the University of California, Berkeley.

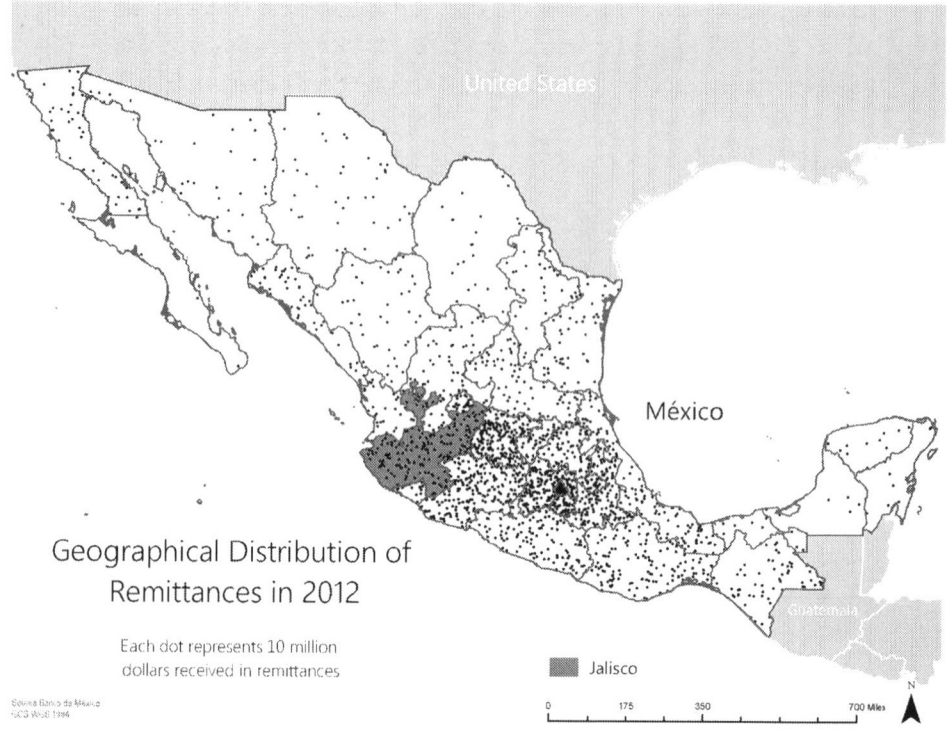

Geographical Distribution of
Remittances in 2012

Each dot represents 10 million
dollars received in remittances

Jalisco

FIGURE 0.06. Map of remittances received in Mexico in 2012, following Gamio's
graphic conventions. Drawn by Kelly Strickler.

lies and communities. By contextualizing these durable goods, Taylor
provides material evidence of the exchanges occurring between the
United States and Mexico.

While clothing and durable goods differentiated community members along nascent class lines, the introduction of imported automo-
biles produced more comprehensive spatial change in rural Mexico.[38]
Gamio records that one out of every three migrants in his study
brought a car back to Mexico, leading to the construction of roads:

> The possession of automobiles is absolutely unheard of in the humble
> social class to which the immigrants generally belong. . . . Many sec-
> tions of rural Mexico where the repatriated immigrant goes to colo-
> nize have no suitable automobile roads, and either there is no gasoline
> or else it is expensive or hard to get, with the result that automobiles
> are often useless. The good that results is that the possession of auto-

mobiles stimulates the owners to build roads, however poor these might be due to the humble circumstances of the owners. It would have been better had they brought in more buggies and carriages.[39]

The extent to which repatriated migrants actually built new roads is unknown. This quotation, however, is evidence that the newly acquired modern amenity—the car—caused migrants to perceive a deficiency in their built environment that they attempted to correct through collective action. This makes road building a social process and indicates that remittance roads were among the initial remittance spaces built in rural communities. This view is supported by the fact that fewer than one-third of imported vehicles were trucks suited to rough roads and heavy work; over two-thirds were passenger cars. In a series of migrant portraits taken by Gamio in the state of Michoacán, repatriated migrants posed in their US "Sunday best" in front of a Model T Ford. The same car was used in all of the portraits, providing a photogenic symbol of American modernity as migrant success.[40]

Despite the introduction of dollars and cars, major spatial change did not appear to have taken hold in rural localities and small towns during the period of Gamio's and Taylor's studies. Some migrants were interested in building a home in the American-style, but this

FIGURE 0.07. Repatriated Mexican migrants posing in front of a remitted Ford automobile, photographed by Manuel Gamio in 1937. Courtesy of the Bancroft Library at the University of California, Berkeley.

desire was quickly overcome by the logistical and practical difficulties of doing so. In Arandas, Jalisco, Taylor records a return migrant's musings regarding a new home: "I would like to have a house in American style. . . . But . . . here we build thick so no bullet can come through, and no windows, so when the door is shut, no one can come."[41] Migrants who did build American-style houses quickly reverted to their old customs and sought refuge in traditional-style homes. A local nonmigrant in Arandas told Taylor: "When the Mexicans come from the United States they are converted. They have better manners, dress and more money. They learn to wash their faces. . . . Many live in a *jacal* [traditional house], and upon return, make a new house. . . . But after [a norteño] has been here for a time, he loses his learning and his wishes and makes his living as before."[42]

Taylor and Gamio also record migrants' sporadic and largely unsuccessful attempts to elevate their economic status. According to Taylor, the majority of emigrants "spent their money as fast as it was earned," restricting material changes to ephemeral things they could buy or consume.[43] Taylor recounts several cases of migrants who unsuccessfully attempted to change the structural conditions of their lives: "Probably the emigrant most fired with enthusiasm for an altered model of life was the young Pennsylvania steel worker who had purchased land, oxen, and horses. His works showed both the hopes and the difficulty of realization: 'I have many desires to do things in the style of the United States. For example, I would like to have a pump for irrigation so I could have better crops every year. Here we need money for machinery for our farms; we have oxen and no machinery and can't do much without money.'"[44] The necessary institutional, economic, and political support to bring infrastructure to such places did not exist. Experience working in the industrial North did not help migrants improve conditions at home, because the skills migrants learned in the United States were specialized. This was antithetical to how work was performed in Mexico, where self-sufficiency, not efficiency, was the guiding principle and where the craftsman or builder remained an autonomous figure.[45]

While migrant ambitions to change Mexico may have been tempered by logistical constraints, from the perspective of some nonmigrant inhabitants in Arandas, migrants were perceived as a threat to patriotism. Taylor records the voice of a leading merchant in Arandas: "Every Mexican who goes, likes the United States better than Mexico. He gets a better life there than here. After 100 years, it will be good-bye to Mexico. I am afraid they will like America better than Mexico. We are making 'war' so they won't become Americanized. They will not like the Mexican flag; they have no love of country, and that is a great danger to Mexico."[46]

While this merchant is certain that migrants "like America better than Mexico," Taylor argues that migrants were actually ambivalent regarding their preference of country: "But with a large proportion of the returned emigrants, the happier life in Mexico was more than counterbalanced by the higher material standard of living in the United States. Many asserted that they were happier in Arandas, and almost in the next breath, that they would go back to the United States if work was plentiful, and would gladly live there the remainder of their lives, apparently seeing no contradiction in their statements."[47] While Taylor was researching migrant housing conditions in California, he approached a couple living in a self-built shack under a tree and asked the owners why they did not invest more in their housing. They replied that they did not know if they would stay and that they might return to Mexico. He then asked, "How long have you been here?" to which they responded, "Thirty years."[48] Taylor notes: "Since it [Mexico] was immediately adjacent geographically, it was also close psychologically in the minds of Mexican immigrants in the United States."[49]

In more recent decades, migrants who might "like America better than Mexico" have built places and brought objects back to Mexico in part to create at home the "better life" found in the United States. Seventy years after Taylor's study, Guadalupe Gómez, a Mexican migrant and political organizer in the United States, noted: "We have been those who are neither from here nor there. Now we will be those who are both from here and there—both things at the same time."[50] Migrants are resolving decades of ambivalence by constructing buildings and spaces in Mexico (and the United States) that reflect new lifestyles acquired through transnational migration. Because of migration, the largest city in the region of Los Altos—the city adjacent to Arandas, where Taylor conducted his research—is known as "the migrant city." The upper-class neighborhood called Beverly Tepa is named after Beverly Hills. The desire to own a wristwatch has been replaced by more extravagant ambitions with higher stakes, such as owning a home in Beverly Tepa. Due to the daily costs of migration and remitting as a way of life, men and women want to transcend space and time: by building there here and here there, they psychologically dwell in both places at once. But for this not to cause pain and suffering, men and women would have to be superhuman, able to be both here and there at the same time, to *transcend* space and time.

Remittance Space as a Framework for Architectures of Migration

Remittance space is the sum of individual migrants' and their communities' construction practices and narratives, as well as the macro processes, institutional regimes, and symbolic and spatial transformations that are collectively shaped by and shaping remitting as a way of life. With regard to this broad definition of "space," the built environment is an artifact of the patterns and vectors (temporal, social, political, and institutional) that structure migration and remitting. Remittance space is also the enactment, daily use, and collective meaning of the remittance landscape.

The act of remitting itself has specific implications for the nature of remittance space. Remitting is an economic transaction that links two people (the sender and the receiver) and two places (where money is sent from and where it is received). Senders are sons and daughters, husbands, wives, and lovers who make critical life choices to be able to remit. Receivers are often elderly mothers and fathers, or wives, maintaining the original home. In the urban US–rural Mexico remittance corridor, the sender is outside the hometown while the receiver remains inside the hometown. "Home" in this case is both a stable reference point for migrants and a locus for investment, a place where migrants can send the fruits of their labor. These basic relationships give remittance space specific asymmetrical characteristics. For example, from the position of the migrant, remittance space is defined by direct exchange between a mobile, fluid "here" and a fixed, singular "there." From the position of the hometown, the world of senders is a dispersed cloud of individuals all relating back to a common point of origin. Relationships between remittance senders and receivers are personal and intimate. Each remittance transaction—the one hundred or three hundred dollars sent to Mexico on a given Wednesday or on Mother's Day—is a relationship formed, strengthened, contested, or dismantled.

While the individual transaction is personal, the aggregate of all remittance transactions constitutes an abstract flow. This "flow" indicates both a growing number of people remitting and refined remittance-mapping technologies. Since the early 2000s, Banco de México has been developing ways to track remittances more carefully, including working with Mexican consulates in the United States to issue migrant identification cards that they can use to open US bank accounts. As more and more people remit funds, financial and governmental agencies that facilitate flows invent increasingly sophisticated ways to profit from them. Wire transfers impose exorbitant transaction fees.[51] Cement companies allow migrants in the United States to buy bags of premixed concrete for pickup in Mexico. Governments create policies that incorporate migrant remittances into municipal budgets. Remittance flows create international, national, and local markets that further institutionalize remitting as a way of life.[52] The dual nature of remittances—as both an individual act and a financial flow—defines remittance space.

To understand this duality, it is important to first define the physical, geographic, and corresponding cognitive, experiential dimensions of remitting as a way of life. Distance, aspirations, and ambivalence play out in every remittance building project and permeate the remittance spaces produced and experienced by remitters and their communities. Geographic distance is maintained between a person and where he or she came from, and between a person and part or all of his or her family. Distance allows actors to accrue money, gain access to state programs, and learn about and benefit from migrant networks. Geographic distance, however, also produces divergent perspectives, perceptions, and experiences because of people's experiences in disparate places. The geographic, physical fragmentation of families creates a culture of longing. As noted by a priest in a small rural town in Michoacán, "People feel the *frontera*, the distance between their families; some return from the North and cry to me in private because they now have better resources, they finally have cars, but they miss their family, their father and mother."[53] Migrant long-ing can be both concrete (missing family and friends) and abstract (missing "home").

Migrants' legal status vis-à-vis the state also produces profound iso-lation from their communities. Individuals who migrate illegally are members of Mexican society while outcasts in the United States. Ir-regular status means that returning home is dangerous and difficult—known deaths at the US-Mexico border have steadily increased over the last ten years.[54] Attaining legal status in the United States does not necessarily protect migrants from the dangers of traveling home. Thieves wait at bus stops and train stations to rob migrants returning home with money in their suitcase. In migrant circles, it is commonly believed that US and Mexican customs officials who document how much money migrants are carrying at the border work with thieves; as a result, undocumented migrants do not attempt a crossing without good reason, and many go years without returning.

Even if migrants do not carry money home, rumors about their fi-nancial success in the United States can result in personal danger. A migrant from a small town near Ciudad Guzmán, Jalisco, recounted the tragic story of a norteño who had lived for many years in San Francisco and had decided to return to Ciudad Guzmán to live. Upon his return, he and his children were kidnapped, held for ransom, and subsequently murdered. The kidnappers knew that he had been successful in California. The norteño continued, "I still imagine the pueblo is as it was when I left twenty-five years ago. I put my family in danger when we go home without even knowing it."[55] Over time, migrants' ideas of home diverge from what home has become in their absence.

Furthermore, migrants feel an internal psychological distance be-tween their sense of themselves since leaving home and their sense of who they were before. This is not unique to Mexican migrants or to contemporary migration. Rather, this is a story about mobility within established communities. After one leaves home, one's identity and role in the community are destabilized. Leaving behind the norms, rules, and regulations of the institutional and social spaces in which one grew up, the migrant forms a new, second "self" in a new social and environmental context. Exits and entries create new opportuni-ties and changes in social patterns and hierarchies. This "subjective" distance makes it possible for migrants to assume a critical position toward their hometowns. During a village festival, Juan Zamora, the president of a Los Angeles migrant social club, went up to a group of kids and told them not to spit peach pits on the floor. He then turned to me and explained: "They lack manners, they need to change their style of living. Nobody tells them what is right and wrong. . . . When I am here I can tell them, but I am not always here."[56] By asserting his role as cultural mentor, Zamora articulates and emboldens his identity as a norteño who "knows better" than those who have never left the village.

Distance also exacerbates migrants' guilt regarding their initial decision to leave, just as it allows them to reimagine the past. Zamora is caught between memories and remorse: "I miss my pueblo. I yearn for it. But when I go back, the people are changing, the kids are drinking and doing drugs, and all these things we used to do as a community are lost—I feel bad because I was of the first generation to leave, so it is partially my fault that it is not like it used to be."[57] The village is used as a context for actualizing memories of what life was and should be. Zamora's generation of migrants left the pueblo, in part, to help it survive economically. Now they live the consequences of returning to a community transformed by their "abandonment."

The social and economic distance between successful migrants and village inhabitants is also growing. In Vista Hermosa, a quaint town south of Guadalajara, Jalisco, a pair of very successful norteños named Javier and Ruby Villaseñor built a palatial mansion. This practice is not uncommon. Building mansions is one of the ways that those who attain economic success in the United States assert their status in Mexico and put on display their successful journeys as migrants. The couple—once poor farmers in Jalisco and now rich farm managers in Napa Valley's vineyards—employed approximately eighty people over a three-year period to build the house in their absence. The house electrician, who struggled to fulfill his clients' desires to use US appliances and to install circuit breakers modeled after US electrical standards (otherwise absent from houses in Vista), told me a story about bringing his son with him to work. One afternoon, the father and son sat at a dining-room table covered in plastic. The dining room was part of an open-floor plan with a three-story-high domed ceiling overhead. European-style columns supporting the roof ringed the central space. Interior second- and third-floor balconies circled the central atrium, creating multiple vantage points. Imported Italian marble flooring, a plasma-screen TV, a statue of Venus, and an Austrian chandelier were defining interior finishes. In this setting, the electrician's son asked: "Papi, why can't we have a house like this?"[58] Telling me this, the electrician shook his head and his eyes lost focus—how could he explain? While the son, at age six, was old enough to recognize the radical differences between their one-story concrete-block house with few amenities and the migrants' mansion, he was not old enough to understand that his father would have to abandon him, his siblings, and his mother—and risk his life—to have even a small chance at attaining a similar lifestyle for their family. Remittance houses normalize economic distance among community members as they create new aspirations and perceived needs in the youth.

The norteños' desire to create a landscape representative of their new socioeconomic status has created disjuncture and *envidia*, or envy, between migrants and inhabitants who have not migrated. In Vista Hermosa, after years of personal sacrifice, Ruby Villaseñor expressed frustration: "They [the locals] just don't understand; they see us as 'those norteños,' but we are investing in Vista as a gift to the town. We want the things we build to be classy so that the town has a future. . . . Our house is a gift to the pueblo."[59] Even so, remittance houses, like other remittance construction, create divisions within emigrant communities so often assumed to be homogenous.

For many eighteen-year-old boys, migration to the United States is an initiation into manhood, a rite of passage, the next logical step— because of the remittance spaces they have known intimately throughout their youth. According to one rural priest in Michoacán, "Now [migration] is a question of ideology more than of work and money. The United States is Superman. The clothes are better, the houses are better, the money is better. The people around me when I was growing up all had those things. I watched Walt Disney, Superman, and it wasn't the reality that I lived."[60] Even those Mexicans who have never left their hometowns grow up in remittance spaces where they are influenced by popular culture and migration.

Individual aspirations are fundamental to remittance space—they are why people leave, and they are what allow people to sustain a life of psychological, geographic, and subjective distance. Aspirations are

FIGURE 0.08. The glazed ceramic tile and freshly painted surfaces of this remittance house replace the rough edge of the roadway with clean lines. Photograph by author.

often geared toward the hometown. The hometown is the place where progress can be made manifest, the forum for symbolic representations of success. Hometowns are also where migrants find an audience, where the community they assist is located, and where they are recognized as full members of society regardless of their US citizenship status. Aspirations to address a lack, a need, or a desire are intended to open up what David Harvey calls "spaces of hope" for emigrant communities and families.[61]

The practice of remitting to build a house or support an individual migrant's family has evolved into coordinated efforts to rebuild entire hometowns. In this context, migrants take on yet another new identity, that of pueblo benefactors or boosters. Before I started my field research in Mexico, I interviewed the Villaseñors in California. They want their entire hometown (like their remittance house) to reflect their new social position. Over a bottle of wine produced at their vineyard in Napa Valley, they explained that for years they had been pooling dollars with other immigrants in California to refurbish the town. They had landscaped and furnished the main plaza, installed lampposts along the main entrance to town, and built public bathrooms and a colonnaded portico; now they were building an immense multi-sport complex. With resolve Ruby Villaseñor asserted, "Everything is there; all we need to do is change it."[62] Their ambitions to improve the pueblo can be restated as an effort to erase the crumbling adobe and brick one-story facades, dirt and stone streets, and other built-environment features that attest to a history of poverty and neglect.

Those migrants who move directly from rural villages and towns to American cities are immersed in a built environment markedly distinct from their hometowns. Sports arenas, roads, and businesses in the United States inform some migrants' ideas about the kinds of projects they want to build. In Vista Hermosa, a "state-of-the-art" sports arena is intended to rival "those found in the US." A project sponsor's visit to Las Vegas influenced his vision for Vista: "I went to Las Vegas and saw the significance of lights and said, 'Well, here [in Vista] we need to use lights.' The concept of illumination came from Las Vegas."[63] Vista Hermosa—like Las Vegas—is an oasis, but in an expanse of sugarcane. The hope is that dramatic nightlights shining on a state-of-the-art sports arena will draw much-needed attention and dollars to the town. In this appropriation of the image of Las Vegas, what the migrant could not perceive is the complex set of conditions that make electrical illumination a feasible strategy on any scale.

Norteños from Vista now also aspire to represent their pueblo to a global audience. During our initial meeting, after three hours of heated discussion, Javier Villaseñor asked, "How do we put Vista Hermosa on the map?"[64] Vista Hermosa, he and his wife explained, is located in a landscape that has "natural amenities, such as a waterfall and rolling hills," and "looks very much like Napa Valley." In an effort to promote their town and attract visitors, they use its formal name, Vista Hermosa, "Beautiful View," rather than its commonly used historic name, Santa Cruz. However, the town is one of thousands of small, predominantly rural Mexican towns in decline. The Villaseñors' initial motivation—some thirty years ago—to escape rural poverty required knowledge of and preparations for a long journey and foreign employment. Today, their motivation to present their town to the world requires an understanding of, and connections to, global circulations of power and wealth and the tourism industry.

Burgeoning migrant aspirations also shape nonmigrant expecta-

FIGURE 0.09. A residence embellished with an "onion dome" exemplifies the vernacular cosmopolitanism of remittance construction, which represents a world of distant places and possibilities with exotic forms. Photograph by author.

tions for and experiences in their hometowns. Daniel Gutiérrez, a man from Vista Hermosa who works with the Villaseñors, remarks, "They have affected the way I think about what is possible for Vista Hermosa. I see how they do things, like their house, and learn about what is possible."[65] With his sights set high, he too wants to "put Vista on the map." He works with norteños and invests their dollars to achieve this.

The blossoming of the remittance landscape, which fulfills pragmatic needs and mediates migrants' new migratory experiences, provides rich context for what Henri Lefebvre calls representational space.[66] Landscapes themselves take on symbolic dimensions. While specific remittance projects represent different things to different people, the power of the remittance landscape derives from its accumulation of symbols that together make present distant places, people, and points of view. The presence of distance in the immediate environment is the production of a cultural horizon that extends beyond the pueblo. In this period of accelerated built-environment change, the pueblo becomes the subject of an unspecified and unknown possible future. Migrants who take it upon themselves to build join a cacophony of voices defining and proclaiming what that possible future might be.

In the town of Torresillas, Michoacán, norteños constructed a church with a generic neocolonial front elevation and a chancel dome intended to reference the US Capitol in Washington, DC (fig. 0.10). This religious institution, with its reference to the seat of political power in the United States, could be interpreted as an affront to both Mexican nationalism and religious observance. The building is not, however, intended to be a social critique. Rather, according to the priest who took me to see it, it is a representation of thanks to the United States for opportunities to earn *billetes verdes* (greenbacks or green bills).[67] Because of migration to the United States, once-poor villagers can now build a modern church and provide the town with its first public bathrooms. Combining a symbol of US democracy with the architecture of Catholic religiosity also creates a new set of identifications associated with migration as migrants stake claims to both nations. Explicit references to US symbols catalog a particular moment in the region's migration history defined by confidence in America.[68] This is also expressed in material ephemera. In the town of El Grullo, Jalisco, many of whose residents have emigrated to New York, "I ♥ GruYork" bumper stickers decorate cars. By 2011, the certainty and confidence of these representations was threatened by the economic downturn and antimigrant political climate in the United States. As noted by a migrant who has lived in the United States for over thirty years, "The American dream was attainable in the US—*was*."[69] Norteños who "made it" in the United States have been able to build their version of the American dream in Mexico. However, will future generations of migrants continue to use representations of their journeys and transformations symbolic of an American dream that may be out of reach for many incoming migrants?

Ambivalence is another dimension inherent to remittance space. It results from investing in more than one place over an extended period while having the capacity to be in only one place at a time. As individual opportunities and positions in both Mexico and the United States change, migrants reevaluate which place can offer them a better life. Ambivalence takes the form of haunting questions that norteños continually ask themselves: Do I want to return home? When? With how much money? Can I return? What will I be returning to? Do I like

FIGURE 0.10. Above the crossing of nave and transept, this remittance church in Michoacán features a simplified and abstracted copy of the US Capitol dome, with its ringed peristyle at the base and a small ornamental cupola in place of the columned *tholus* of the original. Photograph by author.

who I have become? Do I like what the pueblo has become? Has it been worth it?

The main ambivalence that migrants experience is indecision about where they want to live. Mexicans simultaneously want to stay in their hometown and want to leave it. Once they have departed, they want to return but wish they could forget the shortcomings and burdens of home. The president of Club Lagunillas, Héctor Alarcón, reflected on his own experience of migration:

> I left thirty-three years ago with the illusions of all the youth; I listened to stories about money, came for a time [to the United States], one year, but saw the future here and compared it to there and saw that it was better. After two years I married and had kids and there were ropes holding me. Then came the day that I was neither here nor there. This is not good—it is better to stay in your country, but the options are limited. We could stay poor . . . but we wouldn't have ambition. At least in this country we have rights. We will have a pension.

In Mexico, only government officials have this; in Mexico we need security for the people. . . . What can I do, live with my aspirations or reality? My aspiration is to live in Mexico, but here is reality.[70]

Ideally, Alarcón would be able to attain a salary, retirement, and security while living among his people in Mexico. Because social security payouts in old age result from time spent working in the United States, he lives in a quiet state of crisis. While he dreams of home, the distance between himself and home continually grows. José Ochoa, the president of another club, Club Los Guajes, concludes: "If it was up to me, I would live in Los Guajes, but if I lived there I wouldn't be able to help as much."[71] According to Ochoa, living in Los Guajes is not "up to him." Thus he does not have to give up the Los Angeles business, house, and pool it took him over thirty years to acquire. For him, remitting at least partially resolves ambivalence and indecision about where to be.

The ambivalence about where one wants to be is tied to a deeper ambivalence of identity. A series of binaries now define transnational migrants themselves. Norteños are both hijos ausentes and returning heroes, abandoners and pillars of the community, second-class citizens and upwardly mobile movers and shakers. Locals also feel ambivalence about who norteños are and what they represent.

Subjective ambivalence is masked by a discourse of "generosity." This discourse is linked to how migrants feel about their economic success. Guilt, obligation, familial bonds, and communal purpose drive their generosity. Josefina Hernández, the hometown association president of Club Magdalena, commented that Alarcón, the president of Club Lagunillas, was driven to participate in the club and remit because of "his big heart" and "his love for his pueblo."[72] In spite of other motivations, this sentiment dominates the remittance development discourse.[73]

Building projects embody the contradictions of remittance space. This is most glaringly manifest in the migrants' new homes in Mexico, which represent success and the freedom to build but not economic stability in Mexico or the freedom to live in the new house. Public remittance projects embody another set of contradictions: they provide impressive new spaces for communities that are dwindling in population and spread across national boundaries. Projects also expose divergent priorities between migrants and nonmigrants, disagreements over authority, the commodification of pueblo "traditions," and emergent competition between emigrant communities.

Norteños build, in part, as a way of working through ambivalent feelings about where they belong. Buildings provide evidence that they are returning heroes and pillars of the community rather than deserters. Buildings reinsert norteños symbolically and practically into the hometown community. They require norteños to make a wide range of decisions about what the building will do and what it will look like. They require organizing and fundraising. All this work allows norteño investors to avoid facing harder decisions about where they will live and who they have become, as the building process sublimates these concerns. But with building come new responsibilities and debts as norteños' roles expand from migrant to planner, builder, booster, activist, team leader, role model, executive, and boss, with uncertain implications for the future of the community. The conditions under which, and reasons why, migrants leave hometowns help to define remittance space. Remittance buildings provide a lens to understand remittances as a highly specific social, logistical, economic process with specific implications for the future of the built environment in rural Mexico and the urban United States.

Multisited and Multiscalar: From Rural Mexico to Urban USA

This book explores the contradictions and disjunctures involved in migrant efforts to be here and there at the same time by building here *through* there. As I traveled between different parts of Jalisco, California, and Illinois between 2007 and 2012, I came to see remitting as inherently spatial, geographic, and multiscalar. Two axes run through the organization of the book. The first is time: over time, remittance space has evolved from the private realm of the house to the public realm of the village. The other is scale: from individuals, to family, to emigrant communities, to government policy, to migrant civil society. By moving outward from remitting between families, to collective remitting between clubs and communities, to the government policies that structure collective remitting, my case studies extend from the micro decision to send money home to the macro processes that incrementally shape remittance space.

I use several indicators to identify the costs and consequences of the remittance landscape and the 3×1 landscape. These include the number of abandoned houses, types of remittance architecture projects, spatial arrangements of such projects, their geographic locations, the uses of remittance architecture, the roles of institutional actors in their production, and building styles. Together this evidence exposes the divergence between the remittance landscape as a utopian ideal and as a reality. Putting the production of the built environment under this particular kind of scrutiny challenges dominant narratives about the success of remittances as a means of poverty alleviation. I then "follow the money" back to sites in the urban United States where remittances are accrued and ideas about construction projects and migrant civil society are nurtured.

In chapter 1, I explore remittance house building and dwelling practices. I argue that remittance houses represent a particular lifestyle that is still largely unattainable for their owners and users. The rise of the remittance house increases intrafamilial dependencies based on uncertain remitting practices and is the basis of a *remittance development model* that formalizes and institutionalizes transnational building practices in rural Mexico. In chapter 2, I examine the Mexican government's intervention into remittance building practices through a spatial analysis of its 3×1 policy. I argue that the program's influence on emigrants and their communities in Mexico is antithetical to the program's stated mission. Despite its democratic and transparent nature, 3×1 creates a top-down institutional funnel that channels migrants' informal remittances to government projects that migrants initiate but do not fully control. Ultimately, the 3×1 program extends the logic of the remittance house: stretching communities across disparate geographies can result in material change at home. Yet as the unit of analysis shifts from family to community and an increasing number of people with disparate interests get involved, the complexities and consequences of long-distance building are amplified.

In chapters 3, 4, and 5 I explore paradigmatic sites of remittance construction in three emigrant villages of Jalisco. Chapter 3 examines the gendered nature of remittance space by showing how the construction of a remittance rodeo arena, built in Lagunillas by emigrants to house the Mexican rodeo, supports "ranchero masculinity" while emigration destabilizes gender roles and ratios and throws gendered expectations into flux. Chapter 4 argues that remittance building projects in villages' primary public space—the main plaza (or *jardín*) and surrounding buildings—challenge who constitutes the public and compromise the communal dynamic of public space. This is illustrated by the cultural center in San Juan de Amula, which introduces a new set of cultural norms to a small community by privatizing the once free, outdoor, and communal space of town fiestas and imposing formal regulations on a community organized around unwritten social codes. While the remittance rodeo reifies local traditions, the *casa de cultura* (cultural center) challenges local norms. Chapter 5 addresses migrant ambivalence in old age and the institutionalization of long-distance burial practices. Migrants live in the United States, or in Mexico, with persistent questions about "returning" to their hometowns. In anticipation of old age and death, migrants are building old age homes in Mexico. Examining emigrants' construction of an *asilo anciano* (old age home) in Los Guajes in preparation for their retirement in Mexico exposes the Mexican state's ambivalence regarding its responsibilities toward emigrants. I argue that long-distance building practices require an expanded notion of the public to include new administrative capacities and services that care for norteños now integral to the community but physically absent from it.

The final chapter travels north of the border to address the architecture of so-called migrant civil society in a premier migrant city. Chicago's Jalisco Federation migrant headquarters, known as Casa Jalisco (one out of several state-run migrant meeting halls in Chicago), is allegedly the only example of any building in the United States owned by a state or province (Jalisco) of another country. Unlike embassies and consulates, owned by federal governments, Casa Jalisco reveals the state's reach into American cities. The architecture and objectives of the Casa are directly linked to migrant activism and a migrant industry that spans international borders. These projects structure migrants' experiences of and in American cities and build remitting as a way of life into the fabric of places.

Remittance space is a shifting terrain where clear winners and losers are difficult to identify. It is hard to determine whether migrants are challenging hegemony or reinforcing it in a global age, whether they are undermining traditional hometown social norms or restoring them, and whether the changes associated with remittance space are positive, and if so, why. The remittance projects that migrants (and their hometown communities) have completed are immensely impressive given their circumstances, but the modicum of economic self-sufficiency that they achieve is at a cost that reveals the power of global capital to wreak havoc on rural communities.

1 The Remittance House

DREAM HOMES AT A DISTANCE

In the small town of Pegueros, in the region of Los Altos, Jalisco, Antonio Rodríguez built three new houses, each one an improvment on the last. The first incorporated several sculptural and ornamental features, including an inscription on the entryway lintel, beneath a miniature cupola. It reads (in English), "DEDICATED TO MY PARENTS." On this house situated across the street from his childhood home, the inscription addresses his parents each day when they leave their house to buy food or spend time in the plaza. While they will not see Antonio, who lives and works in Los Angeles, his homage remains. All three houses remain vacant or occupied by a villager who guards and maintains the property. Daily, these arrangements, and the houses themselves, demonstrate Antonio's gratitude to family and the pueblo in his absence.

Located on a rather drab street between two unadorned peso houses, this sculptural home is an exceptional example of what I call the *remittance house*. I use this term to refer to a house built with dollars earned by a Mexican migrant in the United States and sent—remitted—to Mexico for the construction of his or her dream house. More broadly, I use this term to emphasize remitting and migration as key components of contemporary long-distance building practices around the globe.[1] While such houses exhibit similarities, every remittance house is unique and embodies the specific circumstances of the migrant who finances and builds it. Some migrants and their families build informally, adding rooms as the need arises, while others use architectural plans to construct entirely new houses on their land. Understated facades may blend in with the surrounding buildings, or highly ornamental designs may announce a migrant's success abroad. In Mexico, dating back to at least the middle of the twentieth century, the remittance house has crystallized migrant narratives and desires amid shifting cultural milieus. As artifacts of complex relationships,

FIGURE 1.01. Ornamental, hand-carved cantera stone (soft limestone quarried locally) frames the entry of Antonio Rodríguez's remittance house in Pegueros, Jalisco. An inscription above the doorway reads, "DEDICATED TO MY PARENTS." Photograph by author.

these houses are also embedded in the macro processes of globalization and transnational migration.

For at least a century, American immigrants' remittances have dramatically affected the vernacular rural landscapes of their hometowns. As early as 1913, the *New York Times* observed that Italian immigrant laborers "go back when they have accumulated American money, buy property and restore it," with the result that "in squalid villages stand new, clean houses" built by "Italians who have come back from America."[2] Similarly, the Chinese built remittance houses in the late nineteenth century for family members who remained in

China. Today, Turkish migrants in Germany, Portuguese migrants in France, and Central American migrants in the United States use hard-earned wages to build new houses in their hometowns.[3]

The current scale of remitting and the continuous movement of migrants between Mexico and the United States are unprecedented. This fast-growing sector of the economy is spearheading home building for migrants and their families throughout Mexico.[4] However, the consequences of imagining, building, and living in these homes for local communities, family life, and local construction practices and markets have received scant attention.[5]

This chapter explores how the forms of remittance houses not only embed social meanings but also structure social life and relations between individuals, genders, classes, and groups and establish categories or descriptions fundamental to society.[6] Houses—a critical space of migration—reflect and reproduce the social condition of migrants. I examine the meanings and implications of remittance houses through geographically and historically contextualized ethnographies of migrants and their families. Because remittance projects are often informal—paid for in cash without contracts or documentation—I rely on narrative accounts of migrants and migrant families as a primary source for understanding how they spend remittances, the motives that drive them, and the unique history of individual building projects. Architectural analysis of these houses defines the remittance house as a unit of analysis for larger social, political, and architectural discourses about migration and global building practices in rural places. Remittance houses are emblems of the rising social status of once impoverished rural farmers. Yet the houses and the specific forms they take also have unintended consequences that many migrants did not anticipate when building them. For example, the increased symbolic value of the house frequently corresponds to a diminished functional or use value, as migrants living in the United States are unable to occupy them. Similarly, architectural styles and spaces suggest lifestyles that remain unattainable for most. The remittance house can be read both architecturally and allegorically—it is both a house form and a crystallization of the inequities that underpin migrants' lives.

The spaces of the remittance house are also indicators of a profound transformation in rural Mexican society.[7] Perhaps the single

FIGURE 1.02. Unfinished remittance house, San Miguel Hidalgo, Jalisco. Photograph by author.

most striking quality of remittance construction is the social distance embedded in its form. Scholars of the built environment can contribute to the study of how migration is transforming rural Mexican society by analyzing changes in spatial form at both migrants' places of origin and their point of arrival.[8] Social relations stretched across geographies and exacerbated by distance increasingly define local places. The price of improving the domestic dwelling is abandoning it, and investments in the community can end up producing new social and spatial divisions within it. Absence is a necessary precondition for migrants to realize their dream house.

The Village in Historical Context

Jalisco, Mexico, is located about fifteen hundred miles south of the US-Mexico border along the Pacific Coast. It is one of the Mexican states with the highest rates of emigration.[9] Migration to the United States from rural Jalisco dates back to the late nineteenth century. Even before the railroad connected the northern region of Jalisco to California at the turn of the twentieth century, people were heading north on foot.

At the turn of the twentieth century, large-scale agricultural production based on unequal power relations between *hacendados* (owners of hacienda plantations) and indebted *campesinos* (farmers) established agricultural communities. Campesinos in pueblos surrounding the hacienda often planted and harvested land that belonged to the hacendados or powerful families, known as *caciques*. In remote localities, very small subsistence-farming communities, known as *ranchos*, were composed of one or two extended families. In such places, in part due to the neglect of the federal government, most rural inhabitants built modest houses with local materials.

FIGURE 1.03. Map of the state of Jalisco, showing the capital, Guadalajara, the municipalities of Autlán de Navarro and El Limón, and the pueblo San Miguel de Hidalgo. All three communities have long histories of migration to the United States. Drawn by Chesney Floyd.

FIGURE 1.04. A modestly scaled remittance house breaks the continuous mud-brick wall of two adjacent houses that defines the street in Mexican pueblos. The gated entry patio introduces the layered, formal threshold typical in the United States to the Mexican streetscape. Photograph by author.

To study the remittance house I focus on San Miguel Hidalgo, a pueblo in the south of Jalisco established before the Spanish viceregal period. San Miguel's range of building types (from adobe brick huts to lavish remittance houses), its location in a region of Jalisco that has a high emigration rate, and its proximity to the other sites examined in this book contributed to my selection of the site. San Miguel, a pueblo of approximately five hundred inhabitants, was entirely (and remains partially) owned by two caciques. As with many pueblos in Jalisco, San Miguel's built environment reflects its migration history. The impact of emigration to the United States on the community dates to around 1960.[10] Various remittance houses—the types range from one-story cement-block houses to large, ornate mansions—share party walls with preremittance-era adobe brick houses, some of which are hundreds of years old. Although San Miguel is a unique case, it provides information about the remittance house that can be applied across disparate remittance landscapes.[11]

This study is limited to rural places and to individuals who cross the US-Mexico border and work in jobs that are not related to the illegal drug market. However, remittance houses are not only in rural places. New homes built in midsized and large cities need to be analyzed. So do remittance homes built by migrants who have not necessarily crossed international boundaries. Rural Mexicans who have migrated to Guadalajara sometimes build homes in their pueblos of origin that reflect urban Mexican architectural styles. And finally, remittance capital does not result only from economic migrants working legal and ordinary jobs; remittance capital is also increasingly linked to illicit jobs related to Mexico's narco-industry.[12] Narco-architecture is also funded by capital embedded in distant markets and activities and tied to the political economy of both countries. While remittance architecture is being built in both rural and urban localities, and while distant markets support the production of both migrant remittance homes and narco-architecture, I focus on migrant homes in rural locations where the built fabric was relatively consistent before migration and where remittances mark a radical change in what is possible.

Traditional House Forms in Rural Mexico

In rural Mexico, building an adobe house has traditionally been a communal activity performed by men. Until recently, the principal building material in rural Jalisco was adobe brick—a mixture of earth, *zacate* (grass), and horse manure. To make adobe brick, laborers worked in complementary ways: one worker's knowledge of where the *tierra buena* (good earth) was located was complemented by another worker's knowledge of brick-drying techniques. Also, the vulnerability of adobe construction to the elements—notably water, wind, and pests—required a homeowner to continuously tend to his house and to rely on his neighbors to keep it in good condition. These processes reinforced ties between individuals and the immediate environment and created an interdependent community.

While most men in the village were known as *albañiles* (ordinary house builders), some possessed special craft skills: one was able to build roofs and another to craft wooden doors. These specialized skills allowed neighbors to strengthen their standing in the community by extending their help to other families. Similarly, barter produced systems of mutual interdependence in which farm produce could be exchanged for labor and expertise—one farmer's honey would be traded for another's time." This pattern of exchange allowed a seemingly homogenous community to articulate important social distinctions.

Traditional dwellings in San Miguel also exhibit a close fit between domestic space and an agrarian way of life. Typical houses consist of a courtyard (or a large enclosed yard) surrounded by inward-facing living quarters and an interior porch connecting private rooms with the communal space of the courtyard. The courtyard, a multifunctional space, is by far the most frequently used area in the house. In the courtyard a large outdoor *comal*, or wood-burning oven for stewing meat and making bread, a well, and a tub for washing clothes are situated among fruit trees and vegetable gardens. Corrals and stables for livestock, and sheds for tools to make honey or adobe bricks, often constitute an enclosure along one side of the yard. When taken together, these spaces of production allowed families to maintain a level of self-sufficiency.

The exterior wall that encloses the courtyard house also defines the edge of the street. This front wall is fully attached and continuous with neighboring structures, forming an uninterrupted facade. The wall supports a traditional roof known as *dos aguas* (two waters) covered with clay tile, with a ridge that parallels the street and extends seamlessly from one house to the next. The wall and roof create a continuous fabric that separates public from private space.[13]

Traditionally, people build and enlarge adobe homes in an incremental fashion. The Rodríguez house, built around 1930, exemplifies this incremental, informal approach to the construction of domestic space. Originally a one-room dwelling, the enclosed space consisted of a communal sleeping area attached to a large unfenced yard. Adults slept on the dirt floor, while wooden boards that rested on the wooden roof beams created a tiny (and dangerous) atticlike space for their seven children to sleep next to piles of corn. During the dry months their five boys slept outside. About twenty years later the family added two additional rooms to provide separate sleeping quarters for boys and girls. Shortly thereafter they extended and enclosed the long veranda or patio on the courtyard side of the rooms, which allowed them to put interior furniture outside, where they spent most of their time. The patio faced the enclosed yard, where the corral and stables for pigs and goats, the well, an outdoor kitchen and oven, and fruit trees orchestrated daily life (fig. 1.06).[14] The construction of the Rodríguez house paralleled the evolution of the family's social structure.

The Rodríguezes did not (and could not afford to) build for an

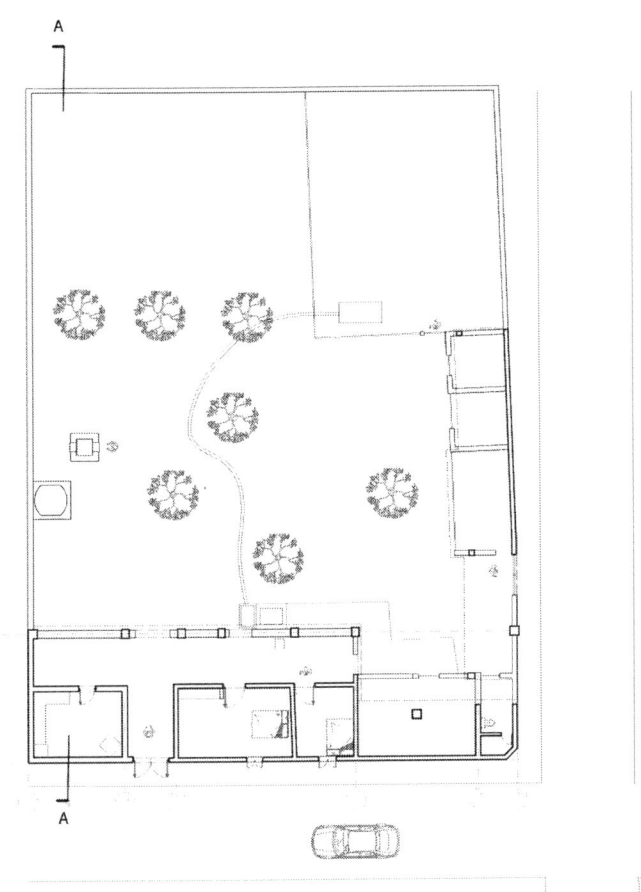

FIGURE 1.05. Plan and cross-section of the Rodríguez house, a typical courtyard house in San Miguel. Remittances funded incremental additions to the original one-room house, built in the 1930s. Drawn by Job Daniel Robles Robles.

FIGURE 1.06. The courtyard of the Rodríguez house contains the functional elements of an agrarian homestead: a well, a *comal* for baking, laundry lines, fruit trees, stables, a corral for pigs and goats, and a chicken coop. Photograph by author.

imagined future. When many children were born, they added rooms to house them. When the livestock overtook the yard, they added spaces to contain the animals. After a particularly profitable summer harvest, they enclosed the patio to shelter the family from the rain. Farmers did not have the luxury of building at one time houses that met all of their needs, in part because building required resources contingent on external factors: rainfall, seed quality, prices for farm products, the farmer's health, disposable cash, the cacique's demands, and limited time to make bricks and build. These logistical constraints dovetailed with religious beliefs. The colloquial saying "If you plan for tomorrow, God will damn you" was (and is) professed by devout Catholics who left "planning" in God's hands. The lack of architectural plans, the continuous and open-ended approach to building, and the contingent nature of opportunities contributed to an environment in which a set of buildings, or in this case "the home," was seen as something changing over time rather than as a finished product.

Available materials, shared facade elements, and a desire for uniformity have lent traditional Mexican pueblos a marked continuity and homogeneity of appearance. Locals wanted adobe brick made from the same earth. The exterior wall and the roof, made of a fired adobe tile known as *teja*, connected the disparate homes visually and materially, creating a uniform aesthetic. Individual houses resembled one another.

Since the 1930s, village life has been increasingly disrupted by a series of factors affecting Jalisco's countryside. Critical droughts in the 1930s and the violence of the Cristero War (1926–29), which pitted the federal government against the Catholic Church, ravaged small towns. The Bracero Program (1942–64), under which Mexican farmers were hired to work in US fields, and the geographic isolation of pueblos from the new highways built in the 1940s and 1950s, propelled hungry and desperate men north.[15] These environmental, political, and social upheavals affected building practices.

Waves of successive migration during the twentieth century meant that fewer men and women were available to erect buildings and till the land. As soon as they were able, men who migrated north sent dollars as a substitute for their labor on the land. The flow of men shuttling back and forth between Jalisco and the United States produced a parallel, opposite flow of dollars sent home to support families.

By the 1970s and 1980s a noticeable trend in new home construction, linked to remittances, emerged in southern Jalisco. In 2006 alone, Jalisco received $2 billion from men and women who are now identified proudly in Mexico as *paisanos* (countrymen). They are no longer called *migrantes* or *pochos*—terms historically used to characterize people as being willing to abandon their land, traitors to their home country.[16] Although no one knows exactly how much of the remittance money is used on home building, the influx of dollars has resulted in a building boom across rural Jalisco.[17]

Since the early 1980s, local infusions of capital have changed the way that campesinos conceive of the building process. Now, rather than merely providing much-needed shelter at a minimum cost, building can involve changes that make families more comfortable or beautify their houses. Migrants also build for retirement, to define themselves as successful to their family and community, or to express themselves. In this region, very seldom do migrants view new homes as economic investments. A lack of potential buyers and the possible

FIGURE 1.07. After building several remittance houses in the 1980s and 1990s, don Miguel now lives year-round on the rent he collects from one (right). His neighbor owns a gardening business in California and leaves his remittance house (left) vacant most of the year. Photograph by author.

damages to property and goods that result from renting discourages owners from selling and renting remittance houses.

Disposable income—the building capital available to a migrant family—limits the extent and quality of construction in a project. Small capital flows may result in a decision to undertake small-scale remodels, such as simply replacing old windows with new ones. More income may result in more substantial building projects: demolishing an old adobe house to build a dream home or building on newly purchased land. In either case, migrants want to build rather than buy a house, and they want to change building materials and forms as well. Old materials—adobe, zacate, and wood—are adandoned in favor of more permanent industrial materials: fired brick, steel, aluminum, cement, and glass. The migrants draw design motifs from a wide spectrum of personal experiences to create unique homes.

Motifs in Remittance Construction in Rural Mexico

A migrant's decision to fully or partially detach his or her remittance house from continuous exterior walls and rooflines is the most immediately apparent and defining spatial change produced by remittance houses. To build modern houses, which may have multiple stories, two-car garages, high ceilings, and suburban US floor plans, migrants must tear down old adobe houses, break from the continuous fabric of the traditional dwelling, and start anew. This decision distinguishes migrant houses from their surroundings. Detached from neighboring houses, the new house will nearly always have an articulated facade painted in bright colors, taking on unusual geometries, either literally or decoratively, and intensified with an eclectic mix of ornamental column capitals, trims, and engrained patterns. Classical, Renaissance, or colonial styles and contemporary elements combine with traditional Mexican construction techniques, craftsmanship, and colors to produce highly varied results. Purple, yellow, or fuchsia houses are complemented by turrets, water fountains, or decorative wooden crossbeams made out of concrete; a single facade may employ details that reference American, Greek, Gothic, Tudor, or neoclassical architectural styles. However, sensing that the four-sided freestanding house is not a part of local conceptions of space, the owners of a new remittance house tend to either fully attach it to the neighbors' party wall at the side-lot lines (but not the roofline) or leave its sides unpainted, windowless, and unadorned. Additionally, some lot sizes are not large enough to accommodate a freestanding house. Often a remittance house selectively references elements of a US suburban roofline. Ornamental parapets in the shape of hipped roofs conceal flat roofs, or these forms are applied directly to the facade.

The second major difference between remittance houses and traditional dwellings is the absence of a central courtyard. The focus of the house shifts from the communal productive spaces of the all-purpose yard to the individual programmatic spaces in the interior of the house. It is possible to abandon the courtyard, where family members once spent all their time, in favor of the individual rooms of the modern home because many intergenerational migrant families no longer live together. Instead, grandparents often remain in their adobe houses close to remittance houses built by absent sons and daughters.

Amenities and new facilities often update the vernacular dwelling or equip the modern home. Modern kitchens known as *cocinas integrales* (signifying built-in kitchen cabinets and modern appliances integrated into custom countertops), garage doors, washers and dryers, televisions, and bathroom sinks are meant to ease daily chores.

FIGURE 1.08. A peso house (left) and remittance house (right). Innovations imported from the suburban United States and adapted to the pueblo vernacular include the carport and patio. The iron fence and gate and the brightly painted facade are typical throughout urban Mexico. Photograph by author.

FIGURE 1.09. The unfinished property-line wall contrasts with the colorful facade of this remittance house built by a family living in Texas. The eclectic facades of remittance houses "flatten" the stylistic elements of US detached suburban houses, appropriating ornamental elements and motifs in a fully attached masonry built fabric. This facade references wooden siding using stucco and concrete. Photograph by author.

FIGURE 1.10. In addition to a garage and a cantilevered second floor, this unusual remittance house incorporates decorative stone window frames that reference the geometry of the dormer windows common in wood-frame gable roofs in the United States. Photograph by author.

Cooking on a gas stove replaces cooking on the comal, and a washing machine replaces extended periods of washing by hand in the yard. Moving the kitchen inside allows for open floor plans and changes the gendered social interactions that once accompanied cooking either outside or in a separate room. The space for informal conversation between women in the yard, or the privacy and female-dominated space of enclosed kitchens, is eliminated in houses that feature a modern kitchen connected to a TV room where husbands or children may be lounging.[18]

Externally, remittance houses import the trappings of suburban domesticity in the United States. According to Hugo Galindo, an engineer who works in San Miguel, "Those who can afford a California-style house get one."[19] Many migrants (and even locals who have never left home) want a front lawn, a pitched roof, a two-car garage, a doorbell, and a mailbox. However, home building and designing in the United States are specific to an American national history of building materials, technologies, construction processes, and an American way of life—all embedded in architectural elements. In Mexico, these architectural elements have a symbolic value that overrides the difficulties of building, living in, and maintaining the houses. For example, some houses have bathrooms that look modern but have no running water; in other cases, families tend a front lawn by pouring buckets of water on it.

In suburban homes in the United States, front lawns are display pieces for passing drivers and pedestrians and can be used recreationally.[20] In rural Jalisco, remote roads have little to no traffic, and grass is proudly maintained for few to see. Furthermore, the lawn ends up replacing the all-purpose backyard rather than being an addition to it, since the house is moved to the back of the lot, displacing vegetable beds and animal pens.

The mailbox is purely symbolic in most rural villages, which do not receive mail from the *cabecera* (head municipality), do not have mail carriers, and are not equipped with post office boxes. Norteños who add mailboxes to their homes are either preparing for a postal future or simply referring to a system that exists in the United States.

Where the mailbox plays a representational role, the addition of the doorbell has a more integrated, functional impact on the space of the home. It also changes the house's relationship to the social fabric of the neighborhood. In San Miguel and several other pueblos around Jalisco, one enters an adobe house through a heavy wooden front door or through the courtyard. The front door is built with a small half-window. Neighbors go up to the window, which is often left open, and call out for the owner of the house. The courtyard and vernacular door allow for casual interactions; they create thresholds between domestic interiors and exteriors that allow conversations without requiring homeowners to invite passersby inside the house.

The doorbell formalizes relationships between neighbors. Houses with doorbells often have windowless wooden doors that must be purposefully opened to see who is calling. The ringing of the doorbell completes the passage across multiple layers of the threshold—gates, lawns, entry porches—that together create spatial barriers for the passerby. Some neighbors are so put off by the doorbell that they refuse to ring it, and some homeowners refrain from answering a ring when they do not know who is calling. The doorbell consequently creates a remittance space that impedes the informal *grito* or street call.

The detached house, the elimination of the courtyard, and the addition of new amenities, facilities, and trappings of US domesticity are intended to update traditional vernacular homes and break with the construction methods of the past. New homes built in this idiom are not necessarily built by migrants. Some locals who have never left Mexico, the lucky few who can afford it, are building in either an American style, the *estilo del norteño* (style of the one who goes north), or a kind of rural contemporary style. They are influenced by remittance houses going up around them, by the urban housing stock they may know from visits to Guadalajara, Jalisco's capital city, and by images they see on television and in magazines. The ubiquity of the remittance house has contributed to a stylistic feedback loop between norteños and their rural counterparts. Dwellers in the remittance landscape (in select high-migration communities in the countryside) are increasingly influenced by other distant places even if they have not traveled to them. In this sense, migration and remitting are a way of life for all inhabitants of the pueblo, whether they individually cross borders or not.

The Remittance Construction Industry

Remittance architecture transforms local economies not only by infusing capital into rural areas but also by fundamentally changing the dynamics of the local economy. The expansion of certain sectors of the construction market coupled with new demands from norteños brings foreign goods into local businesses. Global companies become part of rural localities, and government activity in the construction sector increases. New entrepreneurs in rural construction markets are formalizing informal industries that are now larger in scale and more vulnerable to external market forces.

The remittance economy directly affects the local construction economy through the rapidly increasing demand for fired brick, the main building material used in new construction. The cabeceras used fired brick in the early twentieth century for houses and public buildings. Villages of campesinos did not use this material until the 1950s and 1960s, and even then only a few residents did. In the 1950s, Tonio Ortiz, one of the first *braceros* to return to San Miguel, built the town's first remittance house of fired brick.[21] Ortiz did not alter the

FIGURE 1.11. Tonio Ortiz, San Miguel's first bracero to return and build a house with dollars, stands in his entryway next to his *moto* (an ATV purchased with dollars). He drives the ATV, which replaced his horse, to and from his fields each day. Photograph by author.

basic spaces of the adobe house—he built a two-room house about five yards in front of his adobe house. When he was able to save enough money, he knocked his adobe house down and built an exact replica of it in fired brick on the same lot. Fired brick is preferred to adobe because it requires less maintenance, lasts longer, and carries a symbolic value due to its association with the wealthy.

Early fired bricks mimicked adobe bricks in size—both of them being larger than fired bricks used in the United States. Adobe bricks typically measured approximately 100 centimeters long by 70 centimeters deep by 10 centimeters high. These broad, stout proportions were necessary to bear the weight of the wall. By the 1950s, fired bricks, known as *listones*, were 40 by 20 by 6 centimeters. According to Gustavo Chávez, a local albañil in his eighties, *listón* brick lasts longer than the fired brick made today. "In the past they made brick like you make good bread. They beat it and beat it until it was soft powder. Now they make the brick to break."[22] The substantial listón brick, though smaller than adobe, still functioned as a load-bearing wall component.

The most popular brick used in contemporary modern rural houses, a facing brick that covers structures of steel and concrete, is much smaller than listón. For the same amount of earth and clay used to make one listón brick, manufacturers now produce three *tabique* bricks, which measure 14 by 28 by 6 centimeters and cost about ten cents apiece. According to Rodolfo Sahagún Morales, the largest brick manufacturer in Autlán, a town that supplies San Miguel, "The smaller brick economizes on the use of the clay. For the same amount of good clay you get more brick, and you can build with less brick because of steel reinforcement."[23] Thinner, narrower bricks and slimmer walls appear to benefit everybody—locals, who prefer to buy cheaper bricks, and manufacturers, who can produce more of them. However, locals need to buy more of them, and the value of brick has declined. Furthermore, a new dependency is created on external markets that supply steel and rebar used to reinforce concrete columns and beams. And finally, fired brick houses perform poorly from the standpoint of interior comfort. Whereas adobe brick "breathes," fired brick does not, and to avoid trapping excessive moisture, house designs must account for more ventilation than many traditional homes.

Despite an increase in brick production, old technologies still undergird their production. Rodolfo Sahagún Morales estimates that there has been a 60 to 70 percent increase in *ladrilleros*, or brickmakers, in the last twenty years. In the town of Autlán, brick businesses now support six hundred families. However, laborers sometimes work thirty-hour shifts, watching big earthen ovens heat handmade brick, using old rubber tires for fuel. The ladrilleros—both men and young boys—work in full sun, hunch over as they mix two distinct types of clay and pour them into molds, and breathe noxious fumes emitted by the burning tires. Thus remittance construction supports local people through brick manufacturing, but under hazardous conditions.

Remittance building has also contributed to the expansion of other

FIGURE 1.12. Laborers make bricks by hand, with no shelter from the sun, at the largest brickyard in Autlán de Navarro. Photograph by author.

local craft trades for the production of goods that complement the lavish new aesthetic of the norteños. Locally made custom doors and windows with wrought-iron ornamentation are still preferred to pre-fabricated windows and doors. However, local craftsmen are profes-sionalized and increasingly expensive. It takes an ironworker one day to make a single window that he can sell for five thousand pesos, or roughly five hundred dollars. Ironically, local craftsmen advertise their ability to custom-make doors and windows that appear to be standardized or modern yet are unique pieces that fit unusual open-ings or meet other requests. In this way, the remittance construction industry both supports and shapes local craftsmanship and regionally specific design.[24]

Finally, the numbers and importance of professional albañiles have increased. Before the rise of the remittance economy, most men in the village were albañiles and participated in construction.[25] Now alba-ñiles are professionalized and organized hierarchically from a *peón* to a *maestro de obra*, with four echelons in between. The albañiles are no longer paid in informal exchanges with their neighbors but with pesos. While wages have increased, so have the costs of the materials that wages must buy. Thirty years ago an albañil made thirty pesos a day, which was enough to buy eight sacks of cement. Today one worker makes two hundred pesos, which will buy only one and a half sacks of cement. Albañiles, newly employed by norteños to build extravagant remittance houses, are pushed to the edge—and sometimes past the edge—of their knowledge as they are commissioned to erect structures that they have little or no experience of. Awkward, ill-considered, or nonfunctional spaces are the evidence of this: bedrooms open directly onto the street, second stories are built with doors that open to the sky, rooms intended to be rectangular end up trapezoidal, or kitchen sinks sunk deep into wide countertops force women to bend at the waist to reach for dirty dishes.

Because of the prevalence of mistakes in the designs of remittance houses, norteños are starting to hire architects and engineers and introduce them into the building process, a development that produces tensions and competition with the albañiles who have traditionally played the professional's role. The engineer Hugo Galindo, who was trained at the University of Guadalajara, uses digital catalogs that contain hundreds of photographs of house facades, rear profiles, professional plans, elevation drawings, and even videos to design norteños' houses.[26] The houses in the catalogs were produced in the United States. However, albañiles (who cannot read architectural plans and want to retain their place in the construction process) argue that the architects and engineers are at a disadvantage: they probably have not emigrated to the United States to work and thus do not know the US construction industry firsthand. The argument goes that an albañil who has migrated to the United States and worked in the construction industry is well positioned to know what norteños want.

However, both architects and albañiles—even if they have worked in construction in the United States—are faced with the same major challenge. Nearly all homes in rural Mexico are built with concrete masonry block and fired brick. But most of the designs and new housing types that migrants are imitating north of the border are stick frame construction. As form is divorced from material construction, remittance houses can feel out of proportion, heavy, and monolithic. José López, owner of a business in El Grullo that supplies construction materials to San Miguel, told me, "The houses in the US fall

FIGURE 1.13. An *albañil*, holding a photograph of the suburban US house that a norteño asked him to copy, stands in front of the house (background) under construction in Los Guajes, Jalisco. The photo is of the rear of the original, which will be the front of the new house. Photograph by author.

apart; they are flimsy, built for thirty years. This house," he said, while knocking on its brick and concrete wall, "is forever."[27] López has attempted to bring sheetrock and plywood to rural constituents, but locals do not want wooden houses and criticize the way that buildings are made in the United States. Norteños use photographs of houses that they have taken in the United States or seen in magazines, or point toward other examples in nearby pueblos, in order to replicate the image of the American home without importing its construction materials or methods. In Los Guajes, a norteño gave a local albañil several photographs of a house he wanted replicated. The photographs document a typical ranch-style facade with a monumental poolside rear entrance. According to the albañil, his client told him that the poolside entrance was the front of the house, and in Los Guajes it is the "rear" of the house that faces the street. Beyond a mere aesthetic reorientation, flipping the orientation of the architectural plan influences the internal circulation, layout, and logic of the house, which is wedded to its facade.

Aside from needing more bricks and specialized builders, norteños want items that they have seen or lived among in the United States. These items are not manufactured locally and must be brought to rural Mexico in the back of a truck or imported from foreign manufacturers. This demand has created a niche market for foreign goods. For example, the automatic garage door, imported from the United States and paid for in dollars, was introduced to El Grullo in 1995. Some local nonmigrants also desire foreign goods. A teenager from a small town north of San Miguel wanted hardwood flooring, which she had seen on television and in photographs of her cousins' houses in the United States. Relatives in Los Angeles bought hardwood flooring at Home Depot and drove it fifteen hundred miles in the back of a truck to her house in Jalisco. The symbolic value of the hardwood floor exceeded the time, money, and energy spent getting it to her. It essentially allowed a young woman "stuck" in a pueblo to participate in remittance space and remain connected to her migrating family members.[28] Local businesses are now importing Italian floor tiles and modern bathroom fixtures for both migrant and nonmigrant families.

National and global companies see opportunity in this emerging remittance construction market. Construrama, a branch of Cemex, Mexico's largest cement company, franchises local construction businesses. Cemex thus influences prices and competes with local vendors. Home Depot recently opened branches in Guadalajara, and Famsa, a Mexican furniture company, opened branches in the United States in 2000. Through services offered by these companies, migrants may buy a refrigerator in Texas for pickup in Guadalajara. Although residents of San Miguel would have to drive four hours to get to Guadalajara, this may become worthwhile if the prices there are much lower than at local retailers.

Such services work to formalize a once informal construction process. Recognizing the insecurity of transporting cash across borders in the back pockets of blue jeans (where it is easily and often stolen in airports or bus stations), Cemex allows migrants to open a "materials as capital" bank account. Migrants may deposit money in Cemex branches in the United States, and family members may then withdraw construction supplies from Cemex franchises in Mexico. This transaction mimics remittance wire transaction services spearheaded by Western Union; it allows migrants to control how their money is spent and to avoid wire transaction fees, and it allows companies to control where a family spends its money in Mexico. Famsa offers a similar service for furniture.

In 2002 Cemex took this logic further by opening Construmex, which provided modern house plans for migrants.[29] By 2005 Construmex had sixteen branches throughout American cities. Standard plans with names such as Maya and Anahuac, referring to an indigenous past that affirmed paisanos' rural affiliations, showcased modern single-family concrete homes in the style of US suburban homes. As a Construmex employee noted, "You can build a house where you could not tell the difference between a house here and one there. There is no difference between how a house looks in the United States or in Mexico through our services."[30] This experimental enterprise ultimately failed, and many Construmex offices have closed due to the logistical difficulties of controlling the building processes from a distance. Despite the failure of Construmex's overall business plan, architects are still available for individual consultations, and independent architects have begun offering similar services to migrants from "storefront" architecture offices in cities like Los Angeles.[31]

In turn, the Mexican government has become involved in the remittance house and the construction industry. Vivienda, a program that President Vicente Fox initiated during his administration, is geared toward assisting paisanos in the United States who want to build homes in Mexico. Federal and local governments pool funds to subsidize either acquiring a house or remodeling one that is deteriorating.[32] This program allows multiple levels of government to create alliances with manufacturers (part of the government's portion of the cost is paid in materials and labor) and gives it some control over how remittances are spent. According to the program documents, it helps "populations with the scarcest resources" who are forced to resort to

FIGURE 1.14. In this advertisement for Cemex's Construmex program, the tagline printed on red labeling tape translates, "Here they advise me and I order my materials, there my people build our house."

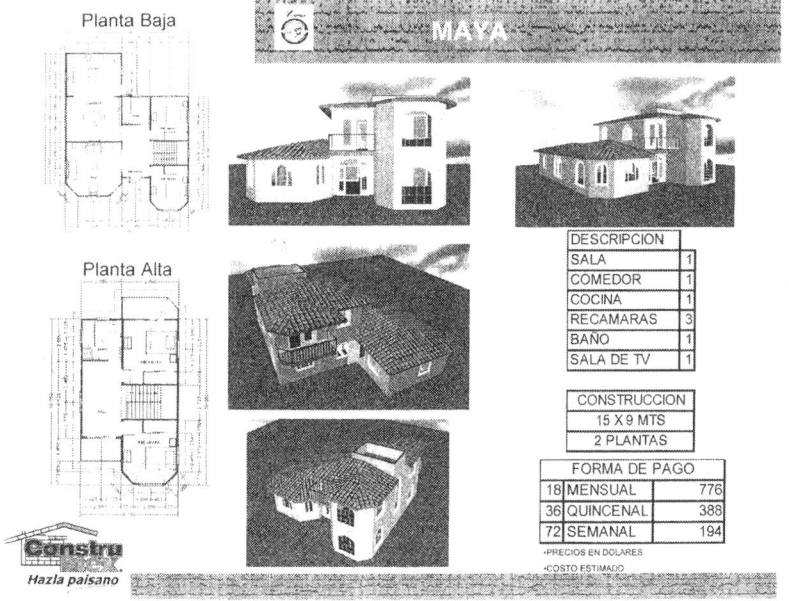

FIGURE 1.15. Plans, rendering views, and payment schedules for Construmex's off-the-shelf Maya house design.

"informal squatting" in "substandard housing." In Mexico, where almost half the country lives in poverty and almost 15 percent in extreme poverty, the government has an incentive to help the poor pay for what could otherwise be construed as the government's responsibility.[33]

In light of these changing conditions, local municipal governments are also changing their land policies. Land in San Miguel is starting to appreciate in response to the quality of houses being built there. This once sleepy subsistence-farming community is becoming a *pueblo de descanso*, or retirement community, for returning migrants and their parents. To collect taxes, the municipal government recently pressured locals to register their houses; 65 percent of the houses are currently registered in the *municipio*.[34]

The expansion of the local construction industry and the increasing competition between multinational companies and local markets are not unique to rural Jalisco—they are defining factors of global interconnectedness. However, the region's dependence on remittances renders it particularly vulnerable not only to global market shifts but also to migration trends and individual remitters' whims. Ignacio Robles Pelayo, owner of a local business franchised by Cemex, admits, "Without migration I don't know how we would survive. We sell the most cement and bricks and windows in December when they [the norteños] all come home for Christmas and make improvements to their houses."[35]

Despite these developments in the local construction industry, shoddily constructed buildings are evidence of the difficulties associated with commissioning a project from the United States. Salvador Uribe, a young man from southern Mexico, worked for several years in the United States as a house painter to finance his own remittance house. Uribe did not visit his pueblo while the house was under construction because he did not have the proper immigration documents. When he learned that the house was finally finished, he made the journey south. Recalling his arrival home, Uribe exclaimed with disgust: "They built me a piece of shit!"[36] The entrance opened directly onto a bedroom, the pipes did not have pressure, and the facade was unadorned cinder-block brick. The building was evidence of Uribe's limited engagement with the builders during the construction process and the difficulties of translating an aspirational architecture based on images and experiences of US homes to those accustomed to rural building methods. Rather than remodel the home or accept defeat, Uribe immediately began building a second home that, he hoped, would be an improvement on the first. The commencement of a second remittance house is evidence of another aspect of long-distance building: for migrants, hope for a better future must exist somewhere — and that place is often the next building project.

Experiencing the Remittance House

The spaces of the remittance house and the larger-scale changes in local construction industries and building traditions influence the daily lives of migrant families. Some families, for whom migration has been a way of life for several decades, have houses that demonstrate a wide spectrum of construction techniques and reflect local experimentation and innovation. In these families, individuals learn over time to better control the construction process. This learning curve can be explored through the building history of the Robles family of San Miguel.[37]

The migration history of the Robles family echoes the experience of many of the family's neighbors. Twelve Robles children grew up in a two-room adobe house with no running water or electricity, a house located in a remote rancho connected to San Miguel by eighteen kilometers of unpaved road. Even after the eventual move to San Miguel, the family could not escape severe poverty. In 1970 Raúl and Sergio, the two eldest sons, eighteen and seventeen years old respectively, illegally migrated to the United States to pick peaches, wash dishes, and muck out stables. Ultimately, all but one of the family's twelve children left for the North. They weathered deportations, dangerous border crossings, and humiliating work experiences. After eighteen years of repeated migrations between California and Jalisco, the children had saved enough money to build new houses in San Miguel.

Today the Robles family boasts six remittance houses built during the last twenty years; the houses line the main entrance of San Miguel. Since 1988, the Robles brothers (principally Sergio and Raúl) have spent nineteen years renovating their mother's house. When the brothers started this project, the house consisted of two old adobe rooms built at the turn of the last century, and a separate two-room

FIGURE 1.16. The *cocina integral* that the Robles brothers built (right) to replace the kitchen in their family home (left). The new kitchen has not been used, as their mother prefers her familiar workspace. Photographs by author.

peso-funded addition built by their father over the course of twenty years. The brothers tore down the old adobe kitchen and rebuilt it in fired brick. Next they added a second story to the father's addition. Then they added a new kitchen next to the old kitchen, equipped it with modern appliances, demolished the corrals, stables, and trees in the yard between the two units, and connected the two units with a large living room and a new roof. By 2007, they had preserved the form of the rest of the old adobe house but had rebuilt it using fired brick, added a modern bathroom, and built a two-car garage. The Robles brothers learned about remittance building through this extended process. By the fourth bathroom they knew whom to contract, what systems were needed to get running water, and how much the bathroom would cost.

Despite their increasing sophistication, the spaces are not used as intended. The mother for whom this eight-bedroom house was built uses her old kitchen and sleeps in her old bedroom. Sergio remarked, "We just finished her new bedroom and bathroom, which was really expensive. We brought state-of-the-art equipment, including safety rails for the bathroom wall so she doesn't fall when showering, but she won't use it."[38] Indeed, most spaces in the house are fully furnished but not used except for the living room, where Ms. Robles prominently displays photographs of her children, grandchildren, and great-grandchildren, most of whom live in the United States. During Christmas, her children and their growing families reunite in San

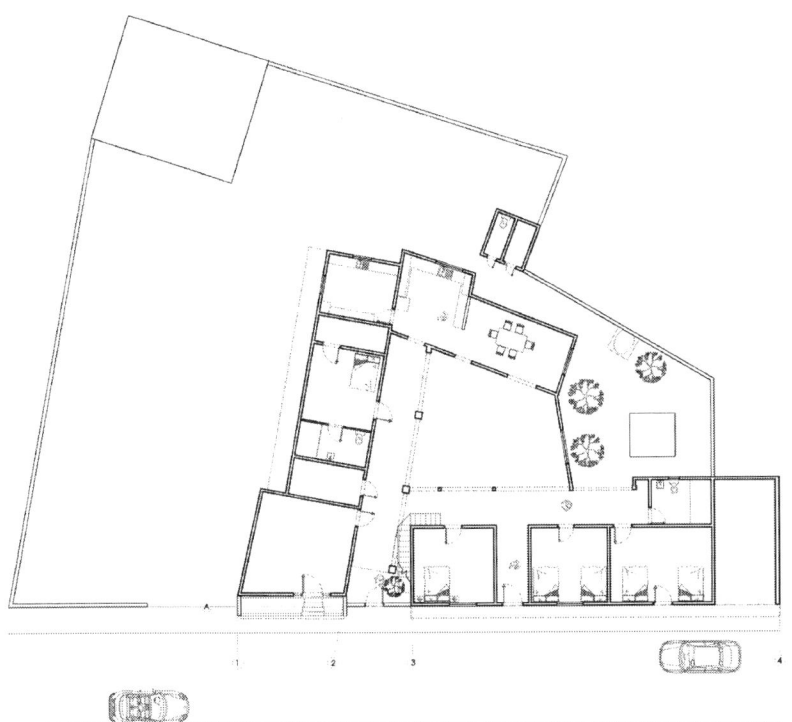

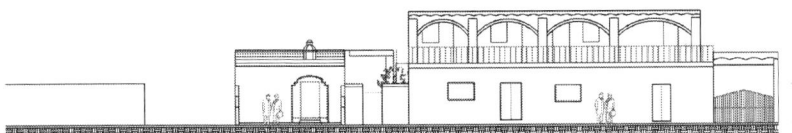

FIGURE 1.17. Plan and front elevation of the remittance house the Robles brothers built for their mother. The house includes a second kitchen, guest wing with multiple bedrooms, four bathrooms with modern plumbing, and a one-car garage (far right). The room on the far left facing the street is used by a Robles daughter as a beauty shop. She and her husband live full time in the pueblo and hope that this microbusiness will support their family. Drawn by Job Daniel Robles Robles.

FIGURE 1.18. Julián Robles's house was one of the first remittance houses built by the Robles brothers. The fenced front setback with a narrow yard planted with grass, patio that doubles as covered parking, and false roof suggesting a gable behind the parapet are common features of remittance houses. Photograph by author.

Miguel; even then there is little use for the mother's house because several relatives have built their own remittance houses.

In the early 1990s, while the mother's house was being remodeled, two other sons—Julián and Abel—built their own two-bedroom houses. With limited resources and little knowledge of construction, they built houses with typical US suburban elements: drive-in garages, narrow front lawns, and sloped roofs. As a result of improper construction and drainage, Abel's half-pitched roof holds standing water and his family fears it may collapse. Meanwhile, he and his family battle allergies exacerbated by mold growing on building materials soaked by water from above. For both brothers, the houses are not as they imagined they would be when they were saving money in California to build in Mexico. Julián built a home with a big living room, a dining room, two bedrooms, and a double garage for his imagined family. But unwed and childless, he does not spend much time at his new home. He sleeps in the bedroom and eats elsewhere—in the field or at his mother's house.

Both houses need major repairs that the brothers cannot afford because they no longer migrate between Mexico and California. Abel and Julián now earn pesos from farming. The average is about eight dollars a day, not enough to buy a single bag of cement. Since they lack the papers to return to the United States legally, going back there would involve danger and hardships. Rather than tilling their own fields, they would be risking their lives in the Sonoran and Chihua-huan deserts, living apart from their family, and working for a boss.

The two younger Robles brothers, Sergio and Raúl, benefited from their involvement in the construction of a remittance house for their mother, and from Abel's and Julián's mistakes in constructing their own houses. In the mid-1990s Sergio and Raúl began construction using architectural plans and architects. Sergio's extravagant home, the only freestanding house in town, is one of the most admired *casas de norteño* in the region. The automatic garage doors, driveway lined with palm trees, and symmetrical Doric columns replicate nearly exactly a house design from the mail-order catalog known as Home Design Services Inc. (a company located in Miami). Sergio originally chose the design because he liked a catalog photograph of it that bears the caption "Alluring Arches Attract Attention." However, the plan of his house departs from the model house type and thus reveals critical distinctions between lifestyles in suburbs in the United States and in rural Mexico. Sergio omitted the attic floor. "What would I use an attic

FIGURE 1.19. The "alluring arches" of the house in this photograph captured the attention of Sergio Robles, who attempted to build an exact replica of the house, down to the landscape plantings, rendering the form of the wood-frame original in brick and concrete. Photograph by author.

for?" he asked.[39] He also commissioned a room-size safe in the master bathroom. The thick walls keep all his valuables protected: he lives in the United States eleven months a year.

Raúl Robles also used an architect-designed plan for his remittance house. His plot, sandwiched between two other courtyard wall houses, was not wide enough to allow the house to directly face the street. To maintain the original design of the facade, he rotated the house 45 degrees, creating a triangular front yard and oddly shaped rooms.

Both brothers use ornamentation and detail to bring the experience of an American suburban home to rural Mexico. They both have a cheery "Welcome Home" doormat at the top of their front stairs as well as wood furniture that they carried across the border. The plantings in Sergio's front yard approximate those visible in the Home Design Services catalog illustration. He displays *Home Life* magazines in his house. Both brothers equipped their remittance houses with modern light switches, stereo systems, and large televisions. These objects create material and symbolic connections to US prosperity and provide fodder for local discourse about the details of modern house design as well as the luxuries of migration.

Although Sergio paid only $600 for his plan, his rough estimate of the cost of building the house was $250,000: "I am not sure how much I spent; I sent all the money to my brother and he bought everything."[40] His house cost more money than any other building in town, including the church. It is more than four times the cost of his two other brothers' more modest remittance houses. These differences illustrate the impact of specific migration experiences. Both Sergio and Raúl were able to build such extravagant houses because they are no longer menial laborers. They now own two successful carpentry businesses in the United States. Furthermore, because these brothers were granted citizenship through the 1986 amnesty program, they may travel safely from California to Jalisco to tend to their houses and visit their family members still living in San Miguel.[41]

Despite the apparent quality of the Robles brothers' houses, their success in a broader sense remains ambiguous. The brothers, who maintain houses in California and Jalisco, are confronted with the expectations of their US-born children, who want an American standard of living and a world of opportunity in both places. The brothers work eleven months a year to meet these demands while their beautiful homes in Jalisco stand empty. The choice is clear: living in a remittance house year-round would mean losing the ability to maintain it.

At the same time, the prices paid for such rewards have been real and high. Before obtaining citizenship in the 1986 amnesty program, Raúl was deported multiple times, losing all his money and belongings each time. During one illegal border crossing he almost lost the finger that he used for hours to prevent the trunk of a car from closing so that fresh air could come in. He washed plates in restaurants and did hard labor before he landed a job in the same carpentry factory as his brother Sergio. He endured all those trials and more before he could become the owner of a small carpentry business like his brother Sergio. His life, full of humiliating and dangerous circumstances, has been systematically invested in creating a remittance house. And though it probably reminds him of his struggles, the young and eager men and women of San Miguel who see it imagine success in America rather than hardship. Beautiful and harmonious representations often hide the arduous physical labor involved in the production of space.[42] For many youth in San Miguel, the remittance house reinforces the desire to cross the US-Mexico border, overriding the difficulties of crossing the border and the insecurity they will inevitably have to contend with in the United States.

The Remittance Development Model: Distance Built into Emigrant Communities

The ubiquitous brightly colored facades of remittance houses against the backdrop of Jalisco's farming communities provide evidence of the increasing dominance of migrants' remittances as drivers of change in rural Mexico. The Mexican government's reliance on entrepreneurial individuals as economic engines in rural areas constitutes the basis for what could be called a "remittance development model." In this model the state plays an increasingly marginal role in rural development, while migrants claim the mantle of civic benefactors with its attendant rewards, risks, and responsibilities. This relationship is formalized by federal programs like 3×1, which matches migrants' funding with municipal, state, and federal dollars for public and infrastructure projects.[43] While remittance houses are generally built informally with private funding, they are emblematic of broader shifts in rural Mexican society.

Remittance houses do more than signify a transition to a fundamentally different process of development, they also provide insight into the nature of the remittance development model. Where state-financed development is strategic and normative in its orientation, development driven by rural migrants is often tactical and based on personal aspirations. Migrants are reacting to local conditions, driven by necessity or ambition, or motivated by familial and civic pride. This orientation to the personal and local is evident in the form and appearance of remittance houses, which migrants distinguish by using the best available materials and by emulating the latest styles of US residences.

More important than the distinct types of development associated with remittances is the evident distance between the aspirations and the realities of migration and remitting. People who migrate to improve their lives must risk a dangerous crossing at the border, endure second-class citizenship in the United States, and live apart from their closest family members with no health care or police protection. Some undergo all these trials to build houses that are left unfinished, are completed but not functional or comfortable, are lived in by part of the family while the remainder is in the United States, or are completed but abandoned or not maintained. Families in Jalisco that manage emigrants' remittance investments may squander the money or use it for an emergency. Remittance flows stop when a migrant dies, loses his or her job, assumes more responsibility toward relatives in the United States, or becomes ill or incapacitated. Remittance flows also stop when a migrant moves back to Mexico. Scores of houses strewn across the landscape in rural Jalisco expose the discontinuity between the remittance house as imagined and the remittance house as built. Distance is built into the remittance house through its production.

Just as the distance between a migrant and his or her hometown is implicit in the remitting process, the government's reliance on migrants is correlated with a general lack of support for migrants and their families. Successful migration and remitting do not guarantee a happy or peaceful retirement for those who return. The Mexican fed-

FIGURE 1.20. According to locals, the structural columns of this apparently abandoned remittance house have awaited a roof for many years. Photograph by author.

eral government sporadically and unreliably provides meager assistance to the elderly through Desarrollo Integral de la Familia (DIF, the National Agency for Family Development). However, it does not provide retirement benefits or guarantee social security. As a result, some or all of the family members must stay in the United States to continue remitting—fundamentally redefining the nature of "home" by embedding persistent geographic distance into daily life even after the initial goals of remitting have been achieved.

The global financial crisis of 2007 to 2008 that began in the United States exposed the dangers of this model. Since 2006 (the peak of the US housing bubble) remittances to Mexico have declined. According to data from the National Survey of Household Income and Spending in Mexico, between 2006 and 2008 over 250,000 families that had previously received remittances from family members abroad saw those funds dry up. The Inter-American Development Bank reported that in 2007 a reduction in remittances left at least two million people without the financial help they had once received. Many families still receive remittances, but the amount is less than before and has slowed the rate of construction. The Mexican newspaper *La Jornada* reports: "Less money from migrants equals a decline in consumption in many regions of the country and affects the albañiles who build houses for the migrants." The reporter asks: "What happens when an albañil loses his work in the United States? Well, it is probable that four or five albañiles lose their work in Mexico. The drop in remittances, according to the experts, has affected overall the Mexicans who work in construction, a branch seriously affected by the economic crisis of our northern neighbors."[44]

Risks are not borne by migrants alone. Geographic distance and fragmentation affect people throughout rural Mexico. Decaying vacant houses, which produce voids in the social and spatial continuity of the street, are a liability for locals because thieves have learned that the houses are often full of new and expensive goods. Houses are also a burden for families who have sacrificed everything to achieve them but cannot afford to live in, maintain, or protect them, but do not want to abandon them completely. The spaces of these houses also change social norms and customs: the new settings tend to isolate migrant families behind yards and fences and create animosity in a community of people by disrupting their common history. Furthermore, the remittance house creates inequalities between those who emigrate and those who never leave Mexico. As the remittance process is increasingly institutionalized and formalized, these disjunctures and disparities intensify.

Currently, just after the turn of the twenty-first century, the remittance house is still the most prevalent type of built environment change implemented by migrants "from below" in rural Mexico. As simultaneously a pragmatic strategy to meet families' basic needs, a repository of hard-earned capital accumulation, and a symbolic site for self-expression, the remittance house influences the imagination and daily life of both migrants and nonmigrants. But vacant and abandoned remittance houses remind us that migrants' building projects do not turn out as intended. As migrants initiate larger projects with public implications, the remittance house provides a useful conceptual template for understanding the stakes, contradictions, and ultimate success or failures of public remittance building as a form of development from below.

2 Tres por Uno

THE SPATIAL LEGACY OF REMITTANCE POLICY

Today the Mexican landscape is undergoing a building boom on multiple scales. For decades, Mexican migrants located in the United States have spent hard-earned dollars on building both private homes and public projects in their hometowns in Mexico. What was at one time an informal process of remitting directly to one's family is now a process increasingly formalized by the Mexican government, corporations, and migrants themselves. The impact is vast—from how remittances are used to the spaces this money produces in rural places. This chapter provides an institutional context for the current moment of remittance space by examining the Mexican government's Tres por Uno (3×1) program. This program has played an important role in transitioning remittance building from individually conceived, privately funded, smaller-scale projects to larger communally produced and funded ones.

In the early 2000s, migrant-government collaborations were formalized through the creation of 3×1.[1] In this program, migrant remittances pooled and sent by hometown associations (HTAS) in the United States are quadrupled by federal, state, and municipal funds for regional development. Since the inception of the program, there has been an ongoing exchange between the voluntary actions of transborder migrants to improve their hometowns and Mexican government agencies' development agendas. In this way, informal remittance building and planning practices spearheaded by migrants have been formalized by the state. In turn, the state's formalization of the remittance economy has redefined the context for remitting and has created new incentives for migrants. While most migrants still remit directly to their families, since the early 2000s scores of new HTAS have formed in the United States. The new HTAS are closely involved in the development of their hometowns, defining the town's needs and

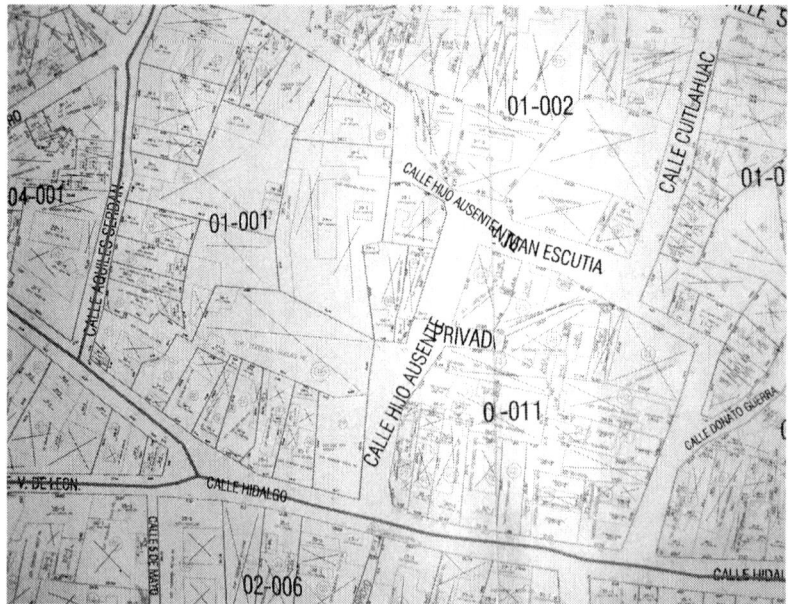

FIGURE 2.01. Street names recorded on the municipal parcel map of El Limón, Jalisco, demonstrate the importance of migration, and migrants, to the community; Calle Hijo Ausente (Absent Sons and Daughters Street) runs through the heart of town, intersecting Calle 5 de Mayo (commemorating Mexico's victory at the battle of Puebla), Calle Cuitláhuac (an Aztec ruler), and Calle Hidalgo (the priest who declared independence from Spain in 1810).

shaping its landscapes, while the Mexican government is increasingly invested in the organizational structures and daily lives of its emigrants in the United States.

At first, 3×1 appears to be a transparent mechanism that unlocks the potential of migrants to envision, fund, and carry out their own agenda. Closer inspection, however, reveals a dialectic between migrant and institutional power in which migrants participate in the ancillary programs and institutions established by the government to transform environments in a way consistent with existing power structures but increasingly funded by individuals and communities. In this sense, migrant participation in 3×1 constitutes a formal strategy of exporting labor (low cost due to lack of protections and rights for undocumented workers) in exchange for "US" investment in rural hometowns and the construction industry that builds the projects.

No other Mexican models of development, past or present, have re-lied explicitly on migrant remittances.[2] Federal program regulations structure 3×1 transparently as a democratic development policy that aids Mexico's poor migrants who want to better serve their home-town communities. And through its US consulates, the government collaborates with migrants to create powerful and effective migrant networks that can be used for future nationwide agendas. The 3×1 pro-gram is structured to avoid the clientelism endemic to Mexico, clien-telism associated especially with the Partido Revolucionario Institu-cional (PRI), the political party that governed Mexico for over seventy years until Vicente Fox (PAN) won the presidency in 2000. Histori-cally, politicians have used the promise of building projects as one of many strategies intended to secure patronage. Ten years into the pro-gram there is mounting evidence of the uneven results of 3×1; some migrants have realized projects that forge new pathways for, and meanings behind, building projects, while other migrants have had their projects fall prey to local politicking, corruption, and in-fighting.

Not long after its inception, scholars were quick to argue that the program allows the state to co-opt migrants' efforts to support their communities as a strategy to achieve rural development at low cost to the government. Migrant contributions came to represent a sort of subsidy for public works that is not required from better-off sectors of Mexican society.[3] Scholars and migrant activists also argue that de-spite its unique structure, the program is reproducing Mexico's en-trenched clientelistic systems.

The formalization of migrant organizations and their remitting practices affects what is built on the ground, which shapes daily life in rural Mexico. I argue that the formalization of remittance build-ing is linked with the Mexican government's social construction of *migrants as benefactors*: migrants whose apparently limitless gener-osity propels them to sacrifice their hard-earned dollars to improve the quality of life for people in their hometowns through public build-ing projects. I examine relationships between individual and collec-tive action, informal and formal processes, and grassroots activism and government programs, not just in opposition but also as defining a continuum of strategies in remittance development. These relation-ships directly influence and shape places and people's experiences of them.

This chapter builds on the notion of agency "from below"—a term used by globalization scholars to describe nonelite migrant engagement in grassroots initiatives that involve finding alternatives to low-wage dead-end jobs.[4] For many migrants, limited social, cultural, and economic capital does not keep them from contributing to remittance building. A select group of migrants serve on the boards of directors of the "federations," umbrella organizations that represent and unify various Mexican HTAS. These individuals act as brokers between migrants "from below" and state interests "from above."[5]

Migrant actors from below, transborder activists, state officials, and nonmigrants in emigrant villages are all implicated in a nascent remittance development model. The model is defined by a set of conditions linked to what I call *remitting as a way of life*—saving and sending dollars as an integral part of migrant and migrants' families' social lives and spatial orientations. Although this emergent model extends beyond and predates 3×1, the state's 3×1 program is attempting to harness migrant grassroots social action in its construction of a remittance-state model for community development. Today the model creates the potential for migrant activists to better their communities' standard of living—but at a cost. The use of migration as an engine for rural development, promoted by the state, formalizes migration—and the distances, ambivalences, and cultural change implicit to it—as a component of everyday life in the hometown.

A spatial analysis of the 3×1 program is necessary to understand its implications for the everyday life of migrants and their families in Mexico. Migration is an inherently spatial process due to the geographic distance and fragmentation it produces for migrant families and communities. As explained by Carolina Coria Rueda: "Because my husband and kids have migrated, I feel like I've migrated many times myself. Everything they tell me, everything I see on the news, it's like I've migrated too. But I've never actually gone. But I've gone. I've gone in my own fears and worries, asking God to take care of them without sleeping. I don't know who suffers more: those who cross the border or those who stay behind."[6] In this sense, the 3×1 program institutionalizes a development model that requires geographic distance (between remitters and their hometowns) and fragmentation (among the emigrant population in the United States) to function. These reproduced conditions of distance, fragmentation, and cognitive ambivalence in turn affect the decision making of remittance builders. What gets built? To what end? Moreover, while 3×1 channels money to infrastructure and building projects, it does not account for how the projects will affect place, community, and individual experience over the long term, especially with regard to the administration and maintenance of the project.

The particular idiosyncrasies of remittance construction also make evident the importance of structural conditions on the ground, which influence projects on many scales. Relationships of patronage and power between Mexican towns and their cabeceras (roughly equivalent to county seats), the geography of racial inequality in rural Mexico, the dominance of men's roles in shaping the built environment, and the social and economic history of regional migration patterns produce a spatial and geographic legacy that affects 3×1 projects and their outcomes.[7] These relationships complicate 3×1's goal to democratically address the poor and marginalized populations of Mexico as well as migrants' capacity to transform villages. Spatial analysis illuminates the consequences of normalizing remitting through its incorporation into state-sanctioned policy and formalized migrant networks.

The Scope and Scale of Remittance Development

In 2006, 570 US migrant social clubs were officially registered with the Mexican government's Instituto de los Mexicanos en el Exterior. Three years later that number had tripled to 1,454, and in 2012, 2,398 clubs spread throughout the globe were registered. It is estimated that several thousand informal HTAS exist as well.[8] By 2010, government spending on 3×1 had extended to twenty-eight out of thirty-two Mexican states (I include the Federal District in the 32).[9] By 2007, 3×1 had financed more than six thousand projects with an annual federal budget of an estimated $20 million.[10] In 2008 that amount had more than doubled to approximately $50 million.[11] All these figures have led the president of the Inter-American Development Bank to declare 3×1 a leading axis of economic and social development for rural populations in Mexico.[12]

However, the impact of 3×1 is small when put in the larger context of remitting and migration. In 2011, remittances to Mexico were estimated at $23 *billion*. Over one million households in Mexico benefit from remittances, and 92 percent of Mexican municipalities register migration. The government's federal contribution toward migrant-initiated development projects was thus equivalent to less than one-tenth of 1 percent of the total amount of migrant remittances sent in 2011. Also, 3×1's budget is only a small fraction of governmental programs aimed at social and economic development for Mexico's poor. The most entrenched and widespread program, Oportunidades, founded in 2002 but based on older policies, ostensibly pays families to keep their children in school and covers hospital visits, reaching five million people. Furthermore, whereas 3×1 requires remittances geared toward development to be funneled through HTAs, other countries with state-migrant development initiatives such as Morocco have created formal banks that allow individuals to invest remittances in development projects.[13]

The small proportion of federal contributions to 3×1 relative to overall remittances has caused observers to question the relevance of the program vis-à-vis the substantial political discourse surrounding it. Some migrant activists and scholars argue that 3×1 is little more than a political strategy to win the migrant vote in the United States.[14] Indeed, many Mexican politicians have gained political leverage through the visibility of this program on both sides of the border. However, spending on a policy is only one way to measure its impact. This policy is also about constructing a new *model* for building with remittances in which the state responds to migrants' informal activities on the ground and inserts itself into their building processes. Just as James Scott argues that European colonialism was dependent on mapping distant populations, the Mexican state is attempting to render migration and remittance flows legible so that it can increase its access to and control over migrant resources.[15] To do so, this model targets the building process itself, which is tied to local construction, trade, and the flooding of local markets with globalized products. Moreover, this model is being disseminated in other countries such as Haiti, El Salvador, Guatemala, and Brazil. Thus while the scale of the program is small, its impact on perception and ways of doing business in small towns is significant. Moreover, the tiny percentage of remittances captured by the 3×1 program in 2010 speaks to the program's immense economic potential for future years. Many government policymakers view remittances as an untapped resource.

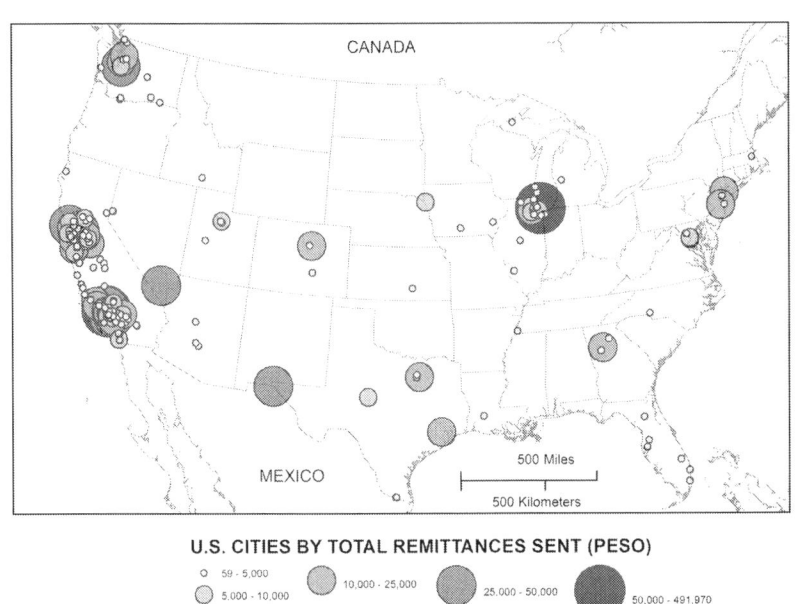

U.S. CITIES BY TOTAL REMITTANCES SENT (PESO)

○ 59 - 5,000   ◎ 10,000 - 25,000   ● 25,000 - 50,000
◐ 5,000 - 10,000   ● 50,000 - 491,970

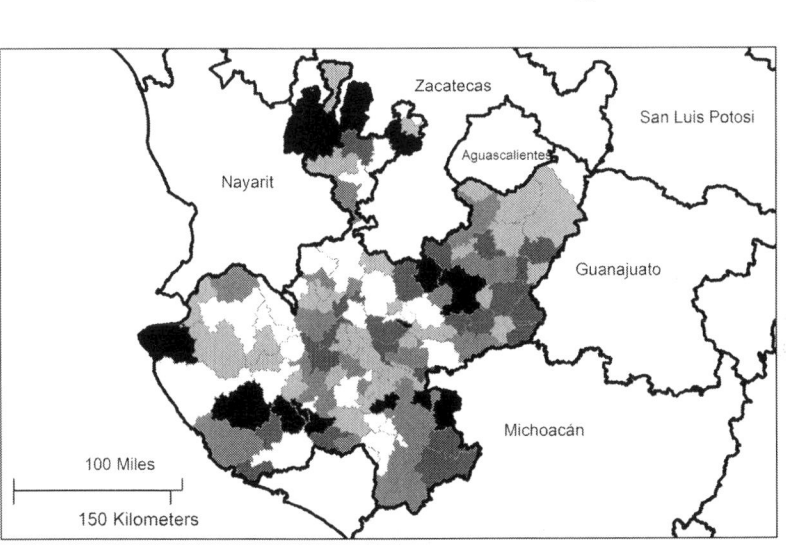

JALISCO MUNICIPALITIES BY TOTAL REMITTANCES RECEIVED (PESO)

☐ 1,200 - 10,000   ▨ 15,000 - 20,000   ■ 30,000 - 61,304
▨ 10,000 - 15,000   ▨ 20,000 - 30,000   * Figures are in "thousands"

FIGURE 2.02. Mapping of 3×1 dollars sent (by US city) and received (by municipality) for projects in the state of Jalisco, 2004-12. Map by Chieko Maene.

Jalisco is among a handful of Mexican states that have captured the majority of 3×1 funds. In 2003 Jalisco created 3×1 Estatal (State), which tries to absorb some of the projects that the federal 3×1 program's budget is too limited to cover. In 2007, 3×1 Estatal spent more than the federal government on remittance projects in Jalisco; it accomplished 546 projects with 94,246,553 pesos, or just under $100,000. Also, from 2003 to 2007 Jalisco captured the biggest percentage of 3×1 federal money out of all the Mexican states participating in the program. The Secretaría de Desarrollo Humano (Department for Human Development, or SEDESOL), which runs the 3×1 state program, reports that since the inception of the federal and state 3×1 programs, over three thousand projects have been carried out, benefiting over 4,153,633 inhabitants out of Jalisco's seven million.[16] It notes, unsurprisingly, that the majority of HTA remittances sent from the United States come from the states of California, Texas, and Illinois. These statistics speak to the impressive reach of 3×1 within Jalisco.

Historic Genealogy of Migrant HTAs

The basic contours of the migrant-state remittance development alliance have been in formation for almost a century. In the early twentieth century, migrant social clubs originated as a response by Mexican migrants to exclusionary practices in US cities. Originally, clubs were not based on migrants' places of origin but rather on the places where they settled in the United States. Like many other immigrant groups, they revolved around providing basic services for Mexican migrants or pooling money to bury the dead.[17]

So Mexican HTAS are not new. They have existed since the turn of the twentieth century alongside the social groups of other immigrant populations, including the Italian, Irish, and Chinese. However, while Italian, Irish, and Chinese clubs in the nineteenth and early twentieth centuries engaged in what is today called "long-distance nationalism" or "diaspora nationalism"—political change in homelands from host locations—the early-twentieth-century Mexican HTAS primarily worked to create support structures for immigrants in the United States.[18] Mexican HTAS' direct engagement with Mexican hometowns increased in the second half of the twentieth century, and explicit state endorsement of and involvement in such action is a more recent phenomenon.

Mexican clubs in the 1920s and 1930s also constructed a sense of national identity among migrants who collectively identified with the Mexican nation as opposed to their specific pueblos. For example, Paul S. Taylor records fifty-one "Mexican Honorific Commissions" registered with the Mexican consulate in Los Angeles in 1929. The goal of all these commissions was "to aid consuls in imparting protection and to aid compatriots resident in the U.S. Also to care and guard in respect and dignity the Mexican Nation."[19] The guidelines proposed taking action in response to grievances from Mexicans working in American fields or factories. The individual clubs within the Mexican honorific commissions had their own guidelines that spoke more directly to community interests. While protection of Mexicans' civil rights was still important, the aim of one such group in the agricultural town of Gilcrest, Colorado (Sociedad Mutualista Obreros Libres de Gilcrest, Colorado), was to assist individuals and families facing illness and accidents, to establish schools and recreation centers to serve Mexicans, to celebrate Mexican national holidays in US areas with large Mexican populations, and to elevate the intellectual, moral, and material level of all its members.[20] Even though echoes of the current HTA and federation structure can be traced back to the 1920s, if not earlier, the first clubs were not regularly collectiing and sending dollars to their hometowns or creating political alliances to support the growth and development of their hometowns. They were, however, forging critical connections with Mexican consulates.[21]

Today's HTA structure in Jalisco can also be traced back to activities in Mexico during the 1940s and 1950s. David Fitzgerald's study tracks the origins of some HTAs to migrant activity in Arandas, Jalisco, that inspired the Catholic Church to initiate policies explicitly addressing migration. In 1944, first motivated by the demoralizing impact that migration was having on family and community values in Mexico, the archbishop of Guadalajara instructed priests to form a Pro-emigrant Section of the Mexican Catholic Union in each parish. This eventually led to the organization of emigrants explicitly around their community of origin, dedicated to its improvements and vitality. Some of these early clubs were based in Mexico's larger cities like Guadalajara because of the internal migration of rural people to urban localities. As people began migrating to the United States, in lieu of Mexico's major cities, organizations spanned greater distances.[22]

Not all regions in Jalisco, let alone the rest of Mexico, had migrant clubs aiding small pueblos this early. The Los Altos region of Jalisco, where Arandas is located, is one of Mexico's oldest emigration zones. While migrants from Arandas were contributing to the construction of their church as early as the 1950s, the organization and collective remitting of migrants from other regions in Jalisco did not begin until much later. In 2012 some small communities were just starting to organize in the United States for change at home, and others had yet to do so.

The historical genealogies of HTAS have been affected by large-scale economic change. Some scholars argue that Mexico's structural readjustment in the 1970s and 1980s, which put many farmers out of work, as well as US amnesty for three million migrants in 1986, not only increased migration to the United States but also resulted in the growth and maturation of social clubs.[23] In contrast to the clubs of the 1920s and 1930s, many of these social clubs were civic, fraternal, informal, or formal associations of volunteers based on their pueblo of origin as opposed to their current residence. In this way they resemble more closely the Italian and Irish clubs of the early twentieth century than Mexican clubs from that time. Clubs use cooperation and social networks to create a common fund for public development in Mexico through collective remitting. Today a club can be loosely defined along a broad spectrum of formality. A club can be three friends meeting in their home or 150 members involved in regimented monthly meetings and hierarchical memberships. While HTAS differ greatly in their effectiveness in completing projects, they help to address the insecure economic conditions of migrants.

While a comprehensive history of migrant club remitting practices has never been written, my interviews with club members indicate that uncertainty was both a motivation for and a constant condition of informal clubs in the 1970s and 1980s in the south of Jalisco. In 1980 the Los Angeles San Juan de Amula Club informally sent remittances for the construction of a *curato*, or small parish building, adjacent to the town's church. The club members collected cash and sent it to Mexico with a member of their hometown. In San Juan, the priest of the town was responsible for allocating remittances and soliciting assistance from a local committee during construction. However, no written records exist to document these cash flows, and oral histories reveal competing narratives about how the money was spent. Similarly, the HTA president José Ochoa from Los Guajes recalled, "For the last twenty years we have given what we could to the church, but nobody there has any idea of how much we spent."[24] The church in Los Guajes did not track remittances or distinguish dollars from other capital flows. Uncertainty regarding exactly how many dollars were received in hometowns contributed to the need for formal cash transfers.[25] The 3×1 program ostensibly structures these transactions, creating a formal mechanism for transparency and accountability where there was none.

Formalization of HTAs

Since the inception of Jalisco's first federation in 1991, the state government has become increasingly involved in the construction of migrant federations.[26] Today various government officials collaborate with organized emigrants in the United States to reach undocumented and documented people who are not affiliated with a club, to organize meetings that broadcast the state's development agenda, and to initiate federations in US cities. The first migrant federation, the Federación de Jaliscienses en Sur de California (Jalisco Federation in Southern California), is still the largest, representing over 120 migrant clubs. The Federación de Jaliscienses del Medio Oeste (Federation of Jaliscienses in the Midwest) followed in 1995. Since then the California federation has split into three, and Nevada and Seattle have formed federations. In 2012 migrants formed a federation in Tennessee. Together, these federations represent hundreds of clubs in the United States. Still, the majority of migrants do not belong to federations. In 2007 Gilberto Juárez González, director of Mexico's Office of Attention to Jaliscienses in the Exterior (OFAJE), remarked: "We still lack contact with Jaliscienses in Detroit, Michigan, Atlanta, and Denver." Aware that they "are the closest contact that paisanos have with the government," OFAJE officials maintain that this lack of contact with other Jaliscienses limits the government's ability to channel dollars from emigrants in these cities to government programs in Mexico.²⁷ In response to this, several Mexican states have opened what are called Offices for Attention to Migrants, or simply *casas*, in the United States. Jalisco has such centers in Chicago, Los Angeles, and San Jose. In essence, federations act as geographic nodes that create openings in American cities for Mexican statesmen and bureaucrats. Without federations, the directors of these Mexican institutions would have to contact the Mexican consulate to research individual clubs and then undertake a massive outreach campaign to inform clubs of the 3×1 program or which remittance transfer centers offer the best rates. Dedicated emigrants who organize as volunteers minimize the state's outreach costs.

Organized migrant clubs often have hierarchical structures. The federation is a tiered system formed by a broad base of loosely affiliated migrants, with several echelons of increasingly active, financed, and politically connected migrants in positions of influence or authority. Those at the top gain most access to Mexican officials and business leaders. This also means that those on the top of this "pyramid" make decisions that affect individual emigrants contributing to the remittance pool.

As migrant clubs formalize, the activities of disparate members become more distinct. Migrants at the bottom of the pyramid participate in the 3×1/HTA nexus through informal gatherings in people's houses and backyards, local restaurants, and parks that allow them to collectively experience nostalgia and contribute to a social project. Meanwhile, transborder activists at the top of the pyramid increasingly work with government officials, attending high-profile functions and meetings that influence how remittances should be spent.

Despite the growing number of migrants involved in and aware of 3×1, there is mounting evidence that as time passes, a shrinking number of individuals exert increasing control over the disbursement of funds. In an effort to promote a democratic and transparent process, the management of Jalisco's 3×1 state program is designed to balance representation by local, state, and federal officials and includes representatives of Mexico's three major political parties. Until 2013, a managing committee composed of twelve representatives made final decisions regarding the disbursement of funds.²⁸ In 2013 the committee was reduced from twelve members to four, with one spot reserved for a migrant representative who is named by a government official.[29] In 2008 Jorge Rosales was one of three migrants who participated in the committee of twelve as a representative of the new Northern California Federation. As he put it, "It's nice to have the power to decide where the millions go; it is kinda cool . . . to say yes, I like that project, or no, not that one."[30] Today that great responsibility is allegedly left to only one migrant representative. The formalization of migrant HTAS into federations is emblematic of migrants' newfound voice vis-à-vis the Mexican government. Meanwhile, new 3×1 hierarchies appear dangerously close to reproducing systems of patronage, rather than instilling democratic values, by putting more and more power in fewer hands.

The proliferation of federations in the United States—resulting, in part, from the geographic distribution of emigrants across the United States—increases the potential for Jaliscienses to engage with state officials through formal channels. As the number and size of HTAS rapidly increase, state employees who focus on the migrant community are stretched thinner, creating competition between pueblos and emigrants for the government's attention and funds. At the same time, Jalisco emigrants do not have a single federation that can claim to represent all emigrant interests—an organization with power to leverage and direct state investment.

Nonetheless, such organization, scholars argue, supports the constitution of a "transnational civil society" in which migrants engage in the public sphere of homelands from host locations, opening a space for migrant critique of the Mexican state.[31] However, these organizations also create public platforms and points of entry for federal and state employees to insert themselves into migrant activities and broadcast their visions for migrants' futures and the futures of their hometowns. Paradoxically, the increasing formalization of migrant clubs can strengthen migrants' political standing *and* foreclose certain possibilities if fewer migrant voices are consequently heard. It is also important that scholars begin to examine the extent to which migrants who are at the forefront of building this "transnational civil society" are challenged by nested patriarchal relationships in rural Mexico. "Civil" societies, while common in the United States, are not necessarily so in the hometowns that migrants intend to transform.

Government Visions of Migrant Goals

Mexican politicians have many opportunities to reach a migrant audience. An annual event held in US cities called Semana Jalisco, for example, unites a wide array of actors involved in remittance development; migrant clubs that raise funds all year long hope to receive public acknowledgment during the event, and hundreds attend. Additionally, federation meetings, federation publications, and the inauguration of 3×1 projects create opportunities for officials to present their view of the "ideal remitter."

In a context where an estimated 95 percent of Mexico's remittances are spent on individual households, government officials go to great lengths to highlight the importance of social contributions with the hopes that individual remitters will become town benefactors.[32] At a federation meeting in California, a migrant who wanted to learn about 3×1 asked: "I want to put a truck farm in Mexico, like there are here. It is what I have worked on for over twenty years. Will you help me with that? I have the experience but not the land. Will the government help me buy the land?" A representative of the government who works with migrants responded, "We are interested in social projects. If the project will help ten families, we are interested, but if it will only help yours then we are not. The idea is to spread the resources we have to as many people as possible."[33]

Conversation by conversation, government employees construct the idea of a social good while at the same time stressing independence from government support. Official 3×1 guidelines announce that the program permits migrant civil society to change the conditions of its communities "without depending completely on the government. . . . Mexico has big business partners in the exterior: its migrants, who allow collective remittances to better the country."[34] It is migrants' sacrifice—"it is their personal money; we are aware that they don't have to do this and that their lives are hard in the United States"—that allows them to partner with the state.[35]

Individuals have responded to these calls. Héctor Alarcón, an HTA president who supported the building of a Mexican rodeo in 2004, now wants to invest in education for the children of his pueblo and in "social projects with a larger impact."[36] Migrants repeatedly announce that they are giving to their *patria* (homeland) and put Mexican flags in their homes or on their cars in Los Angeles. A migrant who has become a remittance-development project director for the Zacatecana Federation, Efraín Jiménez Muñoz, gives speeches arguing for projects "improving the health care and water and sewage systems [that] can benefit the overall well-being of communities."[37]

Perhaps the most important message—repeated in speeches, letters to migrants published in *Semana Jalisco* magazine, and federation ephemera—is an emphasis on migrants' allegiance to the state of Jalisco over their national identity as a way of motivating them to focus on the local. During the 2009 inauguration of Casa Jalisco in Chicago, Governor Emilio González explained: "The remittances toward Mexico have lowered 12 percent, but the remittances to Jalisco have only lowered 6 percent, and it's not that we have it easier, but that we do not forgot our land and we do not forget the people that we left there. . . . Casa Jalisco demonstrates the gratitude of all the people of Jalisco to you that you do not forget us and that, although far away, you all continue having in your heart that fire that characterizes us as Jaliscienses and Mexicans."[38] Previously, in 2007, Governor Francisco Ramírez Acuña declared similar sentiments: "We invite you to preserve, among the new generations of Jaliscienses in California, love of our land, Jalisco, and our motherland, Mexico. . . . I wish to reiterate my promise to be an attentive and transparent governor, conscious of the importance of constructing one sole community, one sole Jalisco; it is not important which side of the border we find ourselves on."[39] Migrants who feel a strong allegiance to their pueblo or their state, not the Mexican nation, are told: "Jalisco is Mexico."[40] Migrants in the United States assert that rather than Mexican American, they are "Jalisco American."[41] This framing of geographic allegiances ultimately reinforces Jalisco as the place that one should identify with and invest in.

Government institutions managing 3×1 also hold events in Mexico to disseminate information about the 3×1 program. A Mexican version of Semana Jalisco has been held in pueblos that "illustrate the most success with the 3×1 program."[42] At one such event in Degollado, Jalisco, in 2007, the program included a Catholic mass and a Power-Point presentation illustrating successful 3×1 projects. The event closed with an extravagant fiesta, a sit-down dinner, performances by several famous mariachi singers, dancing to a professional band,

and Jalisco's "queens" parading around in evening dresses. Club De-gollado (composed of migrants who live in Chicago) put considerable effort and expense into this event. As a reward, the town's success with 3×1 was showcased to representatives of other clubs, municipal presidents from nearby towns, and state and federal government offi-cials, including then-governor Emilio González. The event allowed Club Degollado to demonstrate its fiscal responsibility and strengthen its members' ties to officials who manage 3×1 funds, positioning them favorably for future 3×1 project solicitations. Conversely, the event also created a platform for the state government to disseminate in-formation about 3×1 and garner the trust of local officials throughout Jalisco at the club members' expense. Often it is local nonmigrants or municipal presidents who ask emigrants to look into 3×1 or form a club so that their particular town can benefit from the program.[43]

Rural Jalisco's Spatial Legacy

The formalization of migrant HTAS into larger federations, and the increasing involvement of officials in migrant events, results in proj-ects that have been shaped by (now entrenched) patriarchal and aris-tocratic class structures. Remittance development "from below" tries to overcome, but is ultimately limited by, the spatial legacy of these systems. The specific social relations that define place are social and political systems etched into geographic landscapes that cannot be changed overnight.

Systems of power and patronage operate on a geographical scale. The size, relative proximity, and cultural relationships between towns influence the distribution of remittance funds under 3×1. With the exception of Jalisco's largest city and capital, Guadalajara, Jalisco is composed of a series of cabeceras that maintain delicate, and often fraught, relationships with a regional network of dependent towns or villages. These villages are then connected to even smaller *rancherías*, rural settlements that consist historically of the dwellings of extended families. Generally, the geographically remote towns and rancherías are the most neglected by the state. The cabecera gets money directly from the state and federal government. It then allocates those funds to its dependent localities. Migrants who do not come from a cabecera often complain that the mayor (or *presidente municipal*) has not taken care of their dependents in the rancherías and pueblos, leaving them to fend for themselves. Proximity to Guadalajara also greatly aids a community's capacity to receive funding. Private remittances challenge these conventional systems because migrants send money directly to families no matter where they are located. However, once migrants in the United States join a federation to work on a 3×1 project, at least a portion of their money is funneled through the cabeceras, creating occasions for disputes between migrants, mayors, and state officials and increasing especially municipal control over transnational development projects.

Regional development has also been affected by Mexico's political system. Every six years a new political administration at the executive level is ushered in; municipal presidents are elected on a three-year cycle, and the 1917 Mexican constitution prohibits reelection. Many programs begin and end with the administrations that initiate them, or funding dries up or is redirected, adding instability to the planning of development projects. Although 3×1 is an exception to this legacy, having remained in force continuously since its inception, there are frequent allegations of corruption and cronyism, with municipal presidents or mayors accused of using 3×1 money on cabeceras as opposed to intended ranchos.[44] A migrant from San José de Gracia, Abraham Gabino, does not contribute to 3×1, which he calls "a fraud" because of the fact that migrant dollars are required upfront, followed by municipal investment. Gabino scoffs, "What if he only has one year left in his term? He will just pocket your money."[45] Across Jalisco, relationships between municipal presidents and migrants have become so problematic that migrant activists are strategizing to eliminate municipal presidents (as well as the municipal funds associated with them) from the program.[46]

Mexico's long-standing traditions of discontinuous development programs and corruption have affected not only municipal mayors' practices but also the material development of places, crippling remote localities. Disenfranchised rancherías must deal with the fragmented development of roads, water, electricity, and postal services. Disjointed development efforts and the effects of corruption are illustrated by the construction history of most roads in rural Jalisco. In Magdalena over a four-year period, three different government programs were used to pave six kilometers of rural road. In Lagunillas, the state built approximately half of the main road connecting the town with a nearby highway in 1997. It took local villagers five years to save money and three years to build the remaining half. In 2004 the residents of Lagunillas could finally boast that a paved road connected their rancho with the highway.[47] In these remote places, with limited government support or none at all, locals have built roads, wells, churches, and community centers and installed electrical infrastructure.

The mission of 3×1 is to address Mexico's poor and marginalized rural population—or those most geographically remote from centers of commerce and transit—on the basis of "migrant initiative." However, migration patterns and remittance patterns make it difficult for the state to map rural demographics and poverty. Historically, bad land, drought, and remoteness from cities or towns have pushed people to emigrate. This helps explain why Los Altos, a dry region in the north of Jalisco, has the longest migration history in the state involving the largest percentage of people. Also, the railroads and major roads constructed in the first half of the twentieth century allowed the people in pueblos along such routes easier access to the North. Today Cautla, a remote town that was impoverished in the 1970s, boasts a remittance-financed airport strip and "homes better than Beverly Hills." Onetime villagers have become successful migrant restaurateurs. Remittances and migrant organization resulting from continuous historical migration are slowly changing the characteristics of these once impoverished places.

Disproportionate migration patterns and migration history create unequal distribution of remittances. Some high-migration zones are much better off than their neighbors.[48] For example, San Miguel Hidalgo, a pueblo in the high-emigration municipality of El Limón, showcases several large houses built with remittances and is outfitted with a new rodeo stadium that officially seats four thousand people (and unofficially seats seven thousand), even though the town has a population of only four hundred. Within high-migration zones, these differences also play out in the local environment, where some neighbors are much better off than others. In San Miguel, many of those who still farm, and are considered to be poor by the state, are also subsidized by remittances, while neighboring farmers are living hand to mouth. While the state may be able to identify "marginal" zones on

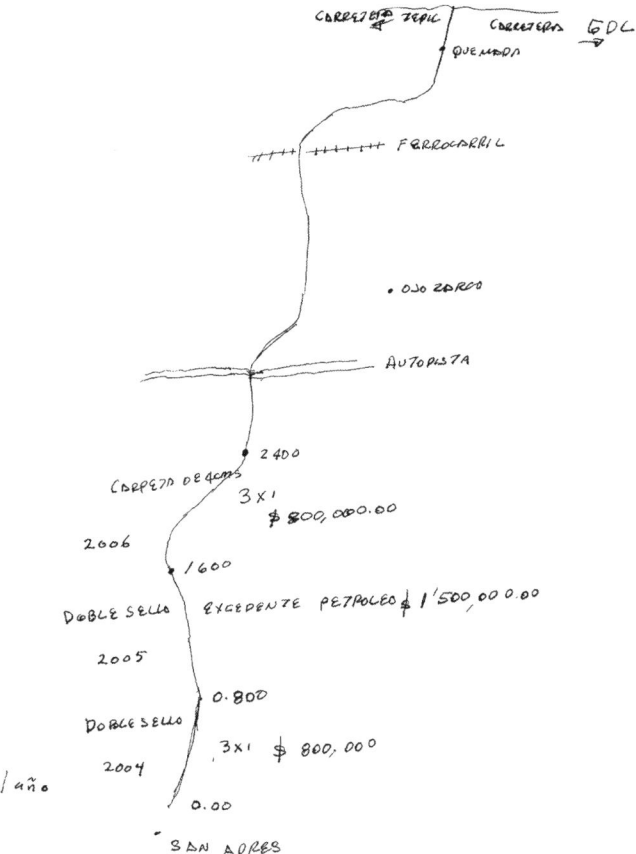

FIGURE 2.03. Cognitive map/diagram showing length, cost, and funding source of three road-improvement projects on the main road leading to Magdalena, Jalisco, between 2004 and 2006.

the basis of indigenous populations and high emigration, it still does not have an effective way to map how remittances have affected such places over time.

Places in Jalisco with a long history of migration also tend to have strong networks in the United States that in turn reinforce differences between levels of remittance funding received by rural communities. Transborder activists rely on these networks to stir up interest in community development and to raise money to remit collectively. Thus strong HTAs tend to come from places with longer migration histories. Migrant activists are also supported by the federation, which creates insider networks that give them access to government representatives and state funds. Among the members of the Federación de Jaliscienses, members of the board of directors are most familiar with the program and have direct access to the officials and HTA members who are elected to approve 3×1 project proposals. Despite the 3×1 mandate that each municipality get equal funds, the distribution of projects is highly uneven, and clientelistic approaches to distributing money prevail.

On a national level, the federal government's stated goal of reaching "marginalized" people through 3×1 refers, in part, to Mexico's indigenous population; but relying on migrants as the drivers of the process has failed to help communities with less established migrant histories. Many indigenous people's migration histories are distinct from, and shorter than, that of mestizos. In Jalisco, indigenous populations have been pushed deep into the countryside on some of the state's driest and poorest lands.[49] Indigenous peoples in Chiapas, Guerrero, and Oaxaca occupy predominantly arid land as well. Poor mestizo farmers also tend to be pushed into far-flung places, and many have lived (and still do) without electricity, running water, sanitation, or basic infrastructure. The truly impoverished are often not able to make the journey to the United States or have been able to do so only recently, which results in weaker migrant networks.[50] For example, Oaxaca's continuous-migration history dates back roughly twenty years, while Jalisco's dates back to the 1920s.[51] Places that have been historically in need—but perhaps not truly impoverished—tend to have longer histories of remitting, which give them more opportunities for involvement with 3×1.[52]

On the receiving end, 3×1's impact is linked to the size of a town's population. Some argue the smaller the community, the greater the impact. In towns with populations of under one thousand, which account for 30 percent of communities receiving 3×1 funding, annual donations represent approximately seven dollars per person, which is seven times the average government investment in public works.[53] In Jalisco, most 3×1 projects are built in towns of fewer than a thousand people.

Migrants' geographic location within the United States also influences their ability to capitalize on and participate in remittance development networks. Due to high demand, in 2004 two SEDESOL offices were created, one in Chicago and the other in Los Angeles, specifically to manage the program. Migrants in all other cities who wish to meet with federal government employees managing 3×1 make trips to Chicago or Los Angeles, wait for rare occasions when officials travel throughout the United States, or make appointments when they return to Mexico. Migrants who live in Los Angeles and Chicago have continual access to SEDESOL officials, which directly influences their engagement with the 3×1 program. In addition to a migrant club's proximity to Chicago and Los Angeles, the geography of particular US states influence migrants' capacity to organize. A government official who works for the SEDESOL office in Chicago notes: "Texas is so divided. The leaders of the Dallas and Houston Federations are divided by three hours. They can't play football together."⁵⁴ Soccer games and other casual engagements create opportunities for migrant leaders to solidify their positions, create mutual bonds, and lobby the Mexican government with a unified voice.

State Migrant Negotiation over What to Build

In addition to corruption, geographic disparities, and the changing roles of migrants, conflicts over the proposed uses of 3×1 remittance funds produce tensions between migrants and the state government's development agenda. The state of Jalisco wants 3×1 to focus on the construction of basic infrastructure. Rural Jalisco has hundreds of miles of unpaved roads; approximately 15 percent of the population does not have running water or electricity. Although these percentages are low compared to those of the poorest Mexican states (in Oaxaca, approximately half of the population does not have running water or electricity), Jalisco is striving to equip all of its localities with basic public amenities. While migrants value and frequently sponsor these infrastructure improvements, their most cherished projects address the visible, culturally important, and symbolic elements of the pueblo. Sports arenas, churches, plazas, and ornamental landscapes more visibly and emotionally signify their devotion to their pueblo.

In one episode in El Limón, Jalisco, both municipal officials and rural nonmigrants expressed anger over two large-scale migrant projects (a cultural center and Mexican rodeo) proposed in pueblos lacking paved roads and running water. According to El Limón's mayor, "The

FIGURE 2.04. A 3×1-funded *portal*, or gateway, to the town of Juchitlán. Photograph by author.

visions that they [migrants] have of development at the municipal level and that we have do not coincide. They want a lot, and they want it visible and looking good to them. In the Presidencia Municipal (municipal office) we are interested in works that sometimes you don't see but that have social importance, like drainage."[55] However, migrants feel that they should be able to spend their money on projects that are important to them. They negotiate distance and the impacts of migrancy on social and cultural traditions through built space. A priest from a small town explains: "The unique marker of identification in the pueblo is the church. People think, 'How am I going to identify with a road or potable water? That doesn't say anything to me, but look at what a nice church we have.'"[56] The symbolic value associated with remittance building is most clearly expressed by large buildings.

In some cases, the federal agency administering 3×1 resolves these local-local or local-state conflicts through negotiation and bargaining. A government employee at the federal level explains: "When the paisanos come home for festivals here, it is very important that their sons who were born there continue to have affection for their communities of origin; they want the garden and plaza to be good so their children maintain affection. The ornamental work is very important to paisanos, more than drainage. So the mayor says, 'We will help with your plaza if you help us with the potable water.'"[57] In essence, the state barters, thus subsidizing state projects with migrant remittances. Jaime Garibay, in charge of 3×1 Estatal, notes:

> My function is to tell them why we need certain projects. For example, the *municipio* of Mezquitic is the poorest. The people from that town who live in Chicago said, "We want to invest two or three hundred thousand [pesos] in the church," but I know the church is fine. They want to make it beautiful. So I tell them that I don't agree, that we should build water plants for four different communities, two health clinics, and electric networks. Think of the people who have no drainage, no electricity; invest some money in bettering the church but put most in improving basic resources. I convinced them that that was what they had to do.[58]

The state has gradually increased the level of funding tied to infrastructure improvements. Government records of all 3×1 federal projects built in Jalisco between 2002 and 2012 document an increase in the number of works dedicated to basic infrastructure. In 2002, 17 percent were infrastructure projects, whereas by 2007 the number of projects dedicated to potable water, sewer systems, electrification, and road paving had risen to 61 percent; by 2011 they accounted for 83 percent.[59] Before 3×1, club members went directly to the townspeople and implemented whatever project they desired. Now complex layers of bureaucracy mediate migrants' desires. The migrants' precious *plaza de toros* or bullfighting ring is not a building project favored by the state. Similarly, when 3×1 started, migrant clubs were excited about building arches to mark their town's entrance and exit. Some arches, such as Juchitlan's, are even marked by a state plaque that lists 3×1's participants. For migrants who work at menial jobs in the United States and live well below the poverty line, the symbolic importance of building inaugural arches or rodeos is meaningful for their daily lives in their hometowns (or their imagined hometown life of the future) but has not been valued in the 3×1 guidelines.

Not all migrant disagreements over 3×1 stem from a desire to build cultural and symbolic structures. Just after 3×1 was implemented across Mexico, migrants in Los Angeles voiced their frustration with the direction of the program in *La Opinión*, the leading Los Angeles bilingual newspaper: "We are not able to have a computer center, give scholarships, collaborate in the construction of churches or a Mexican rodeo, or purchase machinery for the development of farms."[60] Carlos Leal, a previous director of 3×1 at the state level, acknowledges: "At the beginning the federal government wanted to control which projects would be passed without thinking of paisanos. Now it is different."[61] Regardless, tensions among the priorities of migrants, state agencies, and locals remain a fundamental component of remittance construction.

*   *   *

The 3×1 policy has led scholars to question the role of the state in managing its emigrant population and their remittances. While several argue that a defining feature of the neoliberal era is the state's retreat from citizen activities, or that globalization and transnational migration have undermined the territorial integrity of the state, others investigating 3×1 point to the state's increasing involvement with its emigrant population.[62] The Mexican government at multiple levels is actively promoting a reconceptualization of the emigrant: formerly a wanderer, traitor, or vagabond, now a model citizen, hero, and countryman (although someone who plays those roles from a distance). Scholars of 3×1 seek to identify precisely how the state's involvement with migrant clubs has affected migrant agency and their control over remittance flows. While it is important to identify the extent to which the state is influencing migrant activity versus being influenced by it, my interest here is to point out three critical issues that have been overlooked in the 3×1 policy approach.

First, the 3×1 policy is not simply one part of the Mexican state's rural development initiatives, as some politicians have claimed. Rather, it is the heart of a nascent remittance-development model that is setting a precedent for how migrant remittances should be spent and managed in Mexico and abroad. At the core of this model is the construction and valorization of the image of migrant as benefactor, a

discursive strategy integral to convincing Mexico's migrant constituents to volunteer their dollars toward state-sanctioned projects. Second, the policy does not take the social and cultural impacts of building, or consequences of building, into account. Remittance buildings
are the bricks and mortar of villages, and infrastructure projects are
important as well; both types of projects shape daily life for locals. The
injection of remittance capital flows into local building traditions and
industries affects the production of place. Finally, the policy does not
address migration itself as a social and spatial process. The 3×1 program accelerates the ways in which new social patterns created by
migration are built into local landscapes. Migration is a social process
that is changing migrants' worldview, which in turn affects what they
build and why they build it.

The remittance-development discourse, maturing with the blossoming of the remittance landscape itself, reveals that 3×1 is contributing to what Ananya Roy calls the making of millennial development.
In Roy's recent study of microfinancing as a new development panacea
being aggressively implemented by the World Bank and other international organizations, she argues that today development is about
the creation of poverty capital. The poor represent the new frontier
("banking the unbanked") for financial institutions, policy makers,
governmental organizations, and NGOs, who view their financial inclusion as the democratization of development itself. What is at stake
are the humanist intentions behind social development as development becomes subsumed into financial markets.[63] This can be compared to remittance development, where what is at stake is the distinction between migrants' desires (personal and collective) and the
agendas of the state (and other actors involved in formalizing remitting). As the state co-opts migrant grassroots action by harnessing its
energy with programs like 3×1, the distinct agendas of both migrant
activists and politicians (and NGOs and financiers) who work with the
diaspora become blurred and indeterminate.

Rather than co-opting grassroots action, remittance development
provides an opportunity for migrant-state relations to be reconsti-
tuted in both the United States and Mexico because of migrants' roles
in the development of Mexico's countryside. Migrants must be repositioned from the shadows of Mexican society to the center of a migrant

civil society *and* Mexican and American society at large. Furthermore, remittances present an opportunity to build vital landscapes that serve the local community and the migrant community.

As the 3×1 program matures, it has become fodder for disagreements over what role the Mexican diaspora should play in Mexico's development, state politics, and migrant hometowns. Migrant activist Sergio Suárez calls the program "a symbol, a make-believe" because "migrants might sign off on a project so that the municipal president owes him a favor, or to feel pride: 'Look what I did.' Both the municipal president and migrants are, can be, at fault."[64] Migrant activists from Los Angeles to Chicago to Seattle are increasingly frustrated with the program's management and manipulation by interested parties. Debates about the overall success or failure of the program remain unresolved because it has ambiguous and geographically nested implications. In itself a fairly simple "one size fits all" program, 3×1 attempts to create material improvements out of exceedingly complex processes. While capable of mobilizing migrants, the program is not capable of addressing the underlying problems that produce migration and remitting today.

The examination of 3×1 as a development model sets the stage for a material investigation of what this program actually builds. The next three chapters explore three migrant-initiated 3×1 projects in their regional context to examine building with remittances as a fundamentally historic process that inextricably links the social and cultural spaces of rural Jalisco with the spaces of migration and US urbanism.

3 El Jaripeo

THE GENDERED SPECTACLE OF REMITTANCE

New rodeo arenas, forged in the crucible of migration, remitting, and tradition, are rapidly emerging across Jalisco's rural landscape. On the one hand, rodeo rings and stadiums that dwarf rancherías deep in the mountains are what Walter Benjamin calls "wish images," markers of a promise yet to be fulfilled, an inauguration of a new mode of production based on emigrants' investment in places they once abandoned.[1] On the other hand, the new rodeo grounds are evidence of the limits of transnational capital from below, the result of state neglect, and the displacement of migrant desire, with very real implications for individuals' sense of self and the formation and evolution of communities.

The management of a remittance mega-rodeo in San Miguel Hidalgo, a very small village in the south of Jalisco, exposes both the aspirations and the dangers of remittance development. San Miguel has approximately four hundred inhabitants. A handful of the town's norteños—now successful businessmen in the United States—wanted to build the biggest rodeo facility in the region. With the help of 3×1 program funds, they built a recreation center with a *plaza de toros*, a basketball court, a soccer field, and a running track in four months for approximately $500,000. The gigantic and hastily built arena is estimated to have a capacity for up to seven thousand people, easily making it the largest rodeo grounds in the municipality, located in one of its smallest villages.

Drawing sufficient crowds to a rodeo event requires careful planning. For the inauguration of the rodeo in 2008, two wealthy norteños hired La Arrolladora, Mexico's nationally known *banda* from the state of Sinaloa, to draw in crowds. The band cost an astonishing $75,000, or roughly 750,000 pesos, for two hours, an amount that is almost seventy-five times the cost of the local band in San Miguel, and fifteen times the cost of the most popular (and expensive) regional band in

FIGURE 3.01. A young jinete rides a bull as others look on at an informal jaripeo in La Cidrita, Jalisco. Little distance separates performer and audience at this temporary arena, assembled by local men who will take turns riding bulls and watching from horseback, just beyond the steel paddock fencing. Photograph by author.

the nearby cabecera El Grullo.[2] The boosters hoped that these internationally recognized musicians would attract people from the surrounding states of Jalisco, Michoacán, Zacatecas, and Guanajuato, as well as norteños in the United States. In planning both the rodeo arena construction and the inauguration, the norteños were influenced by the Mexican rodeos that they had attended in Southern California. Built in 1979, the Pico-Rivera Sports Arena in Los Angeles is one of the oldest and largest arenas for Mexican-style *jaripeos* (bull-riding events) and *charrerías* (equestrian competitions) in the United States. The arena seats up to five thousand spectators. In contrast to arenas such as the Cow Palace in San Francisco, the Pico Rivera Sports Arena was built for Mexican-style sports events, not American rodeos. Because of its scale, capacity to attract audiences, and use to raise HTA and federation funds, it has served as a model for norteños who are playing new entrepreneurial roles in rural Mexico.

As the inauguration approached, a new day seemed at hand: the pueblo of San Miguel was about to become the center of Mexico's contemporary music scene. A teenage girl from San Miguel predicted, "They will get the plaza full with that band. It's the biggest band in Mexico!" Her mother replied, "Well, if they don't now they never will."[3] A young boy from San Miguel walked around with a cooler each day after school selling *paletas* (homemade popsicles) for two pesos each until he made enough money to buy his ticket to attend his pueblo's event. After spending his spring and summer selling 150 paletas, and being teased by his friends who were securing money from less obvious sources (including norteños' remittances), the boy had the three hundred pesos for his ticket. From individual tactics to group efforts, the event transformed daily life in the pueblo for several months before its arrival.

On the day of the event, many in attendance must have been shocked to see the plaza at only 50 percent capacity. Over three thousand people came to the small rural pueblo, which is over four hours from Guadalajara by car. The massive scale of the venue, however, dwarfed the crowd. Mexicans often say that crowds are the most important marker of success in a fiesta: crowds mean that the dance floor is packed, that the seats are full, that men have to stand to show their chivalry, and that long lines form to use the women's bathroom. Even with its rodeo arena half-empty, San Miguel was inundated with over six times its population—a huge number of people needing gas, food, restrooms, and parking in a town with no gas stations, no formal restaurants, and not a single parking lot. These logistical issues had not been addressed, nor could they have been, by the norteños who sponsored the event. When the day was over, despite all their hard work, the sponsors faced new debts, and the event was deemed a failure by its investors.

This story about a migrant-driven development project in one small town is emblematic of remittance space generally—an aspirational world in which individual migrants risk their hard-earned money to transform the fortunes of their hometowns. But the jaripeo also tells more nuanced stories about change in rural communities. Just as rodeos can generate economic growth, they are also cultural engines, a gendered sport that supports the performance of local rural traditions. The production of the rodeo as a political and economic space, the construction of the rodeo facility as a material site, and the rituals and performances that take place in rodeo arenas narrate the emergence of new identities, the weakening of older collective soli-darities and forms, and increasing political fragmentation. Communi-ties separated by physical, cultural, and economic distances but linked through the circuits of the global remittance and migration industry are *unified* and yet *differentiated.*[4] They occupy what Fredric Jameson calls a "hyperspace," a domain in which local experience no longer co-incides with the place in which it takes place.[5] While the rodeo arena is the location of one of the most parochial of sports, jaripeo or bull riding, it is now a hyperspace that inextricably links the local and the global. In this way the jaripeo is a "working and reworking of moder-nity," a local negotiation of global economic transformations.[6]

As one of numerous dispersed but interrelated spaces produced by remittances, the remittance rodeo arena results from the conversion of the rural peasant into a service-sector laborer. The social mobility he or she experiences, which requires the crossing of international borders, has resulted in the financialization of two regional events in rural Jalisco: the jaripeo rodeo (with its bulls and *jinetes*, or bull riders) and the *coronación de la reina*, or beauty queen contest, often linked to the fiestas surrounding the bull-riding event. These emergent mar-kets based on regional traditions seek to locate a new frontier. In a rural region defined by scarce resources and only limited acquisition of new land, the frontier is envisioned as the expansion and untapped promise of migrant remittances. The increasing scale of the rodeo arenas, the professionalization of the jaripeo's main participants and sponsors, and the insertion of new jaripeo music markets together constitute the commodification of traditional and cultural forms rep-resented in the modified public space of the remittance rodeo.

In the context of remittance development, the rodeo arena be-comes the spatial container for a set of rituals and performances that both dramatize and reveal changes in the social order. Bull riding is a spectacle that can be used, as Bret Gustafson argues, to "visualize power through displays that naturalize gendered, racial, social, and spatial boundaries."[7] The rodeo in Jalisco reinforces the dominance of men in the political and public sphere by representing a rural social order with men at the center. This representation is critical because it cultivates continuity despite a real and imagined sense of regional economic crisis and social instability.

Gender plays a large role in how remittances influence the spaces of the hometown. Typically men have been the ones to migrate from Jalisco, and although women are increasingly joining migration streams north, the gender ratios in rural Jalisco are still lopsided. Scholars study the mothers, wives, and daughters who live off partners' inconsistent and uninsured remittance flows and characterize the village as "female."[8] In Jalisco, colloquial speech refers to the village as a womb or *cuna natal*. The female village can be contrasted to its male-dominated remittance spaces. Men are powering most development decisions regarding remittances in the government and the migrant HTAS. Women, however, are starting to band together and articulate how remittances should be managed and who should manage them. Thus new tensions are born between villagers' gendered expectations and between male and female migrants' visions for remittance space.

The jaripeo provides a lens for understanding contested gender roles in the context of increased migration—and how such changes destabilize routines and rituals. The forms of masculine courage associated with agrarian ways of life are giving way to a new bravery associated with crossing the border, living in a foreign land, and remitting as a way of life. The jaripeo is a vehicle for a migration-based society to reorient itself to a market-oriented entrepreneurial society dependent on emigration. Here tradition is performed and consumed.[9] The remittance rodeo performance is about the consumption of a *ranchero* masculinity (and a *ranchera* femininity) as they are becoming unmoored from the village and are being reinterpreted, reformulated, and manifested in increasingly distant places.

The Mexican government has also played a role in the rise of the remittance rodeo. Neoliberal economic restructuring in Mexico has resulted in the privatization of large government companies as the government dismantles trade barriers, loosens central control of the financial realm, and encourages entrepreneurial activity in lieu of government-funded social programs. While the 3×1 program appears to be out of step with a neoliberal ideology because the government is investing more money in small rural localities, by doing so it encourages norteños to assume new political and civic responsibilities. Furthermore, the encroachment of government agencies in rural zones has triggered a jump in scale in the production of rodeos.

This increased scale, which has resulted in disruption and discontent through rivalry between and within hometowns, calls attention to regional struggles over community, identity, and economic vitality.

The remittance rodeo is a paradigmatic site of remittance space because it is a physical setting where migrants and nonmigrants alike negotiate the tensions produced by migration. To understand how new identities are being performed in particular institutional and structural contexts, I analyze the construction of one rodeo facility in Lagunillas in relation to the political, cultural, and material transformations of rodeos throughout the municipality of Autlán de Navarro.[10] I approach the story of the remittance rodeo in two ways. First, I examine the rodeo as a component of the changing fortunes and trajectories of rural Mexican towns as they shift from an agricultural society to one based on a remittance economy. I address the remittance economy as a new mode of production and disentangle its implications for political formations in relation to authority, power, and entitlement. I then explore how gender dynamics are acted out in the physical spaces embedded within the remittance rodeo. These new expectations, and the shift from community solidarities to individualized notions of access, advancement, and transformation, feed back into the social and economic spaces of the emigrant village. This allows me to move between the specificity of the Lagunillas rodeo to jaripeo space more generally to explore bull-riding as a material site and a discursive arena for migrants, villagers, and officials involved in the rearticulation of social roles and positions of power in regions ravaged by emigration.

History of the Jaripeo in the South of Jalisco

The pre–remittance-era or peso jaripeo was a cultural practice rooted in place. In the nineteenth and twentieth centuries, villages throughout the south of Jalisco held jaripeo events attended primarily by local townspeople. Often the sport was performed during the *fiestas patronales*, or patron saint festivals, which celebrate miracles that have taken place in a given village.[11] Dating back to the colonial period, the jaripeo tradition has been maintained through a succession of political and economic regimes. During the nineteenth century, when the *fiesta de toros* (festivities surrounding bull-riding events) was a critical part of hacienda life, a successful fiesta allowed hacendados to show off their horses and equestrian skills, as well as the skills of the mestizos or campesinos who managed the haciendas and herded, branded, and vaccinated cattle. Over time, these fiestas assumed multiple functions. They enabled the hacienda to raise money and showed the strength and promise of the horsemen who protected the hacienda. A performance born from the grueling experiences of daily life for peasants and hacendados, as the anthropologist Olga Nájero-Ramírez explains, "became particularly significant as a representation of life of the hacienda as one of unity and work for the common good."[12]

In the twentieth century, the dismantling of the hacienda and the construction of *ejidos* (communal land used for farming) and independent villages resulted in newly appointed *ejidatarios*—independent rural farmers who reinterpreted and reinvented the role and meaning of the jaripeo.[13] Ejidos, envisioned by the state as the bedrock of a new family-farming sector in Mexico, were both revolutionary, in that they granted new social status to once-indebted servants, and strategic, in that they allowed the state to secure political allegiance from its rural constituents.[14] New ejidos and abandoned hacienda grounds allowed campesinos and peones to take full ownership of rodeos, corrals, and jaripeo events. The teamwork required by ejidatarios to hold a jaripeo event reinforced the Mexican government's interest in the rise of the ejido as an autonomous and self-reliant agricultural unit. In the context of societal transformation, war, and famine, man's capacity to conquer a bull showcased villagers' success. As is tragically expressed in Juan Rulfo's story "Es que somos muy pobres" (It's because we're very poor), the ownership of bulls or cows during this period created a critical buffer between subsistence and dire poverty.[15]

The jaripeo also supported the state's construction of agrarian reform as a masculine enterprise.[16] State land reforms created not only new political entities but also new identities tied to land stewardship. Ejido lands were passed down from generation to generation within the same family, usually from father to sons, and only male ejidatarios had the right to vote about the use of the ejido's communal lands. While migration throughout Mexico, and within Jalisco specifically, was a major part of life before agrarian reform, many ejidatarios felt that the land they had been granted was land that had rightfully belonged to their family for decades, if not centuries.

The peso jaripeo allowed the poor to perform identities associated with nationality and urbanity. The jaripeo was one component of a more formal Mexican sport known as the *charrería*, which involves several *suertes*, or skill sets, that are performed with trained horses, bulls, and skilled riders who wear formal and elegant suits. Originating in Jalisco, the charrería is one of Jalisco's, and subsequently Mexico's, iconic cultural forms, and competitions take place in Mexico City and Guadalajara.[17] In contrast to the formality of the charrería, the jaripeo is rough and rowdy. It features no formal competition, no judges to score the performance of jinetes, and no requirement of elegant and expensive attire for participants, and is performed throughout rural areas.[18]

An ejidatario, Antonio Gómez, who participated in jaripeo events recalls the spirit of the jaripeo of the 1950s and 1960s:

> Before, they would start the event earlier and it would go for much longer, because the men would play with the bull, rope its legs, throw it down, let it chase their horses. Any person in the audience could decide to get onto the bull. They didn't have the mechanism that they have now to drop the man on the bull and release the bull into the ring. They just jumped on the bull when it was on the ground, had been knocked down. The bulls were local bulls; somebody who owned cows had their bull so the herd would grow, and they would use these, so sometimes the bull was as tame as a cow and other times he was brave or courageous.[19]

Gómez recalls the distinctly informal and autonomous nature of the event. The event did not start or end at a specific time; rather, it would continue at length. In part, this was because the bull riders, and the bulls themselves, were nonprofessional locals. Rather than "protecting their animals," people were "playing" with them in the rodeo ring and throughout the streets of the town. The event was also not limited to the rodeo arena; it also spilled out into the streets. And because it was not bounded by a fence or marked by an entrance, people entered and exited the spaces of the jaripeo as they pleased. Overall, Gómez expresses a sentiment that is echoed by others: the jaripeo was an event that involved the entire village, and "everybody paid attention." The jaripeo that he recalls was a critical part of the cultural development of the landed peasant farmer class. Open to all, it was an arena in which men proved themselves and demonstrated publicly their strength and power while acting in solidarity with other men.

As ejidos and small farming communities struggled to survive throughout the 1930s, 1940s, and 1950s, the building and remodeling of rodeo arenas was a demonstration of their communal capacity, stewardship over land, and perseverance. Rodeo facilities were built from immediately available materials such as quarried stone, wooden planks and branches from fallen trees, or locally made brick. Often these materials would be used to modify a rodeo arena that had been built for hacendados to corral cattle. Even though ejidos were (and are) hierarchical and subject to conflict, ejidatarios' investment in and presentation of a collective identity cannot be overemphasized. Much as in the days of the hacienda, the representation of a collective identity helped to strengthen the position of the ejido relative to other neighboring ejidos and to the state.

Today the impact of emigration, remitting, and changes in national policy regarding rural lands has created a new climate of instability for many rural communities. But emigration and remitting have also held these places together. In the 1960s and 1970s, after the Bracero Program (1942–64), foreign capital allowed Mexican migrant farmers to save and buy seed, invest in cattle, or hire farmhands to work and till their land in their absence. Remittances have also been invested in tractors and other modern farming equipment.[20] The anthropologist Peri Fletcher notes that in Pátzcuaro, a village in the state of Michoacán, early investment in cattle with hard-earned dollars from migration to the United States created a more stable and successful class of farmers.[21] These early investments allowed certain families to break the cycle of poverty that had defined their lives and strengthened local desires for social mobility based on capital accumulation rather than on political or social standing.

From Peso Rodeos to Remittance Rodeos in Autlán de Navarro

By 2007, in the municipality of Autlán, all but three of the region's seventeen rodeo arenas had been remodeled or rebuilt with remittances. The rodeo's importance in the region, the length of time individuals have been migrating, and the diversity of communities in terms of size and political structure resulted in a complex rodeo land-scape. Importantly, in the municipality of Autlán, in contrast to places like Los Altos where remittances and migration have been instrumen-tal since the 1920s and 1930s, migration has been more recent. The ac-celeration of migration and remitting since the 1970s means that con-trasts between the peso rodeo and remittance rodeo are still visible in the landscape.

The first remittance rodeo in the region was built in the 1970s in the town of El Chante to strengthen the existing political structure; that is, ejidatarios (many of whom were not migrants) used dollars to support ejido projects. At this time, the ejido of El Chante was the largest town in the municipality outside Autlán itself and had a siz-able emigrant population. The ejidatarios solicited dollars from their northern contingent at a rate of one thousand pesos per norteño, for a sum of thirty thousand pesos. The rodeo arena materalized the role of the norteño as the external financial unit or "bank." With these funds the ejidatarios were able to build a ten-tiered rodeo grandstand, seat-ing twenty-five hundred people, that they operated and managed. The ejidatario Don Benjamín River proudly recalls: "When we finished the plaza, we took the money we made from the rodeo event and handed the men who lent money their free ticket and their thousand pesos."[22] By asking the norteños (only some of whom had been ejidatarios) for a loan, the ejido had been able to build a rodeo arena that further in-stitutionalized the ejidatarios' position as decision makers and build-ers in the village.

Remittance rodeos developed unevenly in relation to particular migration streams and trends. Two decades later, very small towns in more remote places had adequate emigrant networks to contrib-ute to rodeo remodels. Even then the rodeo arenas were humble in comparison with El Chante's. In the 1990s, the remote rancho of La Cidrita built a wood and steel corral with two thousand dollars that had been donated by approximately twenty norteños (fig. 3.02). This rancho of approximately ninety inhabitants does not have a formal hometown association in the United States or enough norteños to fund the construction of a concrete and brick rodeo arena. Norteños paid for a modest ring of steel beams nailed to tree trunks, and they returned to La Cidrita from the United States for events whose modest profits were used to refurbish the church. The influx of dollars intro-

FIGURE 3.02. Two retired migrants pose in front of the arena in La Cidrita, a remittance rodeo project that they organized and helped to fund. The structure combines fence posts of unsawn locally harvested hardwood and horizontal rails of painted steel channels, paid for with dollars. Photograph by author.

duced foreign materials into a remote village and allowed villagers to accrue profits that were then used to fund renovations. While small in scale, the La Cidrita rodeo ring is nevertheless a transnational civic improvement that stirs local farmers' pride.

From the 1970s, as dollars were used to build rodeo arenas throughout the Jalisco countryside, the men necessary to participate in rodeo events were increasingly absent. In what became "emigrant villages," norteños began to assume the responsibility of implementing and managing the jaripeo remodels *and* events. Community members feared that their geographic dispersion was threatening the continuation of the jaripeo itself. Norteños were poised to assume the responsibility of keeping the tradition alive, however, because they returned with money and desire. Early remittance rodeo arenas built by norteños signaled a shift in how space was produced: that is, they followed the logic of remittance capital itself rather than social relations defined in place.

Building even small remittance rodeo arenas, norteños have found themselves saddled with unanticipated responsibilities due to the implicit assumption that they will also finance future jaripeo events.[23] In the town of El Chacalito, three norteños and one nonemigrant decided to replace the existing eighty-five-year-old stone corral. Their arrangement stipulated that two men would go to the United States to work and send money to El Chacalito while the other two managed the construction process. Since project completion, the pairs have annually alternated the responsibility to pay for and organize the fiestas. One norteño, who now lives in El Chacolito, reminisced about his time working at a restaurant in Los Angeles, "at the top of a tall building with ten floors." He made good money there from 1973 to 1988.[24] Now that he was back in Mexico and earned far less from his rancho, it was harder for him to comanage the jaripeo event. In El Chacalito, norteños who want to continue in their role as patrons of the *fiestas del toro* do not have the luxury of retiring in their pueblo.

These stories have become increasingly common since the 1990s, when the ejidos were economically restructured. In 1993, as a part of national efforts to modernize the Mexican economy and privatize resources, President Carlos Salinas made it possible to formally sell ejido land for the first time in over seven decades through his land-titling program PROCEDE.[25] While this is now a choice, selling ejido land is logistically difficult: ejidatarios must first survey and title it to obtain the necessary deeds. This law has further destabilized the autonomy, communitarian basis, and viability of the ejido, already challenged by Mexico's weakened economy, as some ejidatarios decide to sell and others to retain their land. These changes have in turn complicated issues of "ownership" of shared public amenities like rodeo arenas, creating additional tensions. It remains to be seen whether ejido communities will continue to perform jaripeos while under national incentives to dismantle.[26]

Commercialization and Regional Competition: *Puro Negocio*

With the rise of 3×1, remittance rodeos have both increased in number and grown in scale. Migrants see the jaripeo as an economic engine that will fuel the modernization of their pueblos.[27] Through 3×1 government agencies essentially piggyback onto informal remittance

FIGURE 3.03. In the cabecera of Lagunillas, the presidents of the Los Angeles and Las Vegas HTAS deliver checks to Autlán's municipal president, contributing the migrants' share of the Lagunillas rodeo-arena construction cost. Photograph by author.

financing of rodeo facility construction that has been occurring in the region since the 1970s. In the municipality of Autlán, 3×1 has helped to fund one arena in the village of Lagunillas—discussed above—and two more arenas in nearby municipalities.[28]

In Lagunillas, it was ejidatarios who had originally wanted to build a new rodeo facility. They had talked about the idea for fifteen years, but because of a lack of funds and political consensus, their efforts to initiate the project repeatedly failed. Until 2003 Lagunillas was one of only four pueblos, out of a total of twenty-one in the municipality, too poor to build their own rodeo arena.[29] The other three towns without rodeos were small ranchos of between 100 and 250 people, whereas Lagunillas was an ejido of over eight hundred farmers, schoolteachers, and retirees. Eager to establish their position in the municipality of Autlán, the local ejidatarios of Lagunillas decided again in the 1990s that "this corral [lot used for jaripeos] didn't satisfy us. We wanted

FIGURE 3.04. The formality of the Lagunillas rodeo arena (overlaid with its plan here) is evident in its monumental scale, industrial materials, and ordered spaces. Amenities, including a wheelchair ramp, entrance and exit stairs, nightlights, and bathrooms, distinguish the arena from others in the region. Photograph by author.

something better and started up the idea to build a new one."[30] A local from Lagunillas who travels frequently between Lagunillas and Los Angeles encouraged norteños in California to participate in 3×1 to fund a new rodeo arena. The norteños in the United States were already organized into HTAS, one in Los Angeles and another in Las Vegas, and had been experimenting with different project ideas for Lagunillas. They were inspired by the ambitious plan to build a rodeo facility.

The new facility, built between 2003 and 2007, cost an estimated $500,000 (about sixteen times the amount it would cost to build an ordinary home in Lagunillas) and officially seats twenty-five hundred people. The concrete bleachers, supported by massive load-bearing walls and enclosed by ornamental metal and chain link fences, tower over their surroundings. This monumental and modern structure sharply contrasts with the cluster of dilapidated one-room public buildings, one-story adobe and concrete houses, and largely cobblestone and dirt streets that constitute the village. Locals repeatedly referred to the rodeo as the most modern and comfortable in the region, if not the state of Jalisco.

In addition to the building itself, the jaripeo event held in the new facility contrasts with the informal rodeos recalled by ejidatario Antonio Gómez. Typically villagers, people from other pueblos, and people from the United States drive, walk, or ride horses to the rodeo in procession, especially when it is on the outskirts of town. Clean-shaven young men and groups of teenage girls with their hair pressed and curled arrive wearing new clothing. Men wear crisply ironed shirts, polished shoes, shined belt buckles, and immaculate hats. Once everyone is inside the stadium, elders from the village parade horses around the ring to the sound of brass trumpets and trombones played by the evening's first band. Announcers enter the arena to introduce the names and pedigrees of the jinetes and musicians. Priests may bless the young jinetes who are about to risk their lives. These professional

FIGURE 3.05. Jinetes pray to the Virgin of Guadalupe before the jaripeo begins in Lagunillas. The local branch of the Red Cross estimates that in the municipality of Autlán, bull-riding injuries cause five to ten deaths each year. Photograph by author.

bull riders sport full regalia—sombreros, leather fringe jackets and pants, spurs, vaquero shirts—presenting an impeccable image when kneeling before cheering crowds in the name of the Blessed Virgin.

The rodeo is buzzing with transactions: food and liquor—often locally produced tequila—are brought to one's seat, and the selling of hats and cotton candy keeps the pesos flowing. Hours later the main attraction starts. One after another, the young men jump onto a bull as it is released into the arena. Either the rider is thrown to the ground or he grips the bull tighter, digging his hooked spurs into the bull's ribs as his back and neck whip furiously from side to side. Usually about ten jinetes ride. While their performances are breathtakingly short (from several seconds to a few minutes), the preparation of ten bulls and the intermittent shows by clowns, skilled horse riders, and musicians extend the event several hours. Finally, the evening winds down to the sound of music blasted into the eerily dark and quiet surroundings by a twenty-person all-male band wearing matching silk suits. This scene is repeated endlessly in villages and towns throughout the south of Jalisco and beyond.

Migrants and ejidatarios embrace the rodeo's potential for generating capital and are reconstructing the jaripeo as a for-profit venture. According to a local elder in Lagunillas, in the past attendees "knew what the different moves were called. Now they don't pay attention to these things. They come for the music, to dance, and to drink beer. Before if the bulls were weak nobody would come, but now the bulls don't seem to matter as much."[31] Another elder, don Ignacio, is skeptical: "The old jaripeo was free, not about making money. Now it is all business [puro negocio]."[32] The *puro negocio* aspect of the event hinges on the new professionalization of the jinete, the bulls, the banda, and the beauty queens. Schools throughout Jalisco have been established to train jinetes. Specialized bulls might not matter "as much" but nonetheless are raised specifically to be fierce for the event. Beauty queens are involved in binational fundraisers associated with Semana Jalisco in US cities, and local bands are increasingly implicated in binational music venues and networks. The ejido is not an isolated village but part of a regional network of villages undergoing transformations visible in the jaripeo. In this networked remittance space, rodeo promoters and pueblos compete with one another for audiences and pesos in a region defined by scarce resources.

As multiple pueblos pursue similar strategies for local development through the rodeo, competition takes on novel forms. For example, throughout the last ten years competition between local bands has transformed cultural tradition into an international enterprise. Currently almost every town in Jalisco has a banda of over twenty men who play brass instruments. Young boys aspire to play in the bandas, and those who are successful travel to the United States on work visas to perform for primarily emigrant communities in cities like San Jose, Los Angeles, and Chicago. Successful bandas charge inflated fees, and banda recordings allow youth to escape the space of the village and join YouTube, Facebook, and other Internet sites with user-generated content that serve as vehicles for a transnational apotheosis. Cyberspace can alleviate isolation at certain moments, but it also exacerbates the cultural disjunctures between certain aspects of hometown life and the "modern" world.

Beauty queen contests, a tradition that originated in villages well before emigration, are also implicated in the remittance spectacle and now span international borders. US-born daughters of Lagunilla's emigrants now represent the pueblo as well as the family left behind. Several Mexican American young women compete to raise money; whoever raises the most money wins. As queens, they fundraise in the United States throughout the year and donate their earnings to the pueblo. Beauty queens are also now sponsored by big business: Coca-Cola, agribusiness firms, Azteca TV, and other companies view the binational competition as a way to tap emergent transnational consumerism.

Local ejidatarios are well aware of the economic potential as well as the symbolic importance generated by the modern rodeo facility, and their ambitions demonstrate the importance of the project to them. One asserts: "It is obvious to us who know about it that it is an important rodeo. All of the proper requirements are in place to recognize this rodeo internationally. . . . This *plaza de toros* will cost five hundred pesos for a ticket, and a lot of people will come, from Guadalajara and Mexico. I want to think that we will get to that level, people from Spain! Even though I might sound boastful, we are first place!"[33] The contest has begun, and Jorge Cortéz feels well positioned to win.

While people from Lagunillas are brimming with excitement over their earning potential, other villages nearby scrape their coffers in

FIGURE 3.06. The winner of the Queen Lagunillas competition arrives at the inauguration on the hood of a brand-new Dodge Ram pickup. Photograph by author.

search of money to build, to maintain, or to plan an event in their own rodeo arena. At just ten years old, the Ejutla remittance rodeo arena (partially funded by 3×1) remains unfinished and is deteriorating. The main archway on which Ejutla's name would have been displayed never got built. The bar planned for the lower level was never added, the rodeo seating only partially surrounds the rodeo ring, the stairs are sagging, and the engineered retaining wall is collapsing. Now there is talk of tearing down the incomplete *quiosco* (gazebo). The president of the Ejutla HTA in Los Angeles, Pedro Sánchez, notes that the rough entryway stairs are "especially bad for the ladies with their heels." He is upset about how little support he gets from the people of Ejutla: "Instead of going forward we are going back. If it wasn't for my sons helping me, I wouldn't continue."[34]

Uneven development in the remittance rodeo is rooted in particular migration and remittance histories. Towns with larger migration streams have more potential for remittances, a higher likelihood that some of the norteños will be "benevolent," and thus a greater capacity to produce a rodeo facility that will draw in what money there is throughout the region. Ironically, the towns with the most people absent have the advantage. In Autlán, half-built or abandoned rodeo arenas are reminders of the experimental nature of remittance building. Chiquilistlán's rodeo ring has an almost finished modern concrete stage with steep stairs that was intended for bands, but these bands may never come.

The Contested Terrain of the Remittance Rodeo

In Lagunillas, conflicts that arose over land and project ownership, management, and implementation complicated the construction process. Generally speaking, even though the inhabitants of Lagunillas had originally solicited norteños' help and continued to seek state funds, they received remittance development with ambivalence. Some were hesitant about state-norteño intervention and influence over local affairs, especially the rise of norteños in the local political process and the encroachment of the government onto ejido lands. Nevertheless, norteños are ambiguously both *insiders* and *outsiders*, which casts them as interlocutors between the pueblo and the state.[35]

Furthermore, mounting tensions over social status and power between ejidatarios and norteños are exacerbated by 3×1, which requires ejidatarios and other locals to operate and manage the project on the ground while ownership of the project and the land on which it is built transfers to the state, even if that land is ejido property. While 3×1 is not designed explicitly to be a state-run land grab, it is designed to allow the state to control and ultimately benefit from remittance revenue through ownership and possible management of remittance projects. And in the case of Lagunillas, 3×1 guidelines allow the state to assume ownership over land that has been unavailable to it since the formation of the ejido.

A legal battle over the land has ensued. The ejidatarios of Lagunillas were told that norteños and the government were going to help them build their rodeo arena. An ejidatario, Felipe Quiñones, donated his land for the project. After construction commenced, government officials approached the ejidatarios to have them sign over Quiñones's land. He notes: "I understand that the municipality wants to put the land in their name, but I didn't donate the land for the municipality, I donated it for the pueblo of Lagunillas. I am not trying to keep the land for myself; I just want to make sure that the pueblo controls the rodeo and manages the resources."[36]

According to ejido law, all the other ejidatarios have the right to buy the land from Quiñones before he can sell it to somebody outside the ejido—giving each ejidatario a strong voice in the battle over ownership of the new rodeo. Amid ongoing negotiations the municipal government drafted a contract that stipulates the ejidatarios and townspeople as owners of the arena for ninety-nine years. The ejidatario Jorge Cortéz scoffs: "The municipality is saying we will be in charge for ninety-nine years. As bosses, we can borrow it to use it. Why should I want to be a boss rather than an owner? Why should I feel that I am borrowing it? I am the owner! And my son is the owner! And my grandchildren will be owners!"[37] Ejidatarios are reluctant to give up land granted to them less than a century ago as reparation for injustices and inequities their ancestors faced. As noted by Fletcher, the "importance of land cannot be overstated. It separates the farmer from the peon; it provides a living, even when meager, and is a prerequisite for livestock production. Most importantly, it provides independence."[38] Additionally, ejidatarios have real concerns over the present and future intentions of the state. The region of Autlán has been plagued by political corruption, and until recently the local government shared power with rich caciques; locals do not have confidence in legal institutions. Referring to municipal elections, Cortéz explains: "They assure us that the contract will be respected by the next party. That makes me laugh. How can they know what will happen?"[39] Regardless of the contract, he fears that the incoming municipal administration could claim full ownership of the rodeo arena on behalf of the cabecera.

While three levels of government have contributed to the rodeo arena, it is the municipality that is most invested in it. Municipal officials express concern that if the ejidatarios do not relinquish ownership, the arena will become a private project funded by public money: "What would happen if Felipe died? The rodeo would be his and would go to *his people*."[40] Here officials express a desire to have the rodeo benefit "the pueblo," not only the ejidatarios who retain rights over the land. There is no precedent, however, for how the state would administer a publicly owned arena outside the cabecera to ensure that the profits were distributed.

Both the municipality and ejidatarios have resorted to petty measures to assert power and authority over the rodeo. The architect Eduardo Ramírez, who works for Obras Públicas (the Public Works Office) in Autlán, explains, "This dispute has been going on a long time now, and there are ramifications. The federal government sent a letter to Lagunillas saying that the project was intended to be a public project and that if they do not sign the agreement then they need to pay the municipality and federal government back all of the money that they gave for the plaza [rodeo arena]."[41] While this tactic is official and the letter came from the federal government, it is also a bluff. Villagers have no way of ever paying back the hundreds of thousands of dollars contributed by the state.

Municipal officials attempt to assert powers external to 3×1 guidelines in their efforts to convince ejidatarios to relinquish ownership. As noted by an accountant in Autlán's Public Works Office: "They are a pueblo. They don't have the resources to have a fiesta like Autlán. The money to maintain the building and hold an event is beyond the capacity of the rancho. And they think that migrants will continue helping, but they have other interests and can't continue forever. If they don't hand over the land, we will close the project, not allow them to have events or use it at all. It will become a ghost project."[42] The municipality perceives the temporary nature of migrant remittances and knows that the time will come when the villagers will turn to it for assistance. Additionally, the municipality officially requires the police and Red Cross to attend rodeo events in villages and can close down an event by keeping these civic employees from attending. That authority, however, is undermined by the fact that these "civic" institutions themselves are largely subsidized by private investment, often in the form of migrant remittances.[43]

Just as the municipality attempts to assert control over the rodeo in Lagunillas, the inhabitants of Lagunillas have their own tactics and strategies to claim ownership. Most notably, the ejidatarios have built additions to the rodeo facility that went beyond the project guidelines. In 2007 ejidatarios solicited funds from norteños to build the passageways, corrals, and paddocks necessary to perform a *corrida formal*, or

Spanish bullfight, whose prestige would rival the charrería. Architect Ramírez comments, "It is not normal for ranchos to have *corridas formales*. There is not another example of a rancho that I know of that has one. They were driven by ego; they wanted to be the only ones to have the corrida formal. Norteños too wanted the corrida."[44] This addition cost the ejidatarios and norteños forty thousand dollars beyond the project budget. Additionally, Quiñones built a new house right next to the arena while it was under construction. From this house he could watch over the building process. He also assumed the civic and financial responsibility of running water lines to the site, initially for his house but eventually also for the public bathrooms in the rodeo arena.

Villagers (most of whom who had no experience in or background in construction) managed the construction process themselves, forming a committee that met several times a week for the duration of the work. The committee's president, Darío Valdés, who served as the project manager, recorded each financial transaction by hand in a series of notebooks. Fearing thieves who prey on small communities that install amenities with remittance dollars, they also guarded the rodeo arena while it was under construction, protecting pieces of equipment such as loudspeakers and high-powered lights. The leader of the Lagunillas committee's own family, including his teenage son and his elderly father, ended up taking continual shifts throughout the day and night to watch over the lights and equipment for fear that they would be stolen. With a cot set up in the unfinished bathroom, they slept and ate at the arena for over two weeks.

These measures to assert authority reflect the position of the people of Lagunillas in the construction processes of transnational buildings, whereby 3×1 gives locals power to build but provides no regional planning and only limited expertise. Thus the project and its management are subject to a host of conflicts and inadequacies in the building process. An architect professionally designed the Lagunillas rodeo arena using distant prototypes in Guadalajara, Tijuana, and Spain for inspiration. The arena, "lo más cómodo" (the most comfortable) in the region, is a monumental permanent structure made of poured-in-place concrete. Its details include an inclined ramp and railing for people with disabilities, several grades of concrete seating sculpted by hand with a scalloped template smoothed over the surface to create an even

FIGURE 3.07. During the rodeo, the agricultural field adjacent to the arena (above) is repurposed as a parking lot (below). Most of the cars have US license plates. Photographs by author.

finish, marked entrances and exits, modern bathrooms, and a perimeter sidewalk and fence (fig. 3.04).

Some of these elements make little sense for an arena located several kilometers outside the town. The elderly and those in wheelchairs cannot travel on cobblestone streets that do not have sidewalks, so they cannot attend events unless they can get rides in cars. This apparent disconnect between vision and reality is also manifest in the failure to provide infrastructure to support the project. Quiñones personally paid for pipes to carry water several kilometers from the pueblo to the arena, but he is not promising to continue paying for the water or electricity indefinitely. Fifty percent of the households in this region are still waiting for running water, so investment in the rodeo arena occurs while basic needs go unmet.[45] The committee rents the adjacent agricultural field for parking spaces during an event, however, the farm owner has increasingly demanded higher fees. Astonishingly, in 2012 norteños were investing thousands more dollars to excavate part of a mountain across the street from the arena (which is surrounded on all four sides by agricultural land except for Quiñones's house) to build a multilevel "urban-style" parking structure. When Quiñones's land was donated to build the arena, the impact of building it outside the pueblo was not addressed.

Additionally, the professional architect determined the scale of the arena by creating it to accommodate 2 percent of the regional population of ninety thousand during a period when the population of Lagunillas itself was steadily declining.[46] The rodeo arena accommodates three times the population of the entire pueblo of Lagunillas and depends on a regional audience to fill it.

These conflicts in the ownership, construction, and management processes raise two central questions. First, who or what constitutes the pueblo? Second, who has legitimate authority to make decisions that affect the public space of the pueblo? Lagunillas is considered to be an ejido by both locals and outsiders, but the locals are not primarily ejidatarios. The village contains just over eight hundred people, of whom only ninety-seven are official ejido members. Recent arrivals, called "newcomers," and others born in Lagunillas but whose parents are from neighboring ranchos are not included, neither are women and children.[47] At the same time, the pueblo is also an "emigrant village," and migrants living abroad make decisions about what happens there. The people of Lagunillas estimate that between four and six hundred people from the pueblo live in the United States. According to Felipe Quiñones, ejidatarios have had full control over the management of their rodeo arenas: "The original ejidatarios can act like a business. They have the land, they control it and use it, and they can decide whether or not they want to use the money they make off their land for the good of the community."[48] In emigrant villages where people's roles are in flux, it is unclear how control over resources should be managed and who has the authority to decide.

The Jaripeo as a Gendered Performance

Debates over ownership and authority, typically dominated by males in the community, imbue the jaripeo's performance and its gendered spaces with added significance. Gendered divisions, roles, and expectations in Mexican society are recalibrating to accommodate a seemingly permanent transnational space and all of its irreconcilable difficulties. Within this transnational space, the rodeo is yoked at all times to remitting and loaded at every level with symbolic meaning. Despite the diverse and competing array of people involved in this transformation, it is primarily migrants who find representation in the symbolic space of the jaripeo. Remittances as a new mode of production transform traditional forms of identity throughout the region.

In theory, norteños finance remittance rodeos from a distance to ensure a space for the continued vitality of the rodeo. In practice, norteños' intentions and the negotiation of gendered identities in the spaces of migration reveal the complexities of envisioning, building, and using remittance space. Traditional gendered expectations in the town are expressed by rodeos that put men at the center as performers (the jinete, the banda, the announcers, the horse riders, the bulls) and women at the periphery as spectators. Once a year female spectators command attention as queens who are representative of place and symbolic of male desire. Even then they orbit a spectacle of masculinity. This spatial relationship—men at the center and women on the periphery—enacted publicly, dramatizes men as providers for the family and as leaders of the political process. It is a critical cultural practice for rural society, contributing to local and extralocal constructions of "ranchero masculinity," a hegemonic configuration of gender practices that legitimize men's dominant and women's subordinate positions.[49] This is one of the paradigmatic readings of rural Mexico's patriarchal social order stretching back to the viceregal period.[50] More generally, Matthew Gutmann defines masculinity as anything men think and do to be men, to be more manly than others, and to not be women but to desire them and "conquer" them.[51]

The gendered performance of the rodeo sublimates gender confusion and instability associated with migration for men. When a person for whom ranchero masculinity is an important part of his identity becomes a migrant, two critical things happen. First, the migrant leaves his home. Home is where gendered identities are enacted and fully inhabited, where men are taught how to be men, often by their fathers. When the migrant leaves his house, he also leaves his land. Control over land is linked to male independence; working the land requires the strength of men's bodies, and profits from it reinforce a patriarchal hierarchy. Thus for many men becoming a migrant can be immediately emasculating. It means sacrificing one's home, land, and place in the world for the future.

The journey, the next stage in this migration trajectory, involves crossing the international boundary and, if one lacks proper documentation, becoming criminalized as "illegal." Migrants leave their home to enter the shadows of American cities, the underbelly of the American economy. They cease working their land—which if it is ejido land means they give up their rights to it. For the unauthorized migrant, a new vulnerability immediately creates a divide between those who leave and those who stay.

At the same time, migration is empowering. It is an act that seeks to fulfill desires and dreams, that embodies satisfaction, assertion, and determination. As noted by Douglas Massey and others, for several decades now emigration itself has become a rite of passage into manhood.[52] Furthermore, many Jaliscienses were sanctioned braceros after World War II, and migration can sometimes be a way of following in the footsteps of one's father.

The experience of initial migration is empowering at times and emasculating at others, at once promising and demoralizing. All too often, it does not match up with how individuals imagined it would be or what it would mean. Individuals negotiate this variegated gendered terrain throughout the course of their lives.

Once in the United States, male migrants take on gendered roles that they normally would not perform at home. Men who cook and clean are doing what would be considered "women's" work in traditional Mexican society. Migration scholars have argued that first-generation male migrants lose status and power in the United States because of the particular socioeconomic positions they come to occupy. Over 30 percent of male migrants have service-sector jobs in the United States.[53] Héctor Alarcón, the president of Club Lagunillas de Los Angeles, went from working on farms and building houses in his village, which he considered to be proud work, to cleaning a factory in Los Angeles. Men are also aware that the jobs they hold—in the service sector, construction, and agriculture—are not well respected by many US citizens.

Meanwhile, women have increasingly opted to leave the home and become migrants as well. Whereas in 1990, 80 percent of emigrants from Mexico to the United States were male, by 2006 over 40 percent of them were female. What has changed is that now women are doing paid work—largely in service-sector jobs—and contributing financially to the household. Fewer migrant women in the United States hold jobs than men, and those who do earn less, yet they too remit money to their families at home.[54] Once in the United States, women are also increasingly participating in politics. They partake in HTA activities, making food and organizing migrant gatherings to raise money. They are also increasingly involved in the HTA political structure; the first female president of the Federation of Jalisco was inaugurated in 2008.[55] This exacerbates a divide between women who stay and those who leave, since those who leave are subject to economic pressures that destabilize gendered divisions of labor and are exposed to new gendered norms in the United States that might be contested at home.[56]

Migration scholars argue that these shifts result in a "crisis of masculinity" and the "liberalization of femininity." And studies have shown that men want to return to Mexico, where they imagine their status and power is preserved, whereas women want to stay in the United States, where they gain authority and establish roots.[57] Migration, however, is not always a crisis for men, though it can be a major crisis for women. Robert Smith, who examines the construction of gender in migrants' lives, argues that men make good money in the United States and that their involvement with HTAs results in a sense of power. Furthermore, the men's shift from traditionally masculine forms of work to cooking and cleaning, which are often associated with domesticity, occurs within the logic of migration, whereby earning power triumphs over the means by which money is earned. Those receiving remittances in the village do not look down upon men who cook and clean for their wages. Social and economic status is achieved in Mexico through work performed in the United States, which influences the ways in which migration may cause individual identity crises.

Also, despite women's increased participation in HTAs and remitting, remittance development is male dominated. Men currently control remittance projects because they have the necessary social capital and political credibility to do so.[58] In 2008 a statesman who worked with the 3×1 program noted that rodeo arenas and church remodels were the most common projects solicited by norteños who were presidents of HTAS. Also, in 2007 just 13 percent of Jalisco's Los Angeles HTA presidents were female. The few women who are involved in remittance development often speak of their interest in educational projects, projects that contribute to the social reproduction of civil society. In Magdalena, one of the few female presidents of an HTA has attempted to build a school. Men and women, then, approach remittance construction with different agendas and desires.

Rodeo-arena building allows migrants to translate their hard work in the United States into increased social status and visibility in Mexico. And it allows them to do so through a project that preserves a space for rancho masculinity.[59] Once in the United States, norteños perceive several benefits to being a man in Mexico. For example, though men in rural Mexico do not earn good money, they can drink wherever and whenever they want, and no police officer will arrest or ticket them for driving too fast in the countryside. Time in the United States aids in the reimagining of the village as outside the law—in their minds, migrants link a lawless utopia to their masculine identity, reconstructing a ranchero masculinity that they find little room and time for in the United States.

The rodeo allows migrants to define the symbolic identity of the village from a distance. After the church and its plaza, the rodeo arena is the most highly visible place and symbolic center of the town. Even from a distance, the arena asserts a man's claim on public space in his hometown. Everybody goes there to see the event and be seen during the event. Migrants go there when they come home. While the plaza is quotidian, the rodeo is spectacular. It is what theorist Henri Lefebvre calls a representational space that demonstrates to the other surrounding towns the virility and potency of the migrant men from that town. If one drove on the highway past a village, the rodeo arena might be the only building one could see.

The rodeo also asserts masculinity by being an economic engine. A migrant from Lagunillas, when visiting his hometown, noted: "I am honored to be received with thanks, and to do for the pueblo what nobody ever did for me when I was growing up."[60] Contributing to the rodeo arena instills pride. By bringing an engine to one's pueblo, norteños render their pueblo vital, or hope to. Norteños amend the wrongs of the past by claiming that their pueblo—the one they had to abandon—is now somewhere that matters, somewhere "on the map."

In the case of Lagunillas, norteños were motivated to give an additional forty thousand dollars to build the capacity for a corrida formal because Lagunillas was to have the best rodeo arena in all of Jalisco, if not Mexico. Male ambition manifests. Norteños idealize their past to invigorate their future.

Emigrants' production of jaripeo space protects ranchero masculinity and allows for their continued identification with the fearless bull rider. In some ways, migrants substitute remitting to the family as a form of paternity for a virility that would otherwise be acted out daily. The emblem of that substitution is the professional bull rider. He is the crown jewel of the rodeo. When he rides, time seems to stand still. And he is hired by norteños to perform a vision of rancho masculinity.

Michael Kimmel characterizes the cowboy as "unconstrained by the demands of civilized life, unhampered by clinging women and whining children. The cowboy is a man of impeccable ethics, whose faith in natural law and natural right is eclipsed only by the astonishing fury with which he demands adherence to them. He moves in a world of men, in which daring, bravery, and skill are constantly tested."[61] The American cowboy presented by Kimmel is inspired by the Mexican *vaquero*—for whom the jaripeo is the shining moment. Today the migrant's "faith in natural law and natural right is eclipsed only by the astonishing fury with which he demands adherence to them" as he risks his life to attain and sustain economic and social mobility. William Cronon gives us a different view when he reminds us that "the cowboy was the agent who tied . . . [the] . . . livestock raising zone to its metropolitan market. Far from being a loner or rugged individualist, he was a wageworker whose task was to ship meat to the cities."[62] Structurally, the emigrant is the cowboy. He is the agent linking flows of capital to neglected places.

While the male jinetes dominate the spaces of the rodeo, women—in the role of the "queen"—provide a feminine mirror to these masculine displays. Once a year the local queen is crowned in the rodeo ring. The contestants' frilly and decorative dresses of shining polyester, diamond-studded tiaras, and long-stemmed roses contrast visually with the muscular power and violent movements of the bulls, the clouds of dust, the sweat-soaked hides, and the utilitarian leather and steel spurs of the riders. While the queen is lauded for her grace, beauty, and even intelligence, none of these characteristics wins her the title. The queen is crowned because she earns the most money for the hometown. The competition for the queen is "puro negocio."

This emergent trend has implications for feminine identities both in the rancho and in emigrant communities. The female counterpart to the rodeo spectacle is no longer located in the rancho itself. The participants are often second-generation daughters of migrants from the rancho who live in, and identify primarily with, the United States. The Mexican American queen, in the name of Lagunillas or any other pueblo, comes to the rancho during the yearly festivities and occupies center stage. Her presence telescopes the space of the rodeo, where the actual experience of being in Lagunillas is directly shaped by distant places.

Key to the identity of the transnational queen is the notion of a culturally and spatially bounded place known as "the pueblo." The queen performs throughout the year in the United States to raise money, ostensibly for the improvement of her "hometown." In these performances she speaks of the needs of the pueblo and the important cultural traditions that define it. She even illustrates the pueblo on her folklore gown: elements of the built environment—the quiosco, the church, the cornfields, the rodeo—are painted or sewn on the gowns to verify authenticity and demonstrate the queen contestant's practical and working knowledge of the pueblo. In Los Angeles, queens wear their dresses at a major migrant event known as Semana Jalisco, and "dresses are the most important part of the event, because they represent the folklore and life of their pueblo."[63] In the 1950s, Lagunillas queens represented their town by being "women of the pueblo." Today emigrant children craft representations of the pueblo to construct their heritage and to justify their participation in remittance networks, even though they do not live there.

The new practice of having a US beauty competition does not keep Lagunillas's inhabitants from holding their own competition; rather, it recasts their competition as concomitant to the one in the United States. In 2007 the queens in the United States (one in Los Angeles and the other in Las Vegas) collected over fifty thousand dollars each. Meanwhile, their "original" antecedents in Lagunillas made rounds to restaurants during the Sunday post-Mass meal with tin cans, collect-

FIGURE 3.08. This advertisement in *Semana Jalisco* magazine for the Miss Jalisco USA competition shows contestants in their signature gowns, which portray notable features of the hometowns they represent. The gowns frequently display elements of the built environment, such as church facades and *quioscos* (gazebos or bandstands).

ing pesos for a total sum of nine thousand dollars. The comparison of these two practices reveals what Doreen Massey calls "power geometry," the types and degrees of agency people exert given their social locations.[64] In the consumption and reproduction of a local tradition, Miss Lagunillas USA reinforces the economic and social limitations of her twin rival. This new phenomenon, whereby norteños financially dominate their rural counterparts, is possible because of international migration and global capital and results in new economic disparities at home.

Importantly, while women are participating in one of the key aspects of remittance development by bringing in revenue, they still have little direct power or political influence over development projects. Norteñas are fundamentally changing local modes of production, but they have yet to disrupt hegemonic displays of gendered expectations in the hometown and spaces of migration or to give new material expressions to the evolving relationships between the sexes.

The Transborder Inauguration

The Lagunillas rodeo grounds inauguration of 2007–8 was particularly dynamic because of who was in attendance: a diplomat came from Guadalajara to represent 3×1, the municipal president and his wife came from Autlán, the president of the Federación de Jaliscienses came from Los Angeles. In addition, norteños from several states, HTA members from Los Angeles and Las Vegas, and locals from nearby villages and towns filled the stands.

The committee of Lagunillas worked tirelessly to prepare the town for four days of festivities and the norteños' arrival. They erected an inaugural orange gateway over the road in front of the rodeo arena and decorated the streets and plaza with streamers. The packed festival schedule left no time for rest. The committee hired professional musicians, riders, bulls, videographers, and photographers to make sure that when norteños came home they felt proud of their pueblo, were appropriately received, and approved of how their money had been spent. During the fiesta, villagers publicly expressed overwhelming gratitude toward norteños, giving them trophies and shirts and showering them with praise.

At the beginning of the rodeo event, a trellis made of fresh flowers that read "Bienvenidos" (Welcome) was carried into the arena. Norteños, politicians, and others gave speeches as the audience looked on. A migrant from another pueblo in Jalisco who was also a member of the federation in Los Angeles scanned the arena from inside its enclosure with amazement: "I haven't seen something like this before—this is really something. No, I haven't seen something so big in a pueblo so small."[65] The president of the federation congratulated the HTA members, urging them to "keep winning" by raising and spending more dollars. The diplomat from Guadalajara took the microphone to thank norteños for "keeping the tradition alive." Priests and pastors from afar lauded norteños for "their love for the pueblo." After hours of praise, the presidents of the Los Angeles and the Las Vegas HTAS, the 3×1 diplomat, and the municipal president of Autlán stood under the "welcome" sign and cut the inaugural ribbon into four pieces while the spectators cheered.

Their seamless performance belied the many tensions that had

FIGURE 3.09. Signage on the Lagunillas rodeo fence advertises the Programa 3×1 para Migrantes, publicizing the cost in pesos of the *tercera etapa* or third stage of construction as a part of the government's effort to achieve transparency and accountability. Paid for by migrants and the government, the fence itself is the first to enclose public space in the town of Lagunillas. Photograph by author.

arisen in the production of the event. Women did not participate in the actual ribbon cutting even though they had raised substantial funds through their hard work in the HTA and through the fundraising by the queens. Yet they were not completely absent—women stood on the side of the arena floor with their husbands. This configuration reproduced the dichotomy of men at the center and women at the periphery. However, it also challenged the limited role that women played in the public and political processes in the town; they were occupying the arena for the first time as providers, not just as objects of desire. Today women occupy an ambiguous position as coproducers of remittance space in a society invested in maintaining a patriarchal social order.

The inaugural moment masked new divisions and ruptures between emigrants in the United States resulting from the competition for Queen Lagunillas USA in 2007–8 between Los Angeles and Las Vegas. Both clubs refused to accept defeat by, in part, claiming to "still be counting their earnings." Each proclaimed to have raised over (a stunning) fifty thousand dollars from tens of thousands of small donations. The committee in Lagunillas acknowledged, "There is a lot of tension about which queen won, fighting over who worked harder, those in Los Angeles or those in Las Vegas. The winner is the woman who made the most money, but they are disagreeing about this."[66] The norteños were so focused on who had won that they did not garner any satisfaction from the fact that they had made over $100,000 for the pueblo. The meaningful experience of inaugurating the rodeo and crowning queens was reduced to rivalry over who had more earning capacity in the United States and thus more political power. Norteños sought recognition for work and hardships experienced in the United States which the people who live in Lagunillas did not witness or fully comprehend.

Finally, the conspicuous omission of ejidatarios during the ribbon-cutting ceremony reflects their position vis-à-vis norteños as managers rather than producers of these new spaces. This was manifested in a disagreement between members of the HTAs and the committee of Lagunillas over who got free tickets to attend the jaripeo events. Alarcón explained:

> Now they received us with food when we came; there are people that still need to accept that we are doing something good—that's a reality, we are the ones that did it, not them. When we gave them power, not all the power, the committee didn't give us power. Darío asked, "Should we charge you?" I left it up to them. They gave us twelve tickets even though we have twenty on the board. This made us feel bad. In the *kermés* [potluck fundraiser] we worked, from the youngest kid to the oldest adult. We both bought the goods for groups to sell and paid for them. When we saw that they didn't give us free entrance to our plaza, we felt bad.[67]

The fact that the norteños were not given enough free tickets to even cover the twenty principal members, let alone the three hundred norteños who flew or drove down from across the United States for the pueblo's event, was interpreted by Alarcón as the ejidatario's way of communicating ownership over what he felt was the norteños' rodeo. The Lagunillas committee is invested in asserting ownership whenever possible because the arena was its idea initially, it is on ejido land, and committee members maintain it daily. When addressing who should make decisions about the plaza and event, the ejido committee president passionately exclaimed: "Here is the committee! Here is the committee! Here is the committee!"

Ultimately, ejidatarios must contend with a new social order based on the prominent position of norteños—both men and women—in Lagunillas's public space and events. During the inauguration the role of the migrant as the future at every level of society was institutionalized. The tradition that is now being preserved is remitting. Norteños in absentia have to keep coming back, spending money, and sending money to keep *their* monument alive. The future that the Lagunillas rodeo arena welcomes is thereby a transborder one.

While ejidatarios and villagers have complex responses to this societal shift, norteños face a daunting and ambiguous set of competing responsibilities, allegiances, and desires. As their responsibilities proliferate, so do their ambitions. One goal of many migrants is to resurrect and preserve the jaripeo as a form of traditional culture, yet the forum they have created for performing that version of rancho life is the very place that reveals the extent to which that social order no longer exists. Due to men's absence from the community, their contributions to it are not visible in everyday life; remittances make those contributions tangible, and the remittance rodeo transforms a financial transaction into a material spectacle that acts out traditional social roles otherwise lost.

In this context, the figure of the professional bull rider constitutes a dialectical image. While he harks back to an idealized recent past when men rode bulls and worked the land, today he is not free. He is a young man in rural Mexico making a living by risking his life over and over again. He is the real Benjaminian "wish image" of the jaripeo: a professional working in a modern space, ushering in progress, while shackled to a fixed identity indebted to an almost obsolete mode of production. The rider, a bright star, embodies the aspirations of the men, norteños, who no longer ride bulls because they have *too much to lose.* While they pay for riders, talk about riders, and wear clothing that represents riders, they have too many responsibilities, too much at stake, to risk it all again. The norteños live between a rock and a hard place: the rock of desired financial stability in the United States and the hard place of not being able to protect their cherished ways of life without migrating.

4 La Casa de Cultura

NORTEÑO INSTITUTIONS TRANSFORM
PUBLIC SPACE

Thank you dear Virgin of Guadalupe, for helping me be the same as I always was. It's true, though I'm not sure if you, my Saintly Patroness, have realized the co-incidence, that along with the changes in my appearance (just look at these new clothes) came another way of thinking. I am more tolerant, although I don't always understand or agree. I have changed and I have not changed, Jefecita, but I am still faithful to you, who represents the Nation, even though now I may be Pentecostal, Jehovah's Witness, Adventist, Baptist, or Mormon. What is always important is what I am, and I am still the same devoted person as always, the person who could not live without family, who still asks about the hometown and the dances, even though this huge radio that I have brought—I think they call it a "ghetto blaster"—plays melodies that I used to hate but that now inspire me. I swear to you, dear Virgin, I am the same as I always was, even though I can't recognize myself in the mirror.

CARLOS MONSIVÁIS, an imagined "migrant's prayer"

In December of 2007, I traveled to Los Guajes, Jalisco, a village ap-proximately thirty miles from the state capital, Guadalajara, to see the parade of the *hijos ausentes*, or absent sons and daughters.[1] The rural community of approximately nine hundred inhabitants is geo-graphically isolated, far from the only highway that connects Guada-lajara to the south of the state. Bright December sunlight illuminated the gravel roads and modest homes of Los Guajes. Standing by, as the guest of a prominent norteño named José Ochoa, I watched as a group of about one hundred people who identified as norteños, paisanos, migrantes, and hijos prepared to march from the outskirts of the vil-lage to the town's church. Musicians warmed up on their saxophones, drums, and trumpets in preparation for the procession. Old friends and family members who had not seen each other in years or de-cades chatted gaily. Some American-born children who accompanied middle-aged men and women chose to stand by and watch rather than

FIGURE 4.01. During the parade of the *hijos ausentes* (absent sons and daughters) in Los Guajes, an elderly nonmigrant spectator removes his hat as a sign of respect. Photograph by author.

join their parents in the march. When the crowd had gathered, with cameras ready, the hijos ausentes commenced their procession along Calle Hidalgo. At that moment, the spirited gathering became silent. Individuals wore solemn expressions. For roughly thirty minutes, the participants marched from the eastern side of the village, past Los Guajes's first adobe houses built in the 1800s, to the main plaza. Filling the narrow street and continuing for at least two blocks, the marchers were framed by a crowd of onlookers who identified as Guajeños or *mexicanos* rather than migrantes or paisanos. The movement of the hijos ausentes against the stasis of the Guajeños mirrored the life trajectories of these two groups.

The townspeople treated the hijos as if they were soldiers returned from a foreign war. During the march, they acknowledged them with respect. The norteños marched in silence like a platoon. These were the sons and daughters who returned, gave money to the church, and continually fought to improve the livelihoods of family members who had never left. While called *ausente* (absent), today they were *presente* (present). The march ended in the church, the traditional center of social life in Los Guajes. In the church, the priest publicly thanked the norteños for their "service," for being, in effect, pillars of the community. In the church the hijos were recognized for their sacrifices. After the march and church event, the townspeople prepared a large fiesta for the norteños.

The formality of Los Guajes's parade contrasts with the festive recognition of hijos ausentes as cultural trendsetters in the nearby town of El Grullo. Located in a sugarcane valley south of Los Guajes, El Grullo has a population of approximately twenty-five thousand. Grullenses estimate that another twenty-five thousand from the town live in the United States. In December, El Grullo is converted into an exuberant spectacle of apparent material abundance and activity for the *fiestas patronales*. Music roars from polished SUVS and trucks that circle the church plaza. Booths that occupy the downtown streets sell liquor and food, and the music plays until 4:00 a.m. El Grullo's young people sport the latest fashions. Ringlet curls cascade down girls' backs. Boys' short haircuts are slicked back with gel. Skinny jeans hug hips; other jeans hang stylishly loose from waists.

During the 2008 festivals, one booth that made explicit connections between El Grullo and the United States particularly commanded the attendees' attention. It was called "GruYork," named after the migration corridor between New York and El Grullo—not the largest migration stream between the two countries but one of the farthest geographic distances traveled by Grullenses who go to the United States. GruYork was a DJ booth showcasing contemporary electronic and hip-hop music. A construction-paper cutout of the New York cityscape provided an iconic backdrop for the large speakers and mixing tables. The music drowned out the classical Mexican music and contemporary banda from other music booths lining the block. In a street packed with migrants and locals, by far the most crowded space was immediately in front of the booth where the GruYork DJ played. The DJ engaged the crowd: "Bienvenidos hijos! Bienvenido a tu tierra natal!" (Welcome, sons! Welcome to your native land!). The crowd roared. The DJ shouted, "Where are you from, hijos? How many of you are from New York?" The crowd roared. Whether you were from New York or had never left El Grullo did not matter: GruYork allowed everybody in attendance to identify with the idea of New York.

As portrayed in Carlos Monsiváis's imagined prayer to Mexico's holy Virgin, migrants have changed through their absence; their return brings new distinctions and differences. The recognition of such difference takes place in these annual fiestas and parades. David Fitzgerald calls the process of migrants becoming different "dissimilation," or "the forgotten twin of assimilation."[2] Upon return, migrants want to have a place to go, a place in their hometown that will cater to their needs. Like the annual parades, processions, and fiestas occurring across Mexico, building allows norteños take a literal position in the built fabric of the hometown that will both affirm their pueblo roots and represent their worldly outlook. In addition to performing their identities, some norteños have built spaces within which they can be the audience for an event of their own making.

One such project, the Casa de Cultura, or cultural center, in San Juan de Amula, is bringing new forms of public space and a distinctly "migrant" public to San Juan that is not dependent on their immediate presence. The building is a large open hall and auditorium space where norteños and the people of San Juan can hold important life events such as weddings and quinceañeras (the celebration of young girls' transition to womanhood at age fifteen). Rooms upstairs serve as flexible space for the people of the pueblo to take classes and provide social services. As a new public gathering space built directly adjacent to the jardín or plaza, the cultural center modifies the existing public "nucleus" of the pueblo, which is composed of the plaza, quiosco, church, church garden, and other important civic spaces. This nucleus of the pueblo is a spatial repository of the town's social life.

In this chapter I discuss how new migrant-built spaces affect the public sphere of rural pueblos, producing tensions with existing sociospatial systems such as compadrazgo (the coparenting networks of comadres and compadres established by the Catholic Church and practiced widely throughout Mexico) and the social hierarchy of place.[3] Spaces intended to build connections end up producing differentiation and potentially stirring up discord that reverberates throughout the daily life of emigrant communities. Attempting to build such a place reveals a central paradox of remittance space: migrants desire to reconnect with and relate to their hometown by fundamentally altering it.

In the building of a space to represent the identities and desires of migrants, those very identities are called into question. The norteño's identity is most immediately a referent of his or her involvement in, and connection to, several sites: the host town, the hometown, and the migrant civil society. Migration scholar Roger Rouse has interpreted emigrants' orientation as a cultural "bifocalism," an advantageous position whereby norteños can choose between different ways of being on the basis of the specific context they inhabit at a given moment.[4] Norteños who come from small agricultural villages like San Juan may also know about the inner workings of Los Angeles, and thus have vital knowledge about how to behave in different circumstances to get desired results. Some scholars warn against portraying the experience of migrancy as dividing migrants between "here" and "there," between one set of norms and values and another, and instead emphasize the psychological flexibility and agency that migrants embody. These theories, however, address how migrants respond to distinct environments, not how they produce them.

It is within the context of personal transformation and psychological flexibility that norteños envision new possibilities for the hometown, realized via their hard-earned dollars. Norteños become what Sharin Zukin and Pierre Bourdieu refer to as the makers of the "critical infrastructure" of the cultural economy of place.[5] One way migrants build this critical infrastructure is by constructing a space that implements new cultural ideas, demonstrates new standards of taste, and shapes how people see themselves and their place in the community.[6]

The history of the Casa de Cultura reveals that migrants who experience bifocality are choosing to assert who they have become in the context of their hometowns. In part, their knowledge of distinct places and ways of being propels them to build places where certain ideas take on fixed and calcified forms, places that define and delimit ways of being according to migrants' "multivocal" perspective.[7] In San Juan, the "critical infrastructure" that migrants have built destablizes the local hierarchy of social relations that constitute place and thus challenges cultural constructions of community.[8] The center itself reveals how the people of San Juan and its emigrants have reevaluated their public spaces, and the population they are intended to serve, in the context of migration.

The "Nucleus" of Mexican Pueblos

Throughout Mexican cities, towns, and villages, the physical spaces of the plaza define not only local life but also Mexican urbanism and identity. The spatial morphology of plazas also extend from Mexico City's Zócalo or Plaza Mayor to "Mexican American" towns throughout the American Southwest.[9] According to the historian Richard Kagan, the plaza, as the "the town's chief ceremonial center, site of religious processions . . . and the place where visiting dignitaries were customarily received, . . . served both as *a school and a theater* where the rudiments of [society] were taught."[10] During Spanish viceregal rule, the 1573 Laws of the Indies served as a planning principle to organize the formal layout of towns. Towns were to be, first and foremost, organized around a central plaza that corresponded to the size of the projected population. The church was to be joined to one side of the plaza, governmental buildings to the other. The streets were laid out in a grid pattern, two extending from the plaza's corners and one from the middle of each side. The plaza was to be surrounded on three sides by arcaded walkways or *portales*. The quiosco became another critical element of plaza design since the French "occupation" from the early to mid-1860s. By the late nineteenth century, during President Porfirio Díaz's regime, quioscos became standard features in plazas.[11] They are ornamental structures used most frequently by local bands. These historic features are visible from the plaza of Guadalajara to that of San Juan de Amula and in Mexican-era plazas in the US Southwest.

Throughout small towns in Jalisco, plazas are used for some but not all of the functions common in their urban counterparts. In the absence of large *ferias* or marketplaces, the most important use of the plaza (often referred to as the "jardín") is the staging of community fiestas. Fiestas, whether familial (a wedding or quinceañera) or communal (a holiday such as the local saint's day or Día de las Madres), are notorious for spilling out of the church and taking over the church garden, the plaza, and the surrounding streets. Townspeople explain fiestas as "open to all," a time when "the whole pueblo comes together" to collectively break from daily routines. Fiestas also rely on the compadrazgo system; *comadres* and *compadres* provide assistance, make food, and earn their keep as important members of another's family. In addition to fiestas, plazas are used for small-scale fundraisers known as *kermés* (potluck fundraiser) and what are called *serenatas* or *paseos*. A serenata typically takes place on Sunday evenings when young men walk in one direction around the plaza while young women circle in the opposite direction to the sounds of a local band. This dating ritual has been important to the social reproduction of places.[12]

San Juan de Amula, though an unremarkable village of only five hundred inhabitants, far from the major highways zigzagging across the south of Jalisco, is shaped by historical and social processes that have marked thousands of pueblos throughout Mexico. The identity of the place—as both a physical space and a clustering of social interactions—has been reinforced through the history and legacy of its built environment. Its origins as an Indian pueblo predate viceregal rule, yet there is almost no evidence of this initial settlement in the built fabric. It was identified by the Spanish Crown as an outpost for imperial operations—a cabecera—in the mid-1600s, and thus the Spanish organized the building of the church, its adjacent garden, the plaza, and a street grid loosely according to the Laws of the Indies. The Catholic church and church gardens anchor the plaza. A dense network of adobe houses surrounds the plaza. Many of the external walls of private houses are connected to one another, forming a continuous facade that runs along the street. A network of individual agricultural fields surrounds the domestic zone. The domestic and productive landscapes reinforce the plaza as the geographic and symbolic center of the pueblo and reflect a communal and distributed building process. Due to various local conflicts, including the spread of a virus that decimated the population, San Juan lost its position as cabecera to neighboring El Limón. Still, the legacy of its official function remains in the formal structure of the town center.

Since the turn of the twentieth century, various institutions have competed with the church as organizers of daily life or decision makers at the community level. Today a municipal office, the Casa Ejidal meeting hall, the office of DIF (Desarrollo Integral de la Familia), and the Casa de Cultura form a cluster of institutional, communal, and civic spaces around the original institutional space of the church and the church garden. The single-room municipal office houses a local delegate (under the jurisdiction of the municipal president in the

FIGURE 4.02. The dashed outline shows the areas of the core of San Juan de Amula renovated or built using 3×1 funding, including the church, quiosco, and plaza with a "Children's Garden," the Casa de Cultura, and two resurfaced streets.

cabecera El Limón) who makes some decisions about the use of public space. The Casa Ejidal—once a meeting hall for the members of the ejido—is now defunct and houses mainly tractors in its yard, reflecting the weak position of ejidatarios in the community. The marginal position of ejidatarios is partially a result of the strength of San Juan's Catholic church. The priest argues that the church has assumed the real responsibilities of helping the people of San Juan, who have historically been neglected by governmental authorities.[13] At the other end of the plaza from the church is the Casa de Cultura, newly erected by and partially for norteños who are staking a new claim over the management of the village's public spaces.

The Role of the Church in the Formation of Public Space

The priest individually, and the church generally, has been the most influential figure in determining the use, development, and articulation of cultural values in the public space of San Juan. Whereas delegates, municipal officials, and even community activists have come and gone, Fernando Santiago has served San Juan's parish on and off since the 1960s and remains in office today. Capitalizing on the importance of the plaza, Santiago spearheaded material, social, civil, and religious reforms in the 1960s and 1970s by remodeling the jardín and quiosco as a means to build social cohesion and demonstrate church leadership. Starting in 1961, the priest used the structure and regularity of church sermons to motivate the people of San Juan to save pesos to buy and make bricks that they would then use to build up their town center. For several years, brick by brick, with an outpouring of donated labor from men and women, the plaza and quiosco were erected (fig. 4.04).

Santiago's handwritten captions in his personal photo album tell the story of a symbolic rebirth of a newly self-sufficient San Juan. Below snapshots of the new plaza and quiosco, the captions read: "Shaking off its poverty, San Juan is reborn by its own power. It is the start of a new stage in our history: the construction of the quiosco." Emphasizing the pueblo's autonomy, Santiago wrote, "Without help from the government, with its own power, it made a dream into a reality: the plaza."[14] According to the priest, the new plaza and quiosco were "a place to reunite the pueblo" and "the start of a new stage in our history," one characterized by fraternity instead of poverty and by peaceful gatherings rather than violent conflict. Repeating the words "its own power," the priest emphasizes the town's agency and strength amid debilitating poverty and limited growth.

Since the 1960s, Santiago has maintained some measure of control over how the plaza is used. Fiestas, among the most important spatial expressions of community, also reveal the hierarchical spaces that reinforce community. The priest controls the use of the church, the church offices, the courtyard, and the church garden. Some families have stronger alliances and more resources than others, allowing them to orchestrate more lavish parties. In San Juan, where it is noted that "everybody is family," a system of favors and debts binds community members to one another. Fiestas serve as a social arena for extending and reinforcing ritual kinship relations. While the fiesta is traditionally "open to all," access to church space and families' capacity to provide food for the whole town means that the kinds of parties that families can hold vary.

In San Juan, the building of the quiosco and jardín and the organizing of fiestas that take place there are collective efforts that reinforce the role of the priest as community leader—and thus bolster the status of the church within an institutional hierarchy—as well as the centrality of men in the building process. While women played a critical role by making food to raise funds for bricks, their participation is not memorialized in the priest's album or in local discourse about how the town has maintained its public spaces, while men's roles are. The hierarchy of rural Mexico defined by patriarchy, age, gender, and dependency has been enacted and solidified through its building traditions.

While the priest's strategies have successfully organized community action to improve the plaza and quiosco, they have not succeeded in addressing the need for updated infrastructure and other projects unrelated to the highly visible public spaces of the church. The town's discontinuous networks of roads, sidewalks, and running water demonstrate the limits of incremental community-based infrastructure development. When projects are perceived as benefiting only certain individuals, not everybody in the community participates.[15] Consequently the roads and sidewalks—built and maintained by the families whose houses occupy each section of the street—are often only partially built or repaired, and large sections remain in disrepair. Running water currently reaches only half of the homes in San Juan, leaving some families to use wells or carry water from working pipes. Church members and town leaders have not had the manpower, will, or institutional support needed to get major public works projects under way. In this context of governmental neglect and weak or absent local institutions, flows of remittances have changed the fundamental social, political, and economic hierarchies of San Juan.

The Rise of the Norteño as a Civic Benefactor

In the 1970s, not long after the priest remodeled the plaza, a small group of emigrants formed San Juan's first social club in Los Angeles. The club aimed to give modest amounts of money to the pueblo and to create an opportunity for emigrants to unite in Los Angeles. Vicente Rubio, an early club member, recalls that no more than a dozen gardeners, construction workers, and restaurant workers sent what money they could to San Juan to help out with local needs. They gave their money to the priest, who made decisions about what to build and managed the process. One of the main accomplishments of this early investment was the restoration of the *curato*, or church offices, which had fallen into disrepair because of a cataclysmic earthquake in 1985. Ultimately, using the norteños' dollars, the priest maintained the curato's architectural form, replacing the fragile adobe walls with fired brick.

Despite this initial success, the unreliability of remitting in the 1970s and 1980s eroded trust between club members and inhabitants of San Juan. Club members sometimes felt that their counterparts in San Juan mishandled their contributions. One club member, Ramón Murillo, recalls:

> Always when they do something [in San Juan], we send money from the US. Somebody [in San Juan] is in charge, but we don't have clear records, and so rumors start, they robbed us, this or that. . . . There was a time when people didn't want to hand over money. Once they [norteños] got together there [in the United States] and bought a car for students here [in San Juan]. The pueblo had a new car, but in the end they didn't use it and they sold the car, or . . . Rumors started about people robbing the money, and the people here didn't want to cooperate or do anything.[16]

When norteños decided to donate the car that Murillo mentions, they bought it in the United States and drove it to Mexico themselves as informal insurance against the misuse of their dollars. But ultimately the remitted car could be—and was—stolen or sold. It was not insured or registered and did not belong to any one person who could assume responsibility for it. Ultimately, norteños' inability to control how their money was spent, and subsequent loss of interest by club members, resulted in the demise of the original club.

In the early 2000s, the formalization of remittance-financed projects through the 3×1 program, as well as increasingly sophisticated remittance transfer options, led to a rebirth of the social club. More norteños now have residency papers or US citizenship and can personally monitor the use of their money through frequent trips home. Unlike the informal and incremental projects attempted in the 1970s and 1980s, once the club reengaged, the norteños' civic improvement projects in San Juan's central plaza could now be consistently remodeled and maintained.

San Juan's club has a geographically disperse membership base led by a small group of four. Juan Zamora, Vicente Rubio, Ramón Murillo, and Roberto Gallegos, migrants who have experienced varying degrees of financial success and time in the United States, drive the club's operations. Their work in the HTAS creates a platform for the limited but critical participation of scores of other emigrants from San Juan. According to the HTA president, the hometown organization in the United States represents over 150 families from San Juan. Residents of San Juan estimate that roughly half of the pueblo (that is, five hundred of the pueblo's one thousand people) lives in the United States, with the majority in California, Arizona, New Mexico, and Texas. Club members use phone calls, letters, and even a San Juan website to reach out to this geographically dispersed community.

The core members have developed strategies to cast a wider net around San Juan's expatriots so that they can accrue more remittances. To achieve this goal, influential norteños in the greater Los Angeles region appointed delegates in satellite cities. These delegates were then asked to host and organize fundraising events in their cities. In an attempt to minimize the amount of time norteños and delegates spend fundraising, and to ensure the continuation of collective remittances, the key members initiated an automatic club-membership donation of ten dollars every month. They began with twenty dollars, but according to Murillo, "People cannot commit to such an expense."[17] Zamora, the club president, acts as a collection agent, harassing friends and family for their contributions. "Juan," another club member said affectionately, "is like a fly. He doesn't leave us alone."[18]

The Role of Architecture in Placing the Norteño

Migrant-led transformations of San Juan's public space did not begin with the cultural center. In just three years the leaders of Club San Juan implemented a renewal of the town center that previously would have taken decades to complete with volunteer labor. Eager to capitalize on the Tres por Uno para Migrantes (3×1) program, as well as decades of accumulated knowledge of US economic systems, norteños filled the void left by a weakened church and invested heavily in San Juan's core area. They rebuilt the plaza and quiosco, landscaped a children's garden, remodeled the church, installed running water in a section of town, and repaved two main streets that end at the plaza (fig. 4.02). Ramón Murillo notes, "Since we started the club, when we met, we agreed that the most basic part of a pueblo is its nucleus, its center. To have a good quiosco, plaza, and church—these are the most important things to have. If you are in a pueblo, it is bad if the jardín is neglected. . . . The plan was 'Quiosco, change it. The plaza is in bad conditions, change it. The church is falling down, and why?'"[19]

For migrants, rejuvenating the pueblo by rebuilding its public spaces helps to conceal and ameliorate the consequences of social and economic change resulting, in part, from mass migration. During club gatherings, migrants still reminisce about the town's traditional communal events: crowning the pueblo's queen, day of the *piñata*, and day of the *paseadores* or riders. They describe the ample civic participation and communal celebrations that characterized these traditions, which ceased in the 1970s and 1980s when migration to both Guadalajara and the United States increased.[20] To address the decay of the plaza and the loss of these "bonitas costumbres," or good customs, norteños fixated on the town's aesthetic conditions. They remodeled the very quiosco and plaza built by the priest and his followers that had once represented the unity of San Juan and the centrality of the church. After knocking down the old quiosco and replacing it using contemporary materials and expensive detailing, they resurfaced the plaza, repaved the main road with *adoquine* (small reddish durable tiles), and remodeled the facade and tower of the damaged church.

Building in the town's center brought about unanticipated social change by directly challenging the hierarchy of San Juan's local insti-

FIGURE 4.03. The newly remodeled plaza includes a stone quiosco, stone-paved walkways, raised planters and benches, landscape planting, lights, and a built-in sound system. Photograph by author.

tutions. The priest's absence from the four groups that are supposed to constitute the parts of the 3×1 program (the municipality, the state, the federal government, and norteños) has resulted in his exclusion from decision-making processes regarding 3×1 projects. Offended by the norteños' decision to knock down "his" quiosco and jardín, a church leader and close friend of the priest protests: "The decisions are made between Rubén and the hijos, and nobody in the pueblo is asked or told what is going on."[21] Rubén Parra works for the municipality as treasurer and manages the 3×1 money. Statements made by norteños that the old quiosco was "ugly and dangerous" exemplify a great difference in opinion regarding the significance of specific built environment elements.

The repositioning of the priest Fernando Santiago vis-à-vis the state is fraught because of memories of the Cristero War—the epicenter of which was Jalisco. Santiago, born during that conflict, which took place between 1926 and 1929, is deeply suspicious of the Mexican government because of the costs of that war. Churches in towns near San Juan were destroyed, and the government's army expelled and killed priests. In many ways Santiago views himself as protecting the people of San Juan from the government and filling a vital role as civic leader in the state's absence. Norteños' alliance with the government through the 3×1 program destabilizes his construction of the role and meaning of the government for rural constituents today.

For these reasons, the norteños' interest and offer to remodel the church itself came as a mixed blessing. Since the church was scarred by both natural wear and tear and an earthquake, the priest accepted norteños' proposal to remodel it using 3×1 funds, on the assumption that he would be in charge of the funds. Government pesos and norteño dollars, however, flow directly to the treasury office of the municipality, and Rubén Parra, as the treasurer, was in charge of the money. Aside from being the municipal treasurer, Parra is also the president of the local club that works directly with the Los Angeles club; as a result of his dual positions, he has been a faithful agent of norteños in San Juan, creating tension with Santiago. At the end of the project the priest refused to sign a form that would confirm Parra's use

FIGURE 4.04. A faded photograph in priest Fernando Santiago's personal album shows the quiosco, remodeled in 1961 with funds donated to the church, which was replaced by the much larger stone quiosco conceived of and funded by migrants in 2003. Photograph by author.

of funds to assure the state that the money was properly spent. Signaling desperation, he even accused Parra of purchasing fake marble for the church floors. Today this estrangement between norteños and the priest and his followers lingers. However, as remittance development continues in San Juan, the priest's protest can be little more than symbolic.

Despite all of these built environment changes, it was the construction of a brand-new Casa de Cultura that allowed migrants to add a new program—an event and gathering space not located in the church or individuals' houses—that has had the greatest impact on the public space of San Juan. The Casa de Cultura has no architectural precedents in San Juan or any other pueblo in the region. The project began with a straightforward concept: to create an enclosed event space with plumbing to replace what was called the *casino*, an open-walled lot adjacent to the plaza with no roof or bathrooms. Migrants felt that the informal space was inadequate for holding fiestas, though occasionally it was used for them. When discussing the initial idea of the center at a club gathering, Rubio explained that one night, when he had the shortcomings of the casino on his mind, he dreamed of a beautiful Spanish-style building in the center of San Juan. In the dream he enjoyed a cold beer on the balcony of the building and looked out onto San Juan's verdant hills clustered with fruit trees—much as he imagined the hacendados would have in the nineteenth century. The next day, in the shop of his carpentry business, Rubio crafted a miniature wooden model of a modern structure with a generic neoclassical facade and an exterior two-story Spanish colonial style gallery with Doric columns (fig. 4.05). According to Rubio, "I have seen this sort of thing in Mexican plazas and thought, why not in San Juan?"[22] Rubio's personal transition from poverty to relative wealth has contributed to his belief in the possibility of transforming San Juan.

This instinct to develop public spaces in a Spanish colonial style is common among those who fund remittance projects. For example, in the nearby town of Vista Hermosa, two influential migrants, a husband-and-wife team, explained their idea to build new *portales* along the main axes of the town adjacent to the plaza: "We had to search for an architect who could make columns with the proper dimensions. Many are too fat or short. We wanted them to look more European." This migrant couple has been to Europe, and they brought

FIGURE 4.05. The wooden model of the new Casa de Cultura that Vicente Rubio prepared in his carpentry shop in Los Angeles. Migrants used the model, which combines elements of neoclassical, hacienda style, and Spanish colonial institutional architecture, to build consensus for the project concept in the migrant HTA community. Photograph from San Juan de Amula's website, now defunct.

portales to their hometown not only for themselves (the portales face their remittance house) but also for the "culture of the pueblo."[23] Remittance-financed portales and ornamental columns are now common throughout rural Jalisco. As Rubio notes, he has seen columns in Mexican plazas; columns and portales are iconic landscape elements in all colonial Mexican cities, and remittance building affords migrants opportunities to visually connect their pueblo to the cultural and economic centers of Mexico and Europe.

Rubio used his wooden model to build consensus among influential norteños in the United States to build the center. The club does not have a formal or institutionalized system for determining how its money is spent. Ultimately, deciding how to invest communal remittances depends on the time, resources, and leadership (if the core group deems an idea worthy) of individual club members. They garner support and approval from the broader emigrant network. The recognizable elements of Rubio's cultural center concept won support. Murillo notes: "He made the model, and when we saw it we thought, 'Wow, this is nice.' Well, we all agreed. This appears very big, but finally we said, 'Why not? And as a present for the pueblo . . .'"[24]

Completed in only two years, the Casa is a modern two-story concrete masonry building wrapped in ornamental columns and French colonial–inspired balustrades. The structure fundamentally alters the spatial context of the main plaza. Notably, the Casa is the only two-story public building in town. This is partially because locals have relied on fragile adobe brick as their primary building material. Some adobe houses have been rebuilt with fired brick, but few have added a second story. The Casa, made with reinforced concrete, steel beams, and fired brick, is larger and taller than the church. Upstairs an interior balcony wraps around the primary auditorium, allowing events to be viewed from above and creating private spaces in an otherwise open auditorium. The exterior second-floor balcony also allows individuals to gaze down on those occupying the street or plaza. Before the Casa was built, the church bell tower offered the village's only panoramic view. Otherwise one had to hike up a nearby mountain. The second story creates a public space with a view—a position of authority and inherent distance that was also present in Rubio's dream.

In addition to the unprecedented second story, the building distinguishes itself as "modern" through the installation of automated bath fixtures and other amenities. In fact, San Juan's most modern bathrooms can now be found on both the first and second floors of the Casa. Automatic faucets, and hands-free paper towel and liquid soap dispensers "like the ones you see over there [in the United States]," make for "state-of-the-art" bathrooms inspired by the restrooms in the Los Angeles airport.[25] The auditorium is also outfitted with a drop ceiling of acoustical tiles like those common to office environments in Mexican and US cities. San Juan's only air-conditioning system cools the building during hot summer months. Finally, two automatic garage doors are installed in the west wall to open the auditorium to the street during large events.

With a multitude of potential programs, as an open hall and event space, its meaning is malleable for a diverse set of constituents' needs and desires. Murillo described the Casa's importance for local cultural events: "The auditorium is also important because before if you wanted to have an event, there wasn't a place to have it. They were

FIGURE 4.06. The two-story portico or *portales*, ornamental portal over the entry, hand-carved cantera stone columns, balusters, and factory-built windows distinguish San Juan's completed Casa de Cultura. Both the Casa and the alternating bands of concrete and cobblestone paving were funded through the 3×1 program. Photograph by author.

held in the school, or church, or the jardín, but there wasn't a place big enough to hold events like Día de los Niños or Día de las Madres, or weddings. We used to have weddings outside, but there was no place to go to the bathroom. People would have to ask to use the restroom at people's houses."[26] Norteños also want to hold events at the Casa. Those who live in Los Angeles explain that in the United States they must pay exorbitant prices to rent halls, abide by local regulations that prohibit drinking in public, and limit noise levels for fear that police might break up the event. In San Juan, they say, documented and undocumented migrants alike should be able to hold weddings and quinceañeras in peace. As an added bonus, the building will serve as an educational space, a "present for the pueblo, to change the culture of the youth."[27] All three of these agendas collide with customary social practices regarding how communal space is used and who manages and oversees events.

In the context of town events and fiestas, the new bathrooms and kitchens offer an alternative to the sociospatial practices based in the compadrazgo system of extended familial networks. First- and second-floor kitchenettes allow events to be professionally catered so that food doesn't have to be prepared and served out of people's homes. Similarly, those holding events at the center do not need to rely on the bathrooms of neighbors, comadres, or family throughout town. Also, while the fancy bathrooms succeed at impressing inhabitants, they present a striking contrast between the local context—half of the town is still without potable water—and norteños' aspirations.

The building also makes public events more formal. The presence of the auditorium, San Juan's dedicated performance stage and changing room, encourages planned events rather than the ad hoc performances that used to spill out into the plaza and street. A formal entrance creates a new threshold where event hosts can monitor entry and exit during a "private event" in which tickets can be sold and behavior regulated. These spaces introduce new possibilities into the town and contrast with the open and informal spaces of the plaza.

Equally important to the cultural center's spatial configuration is its institutional administration. The center is a quasi-public, privately managed venue that charges a fee for reservations—an unprecedented innovation in small towns with ejido roots and a strong sense of communal ownership of public space. Families who want to hold weddings, quinceañeras, and other events in the center are charged a five-thousand-peso (five-hundred-dollar) rental fee. This fee has raised suspicion about norteños' intentions. A young woman, Mónica Maldonado, asks, "How can they set a price of five thousand pesos here? Nobody can pay it. They say it is a benefit for the pueblo, but what is the benefit? They built themselves a place to have a party."[28] Families who rent the space are also being asked to rent tables and chairs and hire waiters rather than serve the food themselves or rely on relatives and friends to assist. This shift is not just an unaffordable expense for local families, some of whom earn less than ten dollars a day; it is also a shift that reorients the community away from the compadrazgo system and toward a more entrepreneurial, privatized, and individuated system supported by remittances.

The club also asserts its authority by selectively charging fees or donating use of the center. For certain occasions, such as the municipal tradition of the *reina de tercera edad* (or crowning of an elderly queen), the club has donated the use of the center to the municipality, allowing it to function like a civic hall. But for familial occasions, community members have to rent it. Additionally, norteños who contributed to the cost of building the center get to rent it at a discounted price or use it for free. Currently no other public space in San Juan is privately managed and thus accessible at no cost on some occasions and accessible for a fee on others. Historically the priest has mostly controlled the use of public spaces, and he has not charged a fee. Now norteños delegate from a distance. To facilitate this, Zamora would like to install webcams on the lights in the jardín to monitor what people are doing from Los Angeles. While the norteños assume the authority and power to make decisions that might destablize San Juan, their actions also call attention to the extent to which San Juan's spaces do not adequately reflect what the community has become.

In addition to paying fees, those who rent the space must follow rules established by the norteños. There is no smoking in the building and no drinking on the balconies, and food cannot be carried outside or eaten on the sidewalk or in the plaza. According to Murillo, "Those are the rules, like when you go to a swimming pool you can't bring in food, or you must have a bathing suit—rules to maintain something."[29] These rules introduce new regulated spaces into San Juan. They are also associated with public space in American society, which has social configurations and economic logics fundamentally different from those of rural Mexico. A small poster that hangs in the central auditorium space reads: "No Fumar [No Smoking]." Until now the rural pueblo of San Juan has lacked instructive public text. The need to identify common values and to direct and educate "the public" has not been necessary.[30] The only public signs or text in San Juan, and in many small towns throughout Jalisco, had been painted commercial or political advertisements on crumbling brick walls and occasional street signs. "No Fumar" imposes a social agreement that previously did not exist among community members and lays bare the distance between imported ideas and existing social customs.

As norteños broaden their experience, some recast or come to perceive the people who remain in their hometown as provincial and backward. At the very least, the experience of migrancy contributes to the intensification of perceived binaries: migrant-nonmigrant, have-

have-not, cosmopolitan-provincial. Some norteños, however, idealize inhabitants of San Juan as more connected with the land and closer to God. Others view inhabitants as lacking in the critical perspective that comes from knowledge of life in disparate places. Thus remittance building can be about norteños' desire to correct, amend, or try to preserve "local" ways of life newly perceived as different, retrograde, or ignorant.

The social distance between San Juan "community" members requires constant negotiation. Ricardo Negrete, once a norteño who now lives in San Juan, acts as a mediator between club members and townspeople. He views their differences in relation to the new experiences migrants have in the United States:

> It is different, what they think in the United States versus what we think here. . . . They want to put many laws or rules on the way people here live. For example, they want to have festivals without beer. But that is impossible; then it wouldn't be a party. . . . They don't want people to walk with their food or drinks outside of the building during a party. Here it is common that after people get their food they will take it somewhere else. . . . The club wants people in the cultural center to stay in their seats, like a restaurant. . . . They want this door [points to the main entrance] to be the limit that people can't pass. We like to be outside, but the bad thing about it is that we throw trash on the ground, and then the neighbor has to pick it up or it stays there. That is their point. In the United States, I would be chewing a piece of gum and would look for a trash can to throw it out in, or a piece of paper to put it in. Here, no way.[31]

These rules affect how people socialize, which is an integral part of establishing the social hierarchy of place.[32] They are also adopted from a particular context: in the United States, municipal systems strictly regulate littering, trash collection, and drinking in public space is illegal. Such systems and regulations have evolved over time as a way for governmental agencies to manage cities and towns. While rural Mexico is not devoid of regulatory mechanisms, regulations are not generally enforced. Police do not pay visits to pueblos, municipal trash pickup does not exist, and public drinking is commonplace. Individuals enforce social customs and accepted behavior. However, in this case the individuals attempting to enforce new customs occupy marginal positions in the daily life of the community due to their extended periods of absence.

This dynamic contributes to some norteños' sense of obligation to teach townspeople "better social customs" when they come home for a visit. During the inauguration of the center, Zamora went up to a group of kids and told them not to spit their peach pits on the floor. He then turned to me and explained: "They lack manners; they need to change their style of living. Nobody tells them what is right and wrong. Their parents do the same. When I am here I can tell them, but I am not always here."[33] Zamora asserted his role as cultural mentor when judging the youth as lacking both formal and familial education. Through social interaction he articulates his own identity as a norteño who "knows better." Zamora's judgment also reflects a larger discussion that occurs in norteño circles about the backward culture of the pueblo and people's resistance to what they see as "positive" change.[34]

Norteños also believe that in addition to being an event space, the Casa can bring about much-needed social change through educational programs. A few years after the Casa was built, Rubio expressed a modest goal: "We want to create leaders. If we have classes for eight students and we get one leader, we've won."[35] Aware of the fact that the Casa will not reverse the trends set into motion over the course of several decades, migrants' hopes recalibrate from changing the "culture of the youth" to reaching at least one child. Computers have been installed upstairs with the hope that one day the Casa can provide digital access to college classes through distance-learning programs.

Norteños' interest and investment in the youth is partially motivated by their new opinions regarding local practices that they themselves once participated in. Murillo explained that "much of what characterizes life is that at a certain age you either go to the US or you like to drink beer. This is something practically automatic. What we are trying to do in the auditorium is put classes upstairs, not just an auditorium."[36] Zamora builds on the image of rural youth in crisis by reflecting on his own experiences: "There is a lot of alcoholism in the pueblo. We were that way too, but we came here [the United States] and our lives changed. We all drink, but we were worse. We are trying to help."[37]

People throughout the pueblos and ranchos of rural Mexico share norteños' concerns about the youth of San Juan. Migrants and non-migrants alike worry about the abuse of alcohol and the introduction of stimulants such as crystal methamphetamine. There are many theories for why behaviors previously associated with cities have appeared in the pueblo—Mexico's drug war, which has infiltrated states like Jalisco and Michoacán, has increased the presence of drugs in villages, and cartels sometimes depend on youth to transport drugs.[38] Returning migrants bring "bad habits" learned in urban environments back to the village.[39] In a small town in Michoacán, the priest notes, "teenagers leave young, too young, and sometimes they join gangs or people on the street and come back with drug addictions. Last January, after the festival when migrants come home, some people were in the jardín sniffing glue and snorting coke. In the jardín! And kids were around for whom they are heroes!"[40] In 2011 the pueblo of San Juan experienced its first loss of a teenager to a methamphetamine overdose.

The young people of San Juan witness the effects of global migration, which can take the form of addiction but more often result in new material wealth and social status. Describing an "economy of information," AbdouMaliq Simone explains how rural-to-urban linkages not only facilitate migration but also intensify a sense of difference between the two places. Citizens of rural places become more aware of inequities, which can contribute to a sense of hopelessness or depravity.[41] The imagery of modern urban life that feeds into pueblos through various forms of media also contributes to youths' perception of the pueblo as "stuck in the past." An eleven-year-old girl in Guanajuato expressed anger over all of her friends who suddenly "disappear—they go away" without saying goodbye.[42] Such feelings of abandonment can translate into a desire to also escape, and sometimes the route for that is drinking or getting high.

Inaugural Fault Lines

The inauguration of the Casa de Cultura, ostensibly a festive event to mark the completion of a historic building project, exposed the conflicts implicit in the creation of public spaces and amenities with remittance dollars. Several tensions between norteños' vision and local realities challenged the logic of norteños' efforts. Norteños, because of their investment, felt locals owed them—a debt both of money and of gratitude.

During the inauguration Zamora organized a fundraising opportunity one evening driven by a set of expectations that were out of touch with local economic constraints and cultural norms. Zamora's idea was to convert the Casa into a formal dance club with an entrance fee. He hired a band from Ciudad Guzmán that cost 30,500 pesos, the most expensive band to ever come to San Juan. With a cost of one hundred pesos per person and fifty pesos per Corona, some three hundred people were needed to cover the cost of the band alone.[43]

The "gift to the pueblo," as impressive as it was, became a space of contestation and cause for new controls on the populace. The dance concert—and first ever pay-to-participate event—meant that the entryway was used to check tickets. The entryway became a threshold that divided people into distinct groups. Hundreds of locals who came from surrounding towns to see the center did not actually enter the building because of the fee. Rather, they looked in from the doorway and milled about the plaza. The fiesta—historically open to all—was spatially divided between the public space of the plaza and the private realm of the Casa and dance concert. In the doorway, people loudly debated the entrance fee, exclaiming, "I can't afford it!" Others who might have been able to buy tickets chose to remain outside, where "it is more fun." Some stayed home in disgust, remarking, "I was not invited." The Casa separated people along nascent class lines. The center had become a space of migrant modernity, an emergent space in a little village linked to increasing reliance on remittance capital to sustain daily life.

While locals criticized the private fiesta, norteños and their families were confused and offended by the apparent lack of appreciation for their efforts. Rubio's family from California attended the center's inauguration. His daughter Verónica remarked:

My dad has worked so hard for this town. He plays it down, but he has. I used to come here every summer until I was twelve, then every couple of years; now it's been eight. They work really hard, but the people here don't understand, they *want everything for free*, and that's not gonna happen. Juan gives a lot when he himself is needy. He is hard up in LA. The people in the club are working menial labor jobs, getting paid little, and they still give to the club and their town. The people here will understand this eventually. . . . I think the people here are upset because they think, "Who are these guys that are making decisions from so far away, from the United States?" The club might need to slow down and get everybody on board first. These changes have all happened very fast.[44]

Verónica addresses the rapidity with which the changes in San Juan's public spaces have occurred. She also exposes a genuine disconnect between norteños and locals that is based on a misunderstanding: local inhabitants of San Juan view all norteños as wealthy when in fact many of them are struggling financially. For migrants with little money, remitting is a sacrifice, not an act of philanthropy. Zamora notes, "Those of us who are giving money do not have much to give. Life is hard here; we live day by day."[45] The sacrificial nature of remitting contributes to emigrants' sense of entitlement about exactly how their contribution is used and what it means. But while the people of San Juan welcome norteños' dollars, they often experience norteños' attempts to control social behavior as an imposition.

The fundraiser, meanwhile, did not make any profits and instead put key norteños deeper in debt.

Fracturing Public Discourse and Representations of Place

Building with remittances has contributed to a proliferation of debates about who and what constitute the community of San Juan precisely when the place-boundedness of "community" has been weakening as a result of persistent emigration. As this occurs, the idea of place, and of cultural belonging, takes on new salience.

People who occupy various sites—the local community of San Juan, the spaces of the HTA, and the transborder public sphere—all argue over how the Casa de Cultura should be used and what it means. While some of these participants are interested in the Casa's daily use, others are more invested in the symbolic meanings associated with it. The Casa, as both a material place and a representational space, gives a specific, concrete form to the emigrant community of San Juan. As a representational space of modernity and success, the Casa is idealized as emblematic of progress. Yet it has also become the focus of conflicts between norteños, inhabitants of San Juan, and the priest or other persons with authority and power; these conflicts, in turn, breed mistrust, jealousy, and disappointment. Debates surrounding the use of the Casa expose the fracturing of consensus among different people invested in the pueblo of San Juan.

In the municipality of San Juan, townspeople debate the value of the Casa, many of them viewing it as a missed opportunity for much-needed productive investment. An old man in town who had been involved in managing projects and civic affairs throughout his life remarked: "That white elephant . . . they spent close to 450,000 pesos. They should have spent that money on sources of work. We don't have a *panadería* [bakery] here. Or there are lots of women who sew—we could have a sewing factory, or a canning place for the mango and *ciruela* that rot. . . . They shouldn't have spent so much money on that when we are hungry for work, for sources of employment."[46] For him the Casa, rather than being an admirable state-of-the-art building, represented wasted dollars.

An editorial written by a young man in the neighboring pueblo of La Ciénega suggests that the cultural center in San Juan has evoked widely divergent reactions among locals: "The town is building an ostentatious and pompous house of culture, shows, festivities, and many more things, thanks to the united clubs, the government programs, and the people here. . . . For the representatives and the engineers it will be cause for reverence and elevated pride. For modernity and development it will be a further step toward the triumph of the present over the past. For the peasants, the unemployed, the housewives, and other people, who knows what it means!"[47] Here a Casa that represents modernity and development widens the class divide between engineers and peasants.

Indeed, it is through the center and the activities of the HTA that some local inhabitants have come to perceive others in the pueblo as "backward." Parra, the municipality treasurer, explains: "The people [in San Juan], some are angry. They don't understand why [the Casa de Cultura] has to be so big, what for. Here there is everything, they don't look for more. The fruit is free—we have tomatoes, watermelon—and people don't pay rent. For two hours of work you have enough money to eat, and so that's all they want to work. Those who go to the United

States, it changes their mentality. They have to pay rent; they are a part of a larger system."⁴⁸ Parra's comment contains an implicit critique of the people of San Juan who do not look for more. This is a fault that he feels keeps San Juan stagnant. Without having to go to the United States, Parra gets to benefit from the way that migration motivates and energizes former inhabitants to achieve more. Remittance development may allow him, a twenty-five-year-old man who has no desire to emigrate, to stay in San Juan as the manager of building construction and migrant remittances, rather than to be a farmer without resources.

In the spaces of the HTA, representations are used to define the Casa as a success and to motivate future donations. Slideshows shown at club gatherings in Los Angeles, a calendar that highlights the HTA's built projects in San Juan, and a website managed by an influential norteño frame the building projects as picturesque. During a Los Angeles club meeting, Rubio held up the calendar and explained: "The photographs only show the center of town, which now looks okay, but everything around it is ugly. Little by little we will remake the entire pueblo."⁴⁹ Club meetings in Los Angeles and other US cities are attended by migrants from San Juan, some of whom have not returned to visit the hometown since their initial departure. Representations of remittance projects are displayed to provide those who cannot return the satisfaction of knowing what their hard work and monetary donations have produced. These photographs are shown alongside historic photos of fiestas in San Juan, days at the river, picnics in the mountains, and local pilgrimages. Photographs of celebrations and daily life evoke norteños' nostalgia, which ultimately contributes to their desire to give money to the HTA. Donations justify the distance they endure and the longing they experience.

The Federación de Jaliscienses and the government of Mexico also idealize remittance development. In federation literature, and in meetings that bring together key players in the 3×1 program, the Casa is used as an example of the possibilities of the program. A complete project, architecturally sophisticated and intended to perform a social (and educational) benefit to a "pueblito" in need, is evidence of the success of the remittance-development model more broadly. But the representation of the center as a success in HTA circles and in federation and Jalisco state literature is a willful denial of the discord that the project has produced in San Juan. The power of narrative effectively motivates remitters and propels the production of more remittance-funded development projects.

The New Hierarchy: The Cost of Transborder Ambitions

The norteños' role as leaders of the town and managers of its public spaces comes with burdens and responsibilities, including substantial financial debt. At first, key norteños from San Juan saved what money they could and set it aside for the Casa de Cultura. As the cost of the project grew, they began to borrow money they did not have from a US bank and from norteños who were not managing the club or project but who had some money saved. According to Ramón Murillo, key norteños agreed that getting the building right was more important than adhering to a strict budget: "The project [cost] of the Casa de Cultura was $240,000. We started with $30,000, then $120,000, and now $240,000, because it is a question of details. We started with something, but then people have ideas, and we say, 'Let's do it. If we don't do it, it will be built in any old way, but if we work for these details then it will be made better.'"[50] One critical detail was an air-conditioning system, the only one installed in the municipality of El Limón.

At this point the norteños who invested in this project owe approximately thirty thousand dollars to other emigrants and to a bank in the United States, and their debt has diminished whatever circumscribed financial freedom or mobility they achieved while in the United States.[51] Furthermore, these men now owe money to other migrants in the HTA. Consequently the HTA has changed from a fraternal space involving voluntary donations to a financial space involving accountability and trust. Debts between HTA participants are partially contributing to a loss of solidarity among club members. According to Zamora, 120 members used to contribute monthly to the HTA pool, but after the cultural center was built that number dropped to under 100.[52] In addition to the influence of debt on HTA membership, the *kermés* is losing its popularity as norteños in California increasingly choose to spend their limited capital on other pressing needs. What's more, the club's president and participants are starting to express an interest in helping those from San Juan who are in Los Angeles rather than people in the pueblo. This is a geographical shift in their activist orientation. Around 2010 the website was dismantled, and the club's current status is unclear, likely reflecting some of the distress the club has experienced throughout the Casa's short history.

Several unintended consequences have resulted from the norteños' decision to use remittances to build a cultural center. The president of the municipality has reevaluated and threatened to reduce the already constricted flow of state funds from the cabecera to the surrounding pueblos in light of norteños' demonstration of their financial capacity through the building of the center. According to village inhabitants, leaders of the municipality feel that its responsibility to help the pueblo financially has been entirely fulfilled by its participation in 3×1 projects.[53] San Juan's budget to run a small school and the local delegation or civic office is dispensed from El Limón. El Limón (the cabecera of the municipality) also dispenses a small monthly stipend that allows San Juan to provide food daily for twenty impoverished elderly people who cannot cook for themselves.[54] The municipality may reevaluate its financial obligation to San Juan (which has managed to build a center that outshines all buildings in El Limón) even though the municipality failed to contribute its share of the cost of the center during the first stage of construction. The municipality's abdication of its responsibility has not been reported to the 3×1 state officials. Any club that has conflicts with its cabecera can be blacklisted and prevented from receiving funds for future projects. Rather than address the issue with state officials, norteños paid El Limón's portion out of pocket, contributing to their already rising debt.

Ironically, the norteños' position in this financial quagmire has contributed to their choice to privatize the Casa and thus to introduce a sociospatial model for events that is antithetical to the compadrazgo system. "We built it so fast, and at first we didn't know how much we would need to spend for the lights. We still have to see how much we spend on electricity. We have to set rules, because if there are imperfections we have to pay for them, and where is it [the money] gonna come from if we are only spending?"[55] Renting the Casa will allow norteños to ensure a flow of capital that is not dependent on migrant organization in the United States. Ultimately this is necessary because the hierarchy of San Juan—with norteños at the top—is not fully sanctioned by the government and because norteños lack the necessary funds and authority to oversee the management of public space in San Juan from cities in the United States.

* * *

A critical investigation of the spatial and social consequences of norteños' role as managers of semipublic spaces reveals challenges to the people of San Juan's social, cultural, and spatial construction of community. For norteños, building with remittances requires arduous effort and sacrifice and results in a host of unforeseen responsibilities. This underscores one of the dangers of the remittance model of development, in which individuals who send money to build public projects must act as planners, fundraisers, project managers, accountants, and administrators; a slew of tasks difficult if not impossible for one person to perform. In San Juan, norteños were determined to build, at whatever cost, a building that replicated Rubio's model. Dispiritedly, Rubio admits, "If we had known the Casa would cost so much, we wouldn't have built it."[56]

The building, regulation, and use of the cultural center pits a new economic model against social capital within the pueblo's social structure. A model based on "paying to participate" challenges how the people of San Juan think about public or communal spaces—whom these spaces represent and who is doing the representing. Rouse's study of a disparate group of rural Mexicans affected by transnational migration concluded that in rural Mexico, concepts of personhood emphasize not autonomy or self-expression but occupation of a particular place in an existing field, not "who am I" but "where I stand" in a field of social relations.[57] The interlocking and interdependent system of compadrazgo is challenged by a North American model based on the premise that access to spaces is not about where you are from, your position in the social hierarchy, or the strength of your familial networks but rather about how much money you have.

The cultural center competes with the plaza as the site of town fiestas and gatherings and offers a different social space that is enclosed, has controlled access, and has a specially designated use. The center also seeks to become self-sufficient; the kitchens and bathrooms allow events to maintain autonomy rather than to rely on the surrounding homes. This vision has created a space for norteños in their hometown even if their extended absences have weakened their social ties. It allows individuals who might not have family, comadres, compadres, or friends whom they can rely on to come to the town to get married or to celebrate the quinceañera of their daughter (who most likely is a US citizen) in San Juan.

While it is tempting to look at norteños as detached inhabitants—imposing their desire to hold fiestas on someone else's town, their cultural ideology on a distant relative, or their economic model of space on another's territory—the Casa is also about norteños' attempts to build bridges with village inhabitants and with their own past. The center is intended as a place for youth and as a gift to the pueblo. Such benevolence is supposed to resolve tensions that linger between norteños and those they left behind, since leaving is not only an attempt to forge a better life but also an implicit rejection of the life lived in the village. Influencing young people and giving a gift to the pueblo is a social act that is personally motivated. It is about amending norteños' loss, incurred by their initial emigration. Through building, norteños attempt to *be* at home.

Zamora is conflicted: "I miss my pueblo. I yearn for it. But when I go back, the people are changing, the kids are drinking and doing drugs, and all these things we used to do as a community are lost—I feel bad because I was of the first generation to leave, so it is partially my fault that it is not like it used to be."[58] Zamora's "feeling bad" contributes to his desire to change the culture of the youth—back to how he remembers himself as a child before he (and most of the other grown men in the pueblo) left. He is not alone in his nostalgia for aspects of his childhood, specifically those aspects that cemented his participation in a larger community and his place in a larger field of social relations. The loss of specific practices such as breaking a piñata and playing soccer contributes to his desire to build.

The irony of remittance space is that many norteños have no other place where they are recognized as full citizens. The hometown is theirs as much as anywhere else; it is where many norteños feel they belong. Norteños see the Casa as both a gift to those they left behind and a building that reflects who they have become. And while the Casa is intended to resolve the social and cultural disconnect that emigration fuels, it is a material manifestation of that disconnect. It makes the disconnect tangible by producing a visible, experiential contrast between traditional and new migrant spaces, and between the community of the past and the community of the future. Designed to create a permanent link between norteños and their hometown, the Casa exposes the fragile construction of an "emigrant community" stressed by geographic fragmentation and growing expectations.

5 In Search of a Better Death

TRANSNATIONAL LANDSCAPES FOR AGING AND DYING

Author: Where do you want to be buried?
Javier Villaseñor: I don't know. I have never thought about it. I really don't know . . .
  Mexico.
INTERVIEW IN BERKELEY, California, 2007

I will return. My dream is to open a business there [in Mexico]. I want to return, in two years. Yes, I will return. I hope I return, my heart asks for it.
JUAN ZAMORA, California, 2011

A lifetime of migration complicates end-of-life planning, even for migrants who have achieved some measure of financial success. In 2008 Armando Juárez, a migrant from Quila, Jalisco, was sixty-five years old and contemplating retirement. At age fourteen, Juárez had begun a life of manual labor, farming the land near his hometown. At seventeen, he embarked on a life of migration that included picking cotton and lettuce in border towns, working in hotels and restaurants in the greater Los Angeles area, and driving trucks across the United States. Juárez's most stable job was working at Martin Marietta, an airplane-manufacturing plant in Los Angeles, for thirteen years. After his tenure there, he worked another thirteen years as a licensed truck driver. Throughout his life, he has maintained a connection with his hometown by visiting family approximately once a year for one month. At sixty-five, Juárez needed to decide where to settle down: "I have been working for fifty years. Fifty years of coming and going. I am tired."[1]

Juárez is one of those lucky migrants who have income in retirement. His job at Martin Marietta was a union job. Consequently, he is now collecting a full pension worth $485 a month. Also, because Juárez obtained legal status through the Immigration Reform and Control

FIGURE 5.01. In Holtville, California, near the US-Mexico border, about six hundred migrants are buried without caskets or tombstones at the Terrace Park Cemetery. Activists have come to place flowers and markers that read "NOT FORGOTTEN" at the graves. Photograph by Steev Hise.

Act of 1986, he was able to use a real social security number and is now collecting social security checks for $1,500 a month, for a total monthly retirement income of $1,985.[2] His pension and social security make him rich in rural Mexico, where the cost of living is low. Juárez owns his own house there and does not pay rent or a mortgage. Food is cheap, and daily pueblo life does not revolve around consumption— there is no commercial strip, no fancy restaurants, movie theaters or retail district. Juárez deposits his checks at Bank of America in the United States and then withdraws funds at Banco Santander, Bank of America's sister company, in a town near Quila. In Quila Juárez says he "feels more comfortable" and passes the time with family. While the decision to retire in Quila seems an easy one, his wife, Lupe Martínez, cannot imagine leaving her children and grandchildren who live in Los Angeles.

Lupe Martínez met Armando Juárez in Quila and then followed him to the United States in 1970. Martínez says: "The first two years

I was in the United States, I was in shock. I thought, this is the U.S.? But afterwards I adapted to the life there, and I have never left it. After thirty-one years I am thinking of returning to Quila. My husband is retired and wants to rest. But all my kids were born in the United States . . . and I have seven grandkids. I am accustomed to the American system where you have your house and work. It is hard to imagine leaving."[3]

Migrants like Armando and Lupe Juárez, who have been building lives on both sides of the border for decades, are faced with particularly difficult choices in retirement. Their lives have been defined by their ability to move, the location of their immediate family versus extended family and friends, their contributions to the American labor force, and their need to provide for their children. In old age, migrants like the Juárezes must prepare for decreased mobility, the likelihood of illness, the need for medical care, and ultimately death.[4] The topic of transborder migrants' strategies for coping with old age and the effects of age on identity, migrant clubs, and the spaces and landscapes of migration remains largely unresearched.[5] This chapter addresses the landscapes and spaces of transnational aging and death to answer the following questions: How do migrants transition from active remitting to retirement? How do migrants build structures and institutions to help them manage aging and death? What assistance do the governments of Mexico and the United States provide to aging and deceased migrants?

At the federal level of the Mexican and US governments, there is no formal, coherent, structured system in place to assist either rural inhabitants or transnational migrants in old age. In rural Mexico, people generally live without an official social safety net. Programs that US citizens take for granted such as subsidized health care, social security, pensions, unemployment benefits, and farm subsidies do not exist for Mexicans living in small pueblos.[6] The Catholic Church has been the main institution to offer assistance to rural and poor people, but the scale of migration and its impacts on rural Mexican society are overwhelming the ability of the church to address the needs of the elderly. In the United States, undocumented migrants' irregular citizenship status has made it impossible for them to claim benefits, despite having contributed their labor to fuel the US economy. Of an estimated six million unauthorized Mexican migrants in the United

States, approximately 60 percent lack health insurance, and about 40 percent have no regular health care provider.[7] Migrants who are undocumented pay into a US social security system under false identification and never receive social security checks. Over $21 billion in social security payments has not been tracked to potential beneficiaries.[8] Most migrants also fail to collect any pension from past employers: in 2000, only one in five Mexican immigrants received a pension from his or her US employer.[9] Those who do receive pensions or social security checks often receive them for only a portion of their work history, since many migrants do not begin their working lives with formal and continuous employment. These statistics, coupled with the lack of services used by migrants, reveal the vulnerable position in which many aging migrants find themselves.

In response to the absence of a social safety net for migrant workers, informal and grassroots strategies to assist migrants in old age have developed on both sides of the border. In Mexico, the family unit and coparenting relationships sanctioned by the church and known collectively as compadrazgo fill in the gaps left by the state and are instrumental to the health and survival of the elderly.[10] Families live together, or in a network of connected dwellings, and provide one another with mutual assistance and care. Families pool resources for celebrations and in times of crisis. While the compadrazgo system has sometimes led to envy, jealousy, and conflict among community members arising from broken alliances, forsaken duties, and other conflicts, it also provides critical assistance to individuals in moments of need.[11] In the United States, diasporic alliances and formal social clubs or hometown associations (HTAs) have developed to create structural assistance for migrants who live without a basic safety net. In the 1920s, Manuel Gamio recorded migrants' plight: "I have left the best of my life and my strength here [in the United States], sprinkling with the sweat of my brow the fields and factories of these gringos, who only know how to make one sweat and don't even pay any attention to one when they see that one is old."[12] Because "gringos" did not pay attention when one got old, other migrants did, reformulating the compadrazgo system for migrants hundreds or thousands of miles from their hometowns.

Today the Mexican migrant diaspora has had to contend with both an increasing fragmentation of the family due to migration and an absence of social networks specifically geared toward aging. As argued by the anthropologists Roger Magazine and Martha Areli Ramírez Sánchez, who conducted a study of life stages in transnational migration, babies and the very young can be taken care of by grandparents in Mexico or by parents in the United States or Mexico, but the very old, who are as needy as the very young, are not yet planned for.[13] In the United States the role of community is different; neighbors are not generally comadres or compadres who feel it is their duty to watch over one another. Migrants who have maintained close ties to the social networks of their village must choose between living with their immediate family (who are often in the United States) and living with their extended family and community in the village. Not all migrants, however, have robust social networks in villages to return to.

Organized transnational migrants are attempting to create a structure for migrants' death and burial practices. The first way that migrants have organized is by funding *traslados*, or shipments of cadavers back to Mexico from the United States, an increasingly popular trend among migrants.[14] HTAs, businesses, and Mexican government policies are institutionalizing the practice of migrant burials in one's homeland. More recently migrants have expanded their activities beyond just providing a dignified burial to include planning for a comfortable retirement, nursing, and hospice care in Mexico. In these efforts norteños have found a less than willing partner in the Mexican government, which, while eager to partner with migrants through 3×1, has shown little interest in assisting migrants no longer of working age.

I argue that it will be necessary for government leaders, migrant civil society, and village inhabitants to expand their notion of the transnational public if they are to transform the largely symbolic landscape of aging and death into places where migrants can return and grow old in comfort—should that continue to be a sought-after goal.

In this chapter, by combining a discussion of migrant burial practices with an analysis of one *asilo anciano* (old age home), I am able to compare migrant strategies for dealing with end-of-life issues, as well as to understand the position of the Mexican government toward migrants at different stages of life. An examination of migrant life stories in relation to the cultural landscapes of aging and death exposes both the ambiguous role of the state toward norteños and the ambiguous role of norteños in their communities of origin. Additionally, built landscape elements such as memorials and tombstones and the material culture of funerals, cemeteries, and retirement homes embody the struggles migrants face when trying not only to represent their evolving needs but also to leave a lasting legacy. I analyze the construction of one asilo in Los Guajes to chart migrants' successes and challenges when making preparations for retirement in Mexico. I argue that building an old age home for migrants raises questions about who exactly constitutes the "public" in rural Jalisco, as well as the role of private funding, the municipality itself, and other institutions as the compadrazgo network frays and migrants continue to shape their own futures.

The transnational landscape of aging and dying calls our attention to some of the inherent paradoxes and contradictions of remittance space. Remittance space is largely about building aspirations, desires, and hopes into the Mexican landscape. Migrants are building a better future and a brighter alternative not only for themselves (as represented by the remittance house—see chap. 1) but also for their communities, and especially the youth of the community (as represented by the cultural center—see chap. 4). Efraín Jiménez Muñoz, a self-identified migrant philanthropist and the executive projects director of the Zacatecana Federation of Southern California, argues that the most successful remittance projects are the ones that are "based on a commonly identified need and are a priority for both the community (in Mexico) and the HTA."[15] But not all remittance-building projects fit neatly into this discourse of improvement. The spaces of aging and death are concrete evidence in the physical environment of the institutionalization of remitting as a way of life and an admission of the fact that migrants can no longer depend on extended familial social systems of support in old age.

The Rise and Logic of the *Traslado*

Traslados—the "remitting" of cadavers over long distances for burial in the home country—are on the rise between the United States and Mexico. Being buried in one's hometown is a small measure of certitude, a dignified final act bringing closure to a life of uncertainty.

The return to one's hometown (although after death) finally allows migrants to resolve an ambivalence central to a life of transnational migration: the perennial question of where one belongs. Burials in hometowns allow migrant families to participate in interment rituals that reinforce their position in the hometown despite their physical and temporal distance from it. They also reveal that the hometown is the place with which many migrants ultimately identify, and where they believe a community will remember them.

Today traslados are increasingly common, even for migrants of little means. Françoise Lestage, who conducted a study of traslados in 2008, estimates that one out of every six Mexican migrants who dies in the United States is buried in Mexico. Mexico's Secretaría de Relaciones Exteriores (Ministry of Foreign Relations) reports an average of thirty deceased Mexican migrants "repatriated" from the United States daily.[16] Customs service agents in the Guadalajara International Airport (where the bodies are subject to inspection) estimate that between thirty and fifty bodies are shipped to Guadalajara's airport each month.[17] These bodies are then distributed throughout the region; families in Zacatecas, Michoacán, and Nayarit all collect their dead from Guadalajara's airport. This flow of the deceased requires the cooperation and logistical support of funeral homes and mortuaries on both sides of the border. Carolina Díaz, who works in Funeraria Latino Americana in Los Angeles, which she believes is one of California's first and largest migrant-owned funeral homes, established in 1970, estimates that it ships between nine hundred and one thousand bodies to Mexico and Central America annually, five hundred of them destined for somewhere in Mexico. When I spoke to her in 2008, she said that "the number of bodies has increased in the last five years because the number of Latinos living in the US has increased. The big increase started about five years ago."[18]

According to funeral directors and migrants in both Jalisco and California, a gradual increase in traslados has occurred since the 1970s as the necessary money, technology, and social networks have become widely available to migrants and their communities. This increase demonstrates a fundamental shift in the logic of migration. By addressing a problematic aspect of migration as a way of life—uncertainty over the loss of loved ones—traslados alleviate migrant suffering. Yet at the same time traslados are normalized and made more pervasive. For most migrants, the opportunity to finance a transnational burial is a great improvement compared even with the recent past. In the 1950s, Armando Juárez's father, a bracero working in Texas, passed away. "Back then, it took a month to send a letter, if they ever got it. We couldn't imagine sending the body home."[19] Juárez believes that his father was murdered and is buried in Yuma, Arizona, or "somewhere close by," but he has never been to visit his grave. Juárez's inability to have viewed his father's body in a funeral service contributes to his suspicion that his father was killed.

A lack of closure at the moment of death has been one of the great costs of migration for migrant families.[20] A funeral director in Autlán, a town that provides services for rural communities throughout the south of Jalisco, concurred with Juárez's description of the recent past: "Before 1975 things were very different. There was little communication between here and there: children would leave and people wouldn't know what happened to them. People found out about deaths much later. There was only one public telephone."[21] Because of the uneven development of migration, certain communities still have only one telephone, and some families never learn about what happens to sons and daughters who leave.[22] In the south of Jalisco, however, families now not only learn of deaths but also find ways to bring their loved ones back home.

The traslado is desired because it is a fundamental act of self and community identification as well as a means to resolve norteños' both symbolically and socially ambiguous status produced by continuous migration. Through the burial practice, migrants confirm their allegiance to and identification with their hometown and Mexico. In a transnational magazine called *El Tagüinchi*, a villager is quoted as asking a migrant, "What year did you abandon your pueblo?" to which the woman responded, "I never abandoned the pueblo—daily I carry it in my mind and heart."[23] Migrants' allegiance to their pueblo is further confirmed when they elect to be buried in it. This role of the traslado has been recognized in the cultural form of the *corrido* or popular ballad. Jorge Negrete, in his famous ballad "Mexico lindo y querido," sings, "México, lindo y querido, / si muero lejos de ti / que digan que estoy dormido / y que me traigan aquí" (Beautiful and beloved Mexico, if I die far from your soil, may they say that I am asleep, and have them bring me back to you). This song, well known among the Mexican diaspora in the United States, expresses migrants' longing for and attachment to their ancestral lands. The following lines from the same song instruct the community with regard to the burial itself: "Que me entierren en la sierra / al pie de los magueyales / y que me cubra esta tierra / que es cuna de hombres cabales" (Bury me on the mountain at the foot of the cactus, and cover me with this earth that is the womb of valiant men). Here the imagery of the land is associated with men, and by extension the male migrant: where one comes from makes one who one is. Through the imagining and romanticizing of both the traslado and Mexico, the song confirms migrants' identity as truly Mexican, and Mexico's identity as truly masculine.[24]

Choosing to be buried in Mexico also allows the families of migrants to partake in mourning and funerary rituals, which are a very important aspect of rural society. In rural Jalisco, these rites typically begin with a viewing for a minimum of one full day, during which the deceased remains in the familial home and is on display for townspeople to pay their respects. This viewing is followed by a public procession from the family's house to the cemetery. All members of the village walk behind the immediate family, who follow pallbearers carrying the coffin. Many parties participate in the management of these events. Neighbors and extended family strengthen bonds with the bereaved by arranging the viewing of the dead. They also prepare food for guests, clean the bathrooms, maintain an all-night vigil with the immediate family, arrange for a coffin (which may also include pooling funds to buy it), plan the procession, and coordinate with the priest who performs the service. The community functions as both a funeral home and an extended family. Participation in events is expected and demonstrates respect. For some communities, failure to attend a funeral procession is akin to disrespecting the family of the deceased.[25] Conversely, when a family ships a cadaver to the hometown, the management of the viewing and procession affirms the place of the deceased migrant and the migrant's family in the social fabric.

In the context of migration, the funeral in the hometown is one of the few times when families dispersed across multiple cities in multiple countries reunite. Adrián Félix's ethnographic study of traslados, or what he calls "posthumous transnationalism," finds that when a body is repatriated to Mexico, living family members travel back

with it to Mexico for the funeral. A villager in El Cargadero, Zacatecas, interviewed by Félix recalled the funeral of his son's father-in-
law, who died in the United States. Félix recounts, "It must have been
fifteen or twenty people [who traveled back to the United States]."
The man then added, "But two months ago, one of my sons died over
there, and fifty-two people came. Ten of my children who reside in the
U.S. came, and all of their children and grandchildren. . . . The entire
airplane was full."[26] A funeral director in El Grullo, Jalisco, notes that
the moment of death is "when you see family unity." In this sense, for
transnational migrants the moment of death is tied to the social and
symbolic production of identity, a time when a family's most vital relationships are affirmed and acted out and when the family physically
reunites.

Government, Corporate, and Social Institutions
for Transnational Death

Government programs, businesses, and social institutions are formalizing transnational aging and dying in an incremental fashion. The institutionalization of traslados in effect normalizes "repatriations" and
creates a market for end-of-life services readily available to migrants.
The formalization of traslados and binational funerals has historical
antecedents that date back to the turn of the nineteenth century. Research on the migrant clubs of the 1910s to 1930s by Stanley West, Paul
Taylor, and Manuel Gamio notes that one of the main purposes of migrant clubs (founded by Mexicans, with membership drawn from the
laboring Mexican class) was to assist migrant families who had lost a
loved one or individual workers who became ill.[27] This agenda mirrors
the practices of other migrant groups, such as the Italians, Polish, and
Irish, who also pooled resources to assist one another during times
of crisis or loss. At that time, migrant families had very limited access to government services in the United States. Most laborers did
not have savings that would allow them to buy medicine or pay for a
proper funeral. For example, Taylor notes that the Sociedad Mutualista Benito Juárez of El Centro, California, founded in 1919, and the
Sociedad Mutualista Hidalgo of Brawley, California, founded in 1922,
"primarily assist with doctor bills, medicines, care, and a family
allowance for those who lose their job and a funeral benefit."[28] Some

migrant social clubs donated one hundred dollars, in addition to a collection of one dollar per club member, for bereaved families.[29] Assisting Mexican families during the mourning process was so important that a voluntary collection was taken among club members for families that did not even belong to an association.[30] This money was used to bury individuals locally in the United States—shipping them back to Mexico was not feasible.

Today HTAS use both formal and informal channels to assist migrant families that send their dead to Mexico. Informally, upon notification of the death of an HTA member or his or her family member, the club pools money and donates it to the family. A relative of the deceased who is in the United States may also remit additional funds to family in Mexico to contribute to funeral costs there. Sometimes individuals will even put a collection box with a photograph of the deseased at checkouts in gas stations or businesses in Mexican neighborhoods in the United States, soliciting contributions from the Mexican community at large. At the same time, government officials in Mexico, Mexican consulates in the United States, and the migrant federation in California are creating more formal ways to structure the giving that takes place at the moment of death. Jaime Garibay, a director of the Jalisco government's Secretaría de Desarrollo Humano, which spearheads the 3×1 state program, personally developed a pilot subprogram within 3×1 to assist families in mourning.[31] When a very poor person dies in Mexico, one whose "family can't even afford the coffin," the clubs from that region and the state will help buy the family a coffin.[32] This same program pools funds from club members and the state for migrant families who cannot afford to ship bodies home.

Garibay's pilot program within 3×1 Estatal is emblematic of the Mexican government's rather generous additude toward traslados more generally. Félix's research documents the involvement of Mexico's Ministry of Foreign Affairs and Mexican consulates in facilitating traslados. A consulate employee in Los Angeles interviewed by Félix believes that the ministry began providing consulates with money for traslados in the 1980s, but really committed substantial funds toward the dead starting in 2004. Surprisingly, almost half of the funds dedicated to the consulate in 2004 were designated for the dead.[33] Many consulates determine the amount of assistance on a case-by-case basis, which means interviewing family members and examining financial records.[34] Today HTA members from Jalisco note that when a member of the HTA dies, the family immediately contacts the consulate to obtain financial assistance.[35] Assisting migrant families in times of death allows the Mexican government to make a symbolic demonstration of its dedication to the diaspora in an arena that is relatively straightforward and involves predictable onetime payments.

While the logistics of traslados are complex, sending a corpse to Mexico is both easier and cheaper than sending bodies to other nations. Aside from the death certificate, the Mexican government requires three forms, and the consulate issues its stamp of approval (necessary to repatriate a corpse) without charge. This can be contrasted to Cuba's consulate, which charges two thousand dollars for its stamp, or to El Salvador, which requires eight separate forms to be completed for repatriations.[36] In comparison, the Mexican government makes it easy to conduct such affairs. Jalisco official José Treviño explains, "It is a human right to send bodies back, an unwritten law."[37]

The consolidation of HTAS through the federation has also made HTAS a magnet for businesses that offer services to migrants, including end-of-life services. Funeraria Latino Americana provides a funeral service for migrant families in the United States and plans and executes traslados for a cost of two to four thousand dollars. Migrants who belong to HTAS and federations get a discount of approximately 10 percent.[38] Formalization has resulted in a more efficient and timely process for those migrants networked through HTAS and the federation. Daniel Gutiérrez, an inhabitant of a small town in Mexico, notes that before migrants formed the HTA it took them one month to send a body back, but "now it takes a week or less."[39] Funeraria Latino Americana pays considerable attention to migrants from Jalisco because the Federación de Jaliscienses is one of the largest migrant federations. Funeraria Latino Americana uses Jalisco migrant networks to increase business by buying advertisements in federation publications and by receiving referrals from club members.

Funeral services for Mexican families in the United States and traslados to Mexico and Central America are now being offered by mainstream corporate American funeral homes as well. In Colorado, Service Corporation International (SCI), one of the largest funeral businesses in the United States, has pioneered an office called Fune-

Una mano amiga en esos momentos de Dolor

SERVICIOS LOCALES
CREMACIONES
TRASLADOS INTERNACIONALES
(ENVIAR - TRAER)
ATENDEMOS CASOS DE
CUALQUIER ESTADO DE LA
UNION AMERICANA
PRECIOS ECONOMICOS
SERVICIO LAS 24 Hrs.
ASESORAMIENTO PARA LOS
DIFERENTES PROGRAMAS
DE AYUDA ECONOMICA

llamada sin costo:
1-866-739-9128

3827 Whittier Blvd. Los Angeles CA. 90023
Tel.: (323) 265-7016, (323) 265-7017 Fax: (323) 262-2941

FIGURE 5.02. A full-page ad for Funeraria Latino Americana in the Los Angeles federation magazine *Semana Jalisco* shows a funeral director holding a glass globe containing the white silhouette of a bird. The bird represents both the dove of peace and the airplane that will bring the deceased home to Mexico.

raria Latina to target this emergent market. Unlike Funeraria Latino Americana in Los Angeles, which was started by a family of Mexican funeral providers from the state of Nayarit, sci is an Anglo-American-owned and -operated business. The company is adding Mexican flags to the US flags displayed in certain branches to welcome the Mexican immigrant, who is now a valued customer.[40] By 2011, sci had branches geared toward the Latino market opening across the United States, offering special packages for their target clientele.[41]

The United States–based businesses that help families organize traslados are mirrored by and collaborate with small family businesses in Mexico. Funerarias in Mexico complete the transnational mourning process by assuming all of the responsibilities for the deceased once the body arrives at the Guadalajara airport. Funerarias pick it up, check its identification, prepare the body for viewing, and dig the grave in the village. They then work with the local priest who performs the service.

Traslados appear to be an economical option: even with the added expense of buying a plane ticket to ship a body to Mexico, Mexican funerals cost less than a third of comparable American services.[42] However, the total cost of traslados for migrant families is unclear. Many families first hold services in the United States, followed by another one in Mexico. Family members living in the United States must pay their own travel to return home to Mexico with the deceased. Also, shipping bodies from Los Angeles might be affordable, but shipping from smaller cities and towns across the United States is more expensive. Finally, the symbolic importance of return sometimes prompts families to buy lavish coffins that they cannot afford. This creates additional burial expenses that are distributed among comadres, compadres, and family in the United States.

The Material Culture of Transnational Death

Remittances have transformed the cultural landscape of death and dying in rural Mexico. This is particularly evident in cemeteries, where families dispersed in life can reunite in death and where migrants rest after a lifetime of movement. Cemeteries re-place the displaced, and for this reason they are sites of critical importance for emigrant communities.

The burial of migrants in Mexican cemeteries has material consequences revealing new class divisions in death as in life; new marking and memorializing strategies reveal a rise in disposable income, changing tastes, and an increase in personal and familial expression. In rural cemeteries in the south of Jalisco, migrants' tombstones are generally large, highly ornate, and made of the best-quality materials available to their families (often marble instead of concrete). These tombstones are often adjacent to modest markers made of concrete or wood, emblematic of a different era and socioeconomic status. More recently, migrant families have begun adopting an urban and upperclass Mexican tradition by building small *capillas*, or chapels, with

FIGURE 5.03. While it is not possible to identify funding sources for burial markers and tombs based on appearance alone, here the large size and expensive materials differentiate remittance *capillas*, or chapels, from peso burial markers. Photograph by author.

space for burying multiple family members. Building a capilla is significantly more expensive than setting up traditional grave markers. Whereas grave markers range in cost from free (if built by the family or friends with found materials) to hundreds of dollars for engraved marble headstones, capillas can cost many thousands of dollars.

Migrant remittances and traslados are linked to an increase in consumer choice regarding the material culture of death. Local funerarias in the region of Autlán have incrementally improved the quality of their hearses and widened the range of coffin selections available to families. One business in Autlán, Funeraria Gómez, has four hearses, three of which were driven to Autlán by migrants from the United States. The most recent is a luxurious SUV. The desire for certain types of cars and services in Autlán is influenced by the information flows that accompany migration. As remittances continue to pour into rural communities, the number of expensive coffins sold by funerarias to rural constituents increases, and the selection expands.

Tombstones and capillas are also important ways for families to claim—or reclaim—their status of belonging to the society of the hometown. In the cemetery of Quila, a small pueblo near the cabecera of Magdalena, a notably large capilla was built for a young man born in Chicago whose parents had been born and raised in the pueblo. While he was an American citizen, the parents could not imagine burying him in a city they experienced as hostile and foreign despite the years they had spent living there. Ionic columns mark the facade of his small chapel, crowned by a bell tower that houses a cast stone sculpture of an eagle that is not easily identifiable as either a bald eagle (America's national icon) or a golden eagle (portrayed on the Mexican flag). The choice to commission a generic eagle lets this family acknowledge the important alliances it has with both nations—what both nations have given and taken away.

Migrants also seek to transform burial spaces generally through cemetery design and layout. In the south of Jalisco, several rural cemeteries have been redesigned or expanded by migrants. Migrants' exposure to North American cemeteries, as well as gardeners' work manicuring yards, contributes to the desire to modernize town cemeteries.[43] The president of Quila's HTA, Lupe Martínez, explains why her town is going to remodel its cemetery: "There is no system here. It is not like this in your land [the United States]. Here each person just uses whatever piece of land is not occupied. There is no control. We want more control. We want everyone to do it in a certain way, or at least we want to make it well organized. Currently there is a body on top, one underneath, another over there. . . . It is not pretty the way it is."[44] According to her, changes are meant to bring "order and planning" to what she sees as "disorganized and chaotic" places. In Magdalena, an ex-municipal president has been working with a prominent norteña to renovate and remodel the existing cemetery. The "ideal" cemetery, which they now have in architectural plan, includes a new wall around the perimeter, a formal entrance, a grid of clearly marked interior roads, and plots organized according to principles of geometry, symmetry, and a central axis.[45] Cemetery renovations are popular 3×1 development projects initiated by migrants who imagine they will one day be buried there, an idea that legitimizes their intervention in rural cemetery layouts.

As with other 3×1 projects, the implementation of Magdalena's new cemetery plans has exposed a rift between nonmigrants and norteños. While the wall has been built, the ground leveled, and the north wing of the cemetery marked for plots and roads, locals continue to bury their dead without regard to the indications, plans, or requests that are posted throughout the cemetery. The ex-municipal president explains: "They don't follow the rules. They continue, despite our efforts, to put people wherever they want without regard for our markings and warnings."[46] Creating an idealized cemetery plan is not enough to get rural inhabitants to change long-standing burial rituals and practices.

The cultural landscape of death in rural and small-town Mexico is also about social and cultural dissonance between traditional practices and the building of new spaces by migrants and the revised practices they entail. Migrants and villagers exhibit different mourning practices. In San Juan de Amula, when an elderly matriarch of the Rubio family died, her children came from Los Angeles for the funeral, but a local woman, Raquel Maldonado (not a relative), was shocked to see their behavior. In San Juan, she explained, all close friends and family stay up all night with the bereaved, "no matter how tired [they are]."[47] She stayed awake; meanwhile, the deceased woman's own son, a norteño from California, went to bed. To makes matters worse, the day after the service he flew back home. She described his behavior as "out of touch" with how things are done in San Juan.

Today, as the social fabric of the village unravels, ceremonies at formal *salas de velación* (wake rooms or visitation rooms) are replacing village traditions. The sala de velación is owned and operated by a professional funerary director who manages the entire mourning process, from a one- to two-day viewing to the burial ceremony.[48] Ubiquitous in US and Mexican cities, it is novel in rural Mexico. The hiring of professionals commercializes death rituals and weakens the systems of social reciprocity that bind families together.

Nonetheless, the sala de velación directly addresses migrants' needs. Salvador Luis, owner of a sala de velación in El Grullo, a town that provides services for surrounding villages and ranchos, recognizes that many families overwhelmed by the passing of a loved one are burdened with the logistics of reuniting family members who are all over the United States and Mexico. With this in mind, his sala includes a taxi service to the Guadalajara airport, a drive that takes approximately five hours.

According to Luis, having the casket viewing in a sala de velación creates a structured, efficient, and dignified mourning process as opposed to the emotionally taxing social ritual of holding the viewing in the familial home. Luis explains: "About 30 percent of my customers want the sala de velación; otherwise it is in their house. It is a psychological problem. People are crying, and it is harder if the body is in the house where you lived and shared all your memories—'that's the tree he fell out of.' And you have to sleep there, with the body, while people are constantly around, needing to eat, drink. For your health it is better to have the sala."[49] But while families who provide viewing in their homes may be emotionally burdened, this tradition allows families to strengthen alliances in the community. Aware that the sala de velación, despite its logistical advantages, imposes an additional cost that rural families are not accustomed to paying and requires families to abandon an important social ritual, Luis did not charge for his services for the first six months. "I need to get them accustomed first; then I will charge."[50] While rural families can choose to have their service "free" at home in the village, some norteños do not have a familial home to hold a funeral in, or their connections to the townspeople may have weakened. In such cases, a sala de velación becomes necessary if migrant families in the United States are to achieve a migrant burial in Mexico.

The architecture of the sala de velación is an important part of its appeal to migrant families. In El Grullo, Luis's business, Funeraria de San José, is not more than five years old. Built in a Spanish neocolonial style, the elegant entryway includes arches, a fountain, and green grass. The viewing room for the mourning family is simple and modern, with marble floors and a table where fresh coffee and tissues are kept. The funeral director wants to appeal to the "norteño aesthetic." He attended a convention on viewing rooms held in Las Vegas to get ideas for his sala de velación in El Grullo. While most of the things he learned "are not applicable here because of how we do things," he did replicate a silent water sculpture, now in a garden adjacent to the mourning room, that is "supposed to calm nerves."[51] This sculpture as art—indeed, the entire sala edifice—differentiates the new mourning practice from the old one by creating an aesthetic of mourning and an argument about the necessity (for one's mental health) of luxury. The sala also challenges what Octavio Paz describes as the inseparability of life and death, and the Mexican penchant for bringing death most intimately into daily life.[52] Spatially, having the wake in one's domestic sphere forces the living to reckon with the everydayness of death.

The migrant-funded memorials and tombstones, desired cemetery changes, classy funeral services, and salas de velación have begun to outline a new spatial order of mourning overlaid on the existing one. There is friction as primarily norteño and migrant families initiate spatial changes that correspond to their changing socioeconomic status, circumstances, and needs. Managing death, burial, and mourning practices provides insight into the contradictions of remittance space—the plight of migrants, the creation of new cultural forms, and tensions with tradition. These conflicts and tensions are further illuminated by the broadening spectrum of retirement, aging, and end-of-life services. An analysis of one village's project of building an asilo de ancianos, or old age home, exemplifies norteños' efforts to expand their influence not only over the spaces of their hometowns but also over their own futures.

Actualizing Utopian Space for Transnational Aging

Long before traslados became common, migrants have saved money, used small American pensions, and built remittance houses so they could return to their hometowns in old age. More recently, migrant clubs in the United States have been using the government's 3×1 program to fund the erection of "asilos de ancianos" to house both migrants and elderly inhabitants in rural areas of Jalisco. These old age homes reflect an increasingly coordinated and systematic effort on the part of transnational migrants to manage aging and retirement for themselves and for family members who have remained in Mexico. By doing so, norteños are asserting agency and contesting a history of government neglect. At the same time, they are forming new dependencies and allegiances among rural communities, the Mexican diaspora, and the Mexican state, complicating the notion of "public services" by creating spaces in which transborder migrants can be the beneficiaries of Mexican public services. The migrant-led old age home project reveals the extent to which the Mexican government's position toward its transnational migrants remains undefined. As evident in the project, although 3×1 relies on continuous remitting, the program has failed to recognize remitting as a way of life that creates needs for new services from the government. Once migrants are no longer remitting (and even for those who still are), the state does not have a formal mechanism in place to address their needs; this is especially problematic because migration has challenged the informal social networks that have historically addressed rural constituents' health and well-being in old age.

With a history of nearly eighty years of migration to and from the United States, Los Guajes is a village of approximately one thousand local inhabitants. Residents estimate that its migrants living in Guadalajara, Mexico City, and the United States number three to five times the population of the town itself. Migration from Los Guajes has been persistent and increasing since the 1920s because of the inhabitants' extreme poverty. The town is far from the cabecera, leaving it politically and economically disenfranchised. Two powerful hacienda families owned the majority of the land in the eighteenth and nineteenth centuries; in Los Guajes, a particularly fierce battle waged over land rights during the Mexican Revolution created a class of small-scale private property owners, but peasant farmers did not form an ejido. Following the Mexican Revolution, in the 1930s Los Guajes underwent a protracted drought. During this tumultuous period men began to head north, to both Guadalajara and the United States, to ensure the survival of their families.

Migrant remittances and migrant involvement in civic affairs have contributed to the development of the town at least since the 1970s. A villager described how at that time certain migrants (without structural or institutional encouragement from the state) "returned to put into practice what was learned [in the United States] to benefit the community."[53] The history of migration as development, linked to what geographer Sandra Nichols calls "technology transfers," has been shaping people's roles in the community for decades.[54]

The building of a retirement facility in Los Guajes has coincided with ongoing community development and management funded by its emigrants. Remittance development has been a generally hierarchical process, with specific individuals motivating local material change. In Los Guajes, the first man to assume the dual role of entrepreneur and booster, Pipián Camacho, is credited with bringing electricity to the pueblo, enlarging the school, and building the dam near Agua Escondido and the road that connects Los Guajes to Juchitlán. These infrastructural projects have transformed daily life in Los Guajes. In 1955, when several local families pooled money to buy the town's first truck from the United States, it took nine hours to travel on the road from Los Guajes to Juchitlán. Those who made this journey recall, "We made the road as we went along," by collecting and placing rocks in front of the car to allow passage over muddy terrain.[55] In 1995,

FIGURE 5.04. A marble statue of Pipián Camacho—made from marble excavated in a local quarry financed by Camacho—honors his legacy in the town plaza. Photograph by author.

when the new road to Juchitlán was completed, the commute between towns was reduced to just fifteen minutes. Camacho partially funded these projects and fought with the authorities in the cabecera for resources to implement them; he is credited with "causing the wind of progress to blow" and is lionized by villagers as "a saint."

While Camacho is viewed as primarily responsible for bringing these improvements to the town, a strong migrant community that has been engaged in improving the material conditions of life in Los Guajes has aided his work since the 1970s. For over thirty years, the diaspora of Guajeños have maintained a strong migrant social club based in Los Angeles, Guajeños Unidos USA, with a formal structure and membership and an emigrant directory. It holds two major reunions every year, one in California and the other in Guadalajara. The reunions or *convivencias de hijos ausentes* were created to "mantener unidos los lazos de amistad y fraternidad entre todos los terráneos y con el anhelo de seguir cultivando valores y tradiciones que nos distinguen" (maintain the ties of friendship and fraternity among all Guajeños and with the wish to continue cultivating the values and traditions that distinguish us).[56] In recent years the reunions have served as vehicles for social and cultural reproduction as well as important fundraising venues. With funds raised at its meetings, the HTA has remodeled the village's civic offices, built public bathrooms, installed a quiosco in the town plaza, and fixed the church roof, bathroom, and interior finishes. Once the 3×1 program became available, quadrupling the club's contributions, norteños from Los Guajes paved roads, added new pipes for water, and completed the old age home. Local inhabitants have also facilitated construction projects in cooperation with migrants and other boosters.[57] While local Guajeños do not have dollars to contribute to the building process, they do have valuable time and knowledge of the local construction industry, essential to the execution of remittance-financed building projects.

The spirit of unity that Guajeños pride themselves on has given rise to—and is now shaped by—a unique publication called *El Tagüinchi* (The firefly), geared toward creating an "imagined community" of Guajeños.[58] Since 1993 *El Tagüinchi*, a community-based monthly magazine, has been written by Guajeños in Mexico and abroad, printed in Guadalajara, and sent to Guajeños throughout the diaspora. Each issue presents a biographical history of an individual Guajeño, emphasizing the challenges of poverty and migration and the triumph of the individual over these difficult circumstances. In addition to these heroic and historic narratives, the pages are filled with local sayings or *dichos*, recipes, vernacular words used in the pueblo, photos of the village's buildings, and poems and songs written by Guajeños. A time capsule capturing local cultural traditions as Los Guajes dissolves into a diaspora of Guajeños, the magazine (rather than merely romanticizing the past) helps to produce a cultural identity in the context of globalization, social change, and new transnational lifestyles.

Envisioning an Institution

Los Guajes's asilo de ancianos project was conceived within this framework of a unified diaspora capable of meeting its own needs through infrastructure and other building projects. The asilo project demonstrated the local-migrant collaboration that defines many remittance-funded projects; migrants' roles as nascent developers and locals' roles as project managers have evolved for over thirty years. Ramón

Camacho (brother of the norteño Pipián Camacho), a contributor to *El Tagüinchi*, left the town for Guadalajara as a teenage boy but returned in his forties to live in Los Guajes permanently. Regarding his return, he remarked, "I saw the town becoming sad as more and more people left, so I came back."[59] The initial idea to build the asilo resulted from Ramón Camacho's unique position as both an inhabitant of Los Guajes and somebody familiar with the spaces of migration. Camacho recognized, on the one hand, migrants' and their families' increasing need for retirement assistance due to increasing migration and the transnationalization of family life and, on the other, the very limited role of the Mexican government in providing facilities and services in small towns. Typically, asilos in the state of Jalisco are located in the capital, Guadalajara, or in midsized cabeceras, not in small villages like Los Guajes. Additionally, asilos are geared toward people with mental and physical disabilities, not toward the elderly. Ramón Camacho described the perceived need as follows: "We [Guajeños supporting the project] thought always of helping the people of Guadalajara and the United States that are from here. There are people who want to return but don't have a place to go. They don't have family here, but they want to die on their land. So it is important to offer them a house of rest here and to let them live out their last years happy." The idea came to Camacho when he was visiting a Guajeño in Guadalajara. As he put it: "Don Naranjo died in a one-room house alone."[60] As one of Naranjo's only visitors, Camacho was motivated to create a space that would prevent other Guajeños from sharing Naranjo's fate. His vision was to build an asilo that would provide meals, housekeeping, and hospice care as retirement nursing homes in the United States do.

The asilo project has required long-term collaboration (over fifteen years) and organization by project sponsors. In this effort, *El Tagüinchi* has played a pivotal role as a vehicle to build consensus among the geographically dispersed community of Guajeños about how to invest their collective remittances. The magazine also creates public accountability by recording who invests and what projects they invest in and by publishing images of project results. Thus *El Tagüinchi* creates a historical record of remittances in the absence of other cultural archives. Magazine subscriptions (paid by approximately five hundred people) have also created a continuous revenue stream, which has been combined with the profits from Guajeños Unidos USA fundraising events to fund the construction of the asilo. Individuals who make additional donations to support the asilo are thanked in the magazine's pages.[61]

In addition to providing a fundraising vehicle for the asilo, *El Tagüinchi* has been used to build awareness and an emotional connection between the migrant community and the project. That connection is based on rhetoric designed precisely to engage migrants' sense of ambivalence regarding the management of retirement and to appeal to their longing to return home. For several years the back cover has featured a photograph illustrating the asilo project's progress, accompanied by a quotation, poem, or other text. In 2002 a photograph of the building's brick walls under construction was juxtaposed to the following poem:

"Solo busco una vida feliz"
sin tener que preocuparme por mi alimento de hoy
ni por lo que he de vestir mañana.
No habré de torturarme la memoria
tratrando de recordar los rostros de mis parientes idos,
ni sus gustos, ni sus disgustos.
En mi conciencia no cabrá remordimiento;
lo que hice o dejaré de hacer
pertenece a una parte del libro que ya escribí . . . y gocé a plenitud.
Sólo busco ser feliz los días que haya por vivir.
Y esperaré en santa paz.

["I only look for a happy life"
without having to worry about today's food
or what I will wear tomorrow.
I will not torture my memory
trying to remember the faces of my relatives who are gone,
nor their likes, nor their dislikes.
I will not feel remorse in my conscience;
what I did or what I will leave undone
belongs to a part of the book already written . . . and enjoyed to the
    fullest.
I only look to be happy the days that remain to be lived.
And I will hope (or wait) in blessed peace.][62]

This unattributed poem associates the asilo under construction with the promise of a happy retirement. In some back-cover inspirational pieces the building is given its own voice: "I am maturing for you so that you enjoy me totally; when the time arrives I will be your nutritious food. At that time you will come to me demanding a deserved vacation; with me you will find shade where you can abandon your fatigue."[63] The personified building provides a just reward to those who deserve rest after a lifetime of migration. In several issues of the magazine the phrase below the photograph addresses the dilemma of the aging migrant directly by asking, "Cuándo vas a volver para quedarte?" (When are you going to return for good?).

Despite the revenue from the publication as well as a relatively generous and unified HTA, project sponsors were not able to fund the completion of the project without government assistance. In 2005 Guajeños joined the 3×1 program and began receiving government funds. Before government assistance began, the building had already been under construction for twelve years, and norteños (and to a much lesser extent the pueblo) had spent approximately $190,000. The total 3×1 budget for the 2005–6 year was approximately $60,000, of which the migrants were responsible for $15,000. By 2006 the project was nearly completed, for a total cost of approximately $250,000 spent over a period of fourteen years. This cost can be compared to the $30,000 to $50,000 that families typically spend to build a new house. The asilo is the most expensive building in the village.

An analysis of the building's plan reveals the embedded aspirations and desires of this transnational project. The asilo consists of a ring of cellular dwelling units surrounding an open-air courtyard. The courtyard plan is typically used to build asilos throughout the south of Jalisco, but this one departs in two major ways from traditional plans.[64] First, each room is equipped with its own bathroom and sink, allowing a degree of self-sufficiency. Second, the courtyard itself is roughly square and primarily designed to draw in light and air, as opposed to serving the functional uses associated with traditional courtyard dwellings; no well, fruit trees, brick oven for communal cooking, or other features for outdoor living connect the units to the yard. The modern institutional facilities of the asilo replace these functions of the traditional-rural courtyard. Aside from the individual rooms, the building plan includes a storage unit, a dining room, a kitchen, a laun-

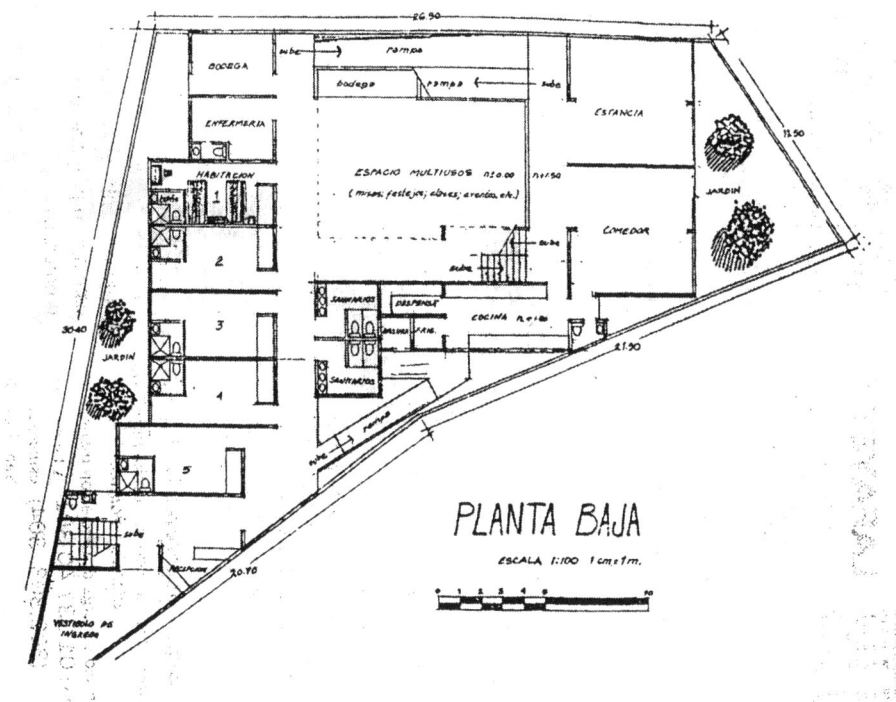

FIGURE 5.05. In the plan of the asilo de ancianos in Los Guajes, printed in *El Tagüinchi*, a trapezoidal parcel prevents efficient deployment of the cellular bedrooms and common spaces surrounding a courtyard or *espacio multiusos* (multiuse space). A new building type in rural areas, asilo floor plans do not follow a single standardized template—note the unusual off-axis entry sequence through a series of vestibules from lower left.

dry room, a medical exam room, and offices for a psychologist, social worker, and secretary. That is, the building is designed as not only a retirement home but also a facility that offers medical services.

The asilo stands out in its built context due to its size, finish materials, and many "modern" fixtures, systems, and amenities. With the exception of the church tower, the old hacienda house, and a few remittance houses, all of the buildings in Los Guajes are single-story structures of either adobe or fired brick, built by albañiles or vernacular builders. Located at the top of a hill, the asilo towers over the church, which traditionally is the tallest and most imposing structure

FIGURE 5.06. One can more readily perceive the incongruous scale and geometry of the Los Guajes asilo from a distance. Larger than the church and several times larger than the *delegación*, or civic office, the building towers over neighboring structures. Photograph by author.

in rural towns. This location creates rooms with views of the pueblo below. The building is finished with metal windows and doors and floored with expensive Spanish tiles. Each bathroom is equipped with new porcelain sinks and toilets. This is a major accomplishment in the context of Los Guajes's housing, where installing bathrooms to replace outhouses or old bathrooms is both difficult and expensive, and where about 20 percent of houses still lack running water.

The New Player in Los Guajes's Remittance Development: The Municipality

Like other remittance-development building projects, the asilo as completed has not fulfilled the original hopes and visions for what it could and should be.

While the asilo's incorporation into the 3×1 program provided a framework for project completion, 3×1 introduced the municipality into Los Guajes's development process, politicizing the project. There is long-standing bitterness between Los Guajes and Juchitlán, as cabecera officials and Guajeños have struggled over resources, power, and authority. Rural constituents in pueblos outside the cabecera have repeatedly complained that the head town controls the region's budget and leaves the pueblos without any funding. As noted in *El Tagüinchi,* the "municipal administration continues serving its town from one purse."[65] According to local inhabitants, the asilo, which is the largest and most modern building in the entire region, not just in Los Guajes, stirred up envy among municipal officials. Ramón Camacho believes "they are jealous, so they don't want to help us, and now they are making us pay for 3×1 projects in Juchitlán."[66] The tensions between the village and municipality intensified as the project became more technical and complex.

The lack of municipal accountability at the state and federal levels has resulted in real financial hardship for norteños sponsoring the project. In 2005, when 3×1 stepped in, the community members of Guajeños had exhausted their resources, and both those managing the project in the village and those sponsoring the project in the diaspora were hopeful. However, the municipal government allegedly did not pay its portion of the $60,000 3×1 budget. To avoid being "blacklisted" by 3×1 program managers at the state and federal levels of government, norteños paid the municipality's portion. In this case, one norteño, José Ochoa, the president of Guajeños Unidos USA, personally donated $20,000 to the project, to cover the cabecera's $15,000 plus $5,000 out of the $15,000 that the HTA had not raised by the 3×1 payment deadline.[67] Ochoa's investment is uninsured, brings no tax benefits, and greatly increases his personal stake in the success of the project.

When municipal officials took over management of the project in 2005 and 2006, they replaced the norteños who had been working on it since the beginning. They failed, however, to make provisions for future management and maintenance of the project. Once the 3×1 funds were spent, municipal officials were not willing to contribute to the cost of running the asilo (which is technically a public service), but it was not clear who was responsible for this cost. Additionally, according to Guajeños, the president of Juchitlán will not approve more 3×1 projects for Los Guajes unless Los Guajes donates money to Juchitlán for its own 3×1 projects. Thus the 3×1 program has incurred a future cost that will not be invested in Los Guajes. Norteño investment in Los Guajes has repositioned the town as wealthy in the eyes of neighboring towns at a moment when HTA members and the town are faced with increasing debt to support their remittance development.

Unable to manage, staff, or maintain the asilo, Guajeños have watched the building sit vacant since 2006. During the final stages of the construction process, the original project builder, Jorge Muñoz, a man from Los Guajes who provided design and construction management services pro bono, was replaced by an engineer from Juchitlán whose main job was cutting project costs. Muñoz describes his design process: "The norteños said build an asilo but didn't explain specifics. I adopted the *estilo del pueblo* [style of the pueblo]. What I like is colonial Mexican architecture. When Juchitlán came in, they pushed me aside and did what they wanted." There have been consequences: "The original project had three stories, but they only built two. The plan has a kitchen, eating room, medical room; all of their needs were taken care of, but this was not how it turned out."[68] Ornate finishes, wooden doors, and arches that were supposed to create an *estilo del pueblo* were stripped from the project, leaving a stark rectilinear form. The main reason the architect's design "was not how it turned out" was that the money and expertise needed to fill these specialized rooms with the medical equipment, desks, and nurses and other staff essential to transforming a building into an institution were not available.[69] Ultimately norteños have paid dearly for attempting an experimental program, a novel effort to produce social change through institution building.[70]

Sadly, the apparent socioeconomic difference between the asilo project sponsors and locals in Los Guajes is being acted out through vandalism of the building. Vandals' main targets are the asilo's toilets and sinks, the amenities that distinguish the facility from most houses in the town. Local vandalism can be understood perhaps as a rejection of norteños' increasing presence in the management of the daily life of Los Guajes. However, according to Ramón Camacho, "kids" who "have nothing better to do" go inside at night and smash the porcelain toilets and sinks and break the windows and doors. In addition to rapidly diminishing the value of the nearly completed building, this behavior is the final insult in a process that has shown migrants the limits of their ability to transform their community and their futures.

The White Elephant

Debates and conflicts surrounding the dormant asilo building outline divergent positions taken by people in the community of Los Guajes and other nearby towns and villages. The main thrust of the debate revolves around the cultural suitability of the project and its intended purpose. As with the overlay of new burial spaces and the integration or separation of migrant burial practices from local customs and norms, the asilo has led locals to question the degree to which it represents a cultural divergence between norteños' and locals' visions of old age.

The conspicuously abandoned asilo has inspired criticism from those who serve the elderly in the region. Silvia Macías, director of the only operating asilo in Juchitlán, faults project sponsors for not taking steps to learn more about operating a home for the elderly.[71] Despite her experience, she said, "they [the norteños] never asked me for advice. . . . They need to get people in there; it doesn't need to be perfect or finished; many elderly are not even washing themselves. Whatever they want is fine—a retirement home, a hotel, a home for someone with money—but they need to say so. They need to set the rules so that people know what the house is about."[72] Calling the building a "white elephant"—a possession whose high cost is out of proportion to its worth, especially in terms of its upkeep and maintenance—Macías discussed the high standard of living implied in the project, which she perceives as a sign that it is not for the people of the region but only for rich norteños themselves. The asilo she runs in Juchitlán is a basic courtyard-type dwelling that houses approximately ten elderly people with mental and physical disabilities and is funded by individual donations and a small monthly quota from the government.[73] The people in her old age home cannot take care of themselves, and she struggles to find money to pay for nurses or helpers to assist them.

Macías feels that the Los Guajes asilo represents a missed opportunity to address the ways in which persistent emigration is putting major strains on the reproduction of social customs and norms regarding the elderly. Communal caregiving is challenged by the emigration of immediate family members. Signs of this strain are evident in the increasing number of elderly people simply abandoned in their homes, without any family members remaining in the towns to care for them. The municipal president of Magdalena, another town building an old age home in the north of Jalisco, notes, "I visited a woman who was without water for two weeks. She was going to the bathroom in her bed."[74] A teacher from the cabecera Ejutla who oversees its asilo project had a similar story: "An old man who is now dead couldn't walk. He had his water nearby, but he went to the bathroom in his pants, in his bed. That is why we need to bring the people from the ranchos here [to the asilo]. Also, families are in the North, and people are now returning with pensions, but who will watch over them? Those who can pay somebody will have somebody to watch over them, and those who can't pay will not."[75]

Even though elderly people are culturally important in traditional society, and even though some are financially supported by remittances, they still face isolation and neglect, which demonstrates the depth of the crisis in the community due to the fracturing of families across geography. In Los Guajes, Josefina Ochoa, the mother of José Ochoa (one of the main donors to the old age home), lives in a remittance house and is provided for by her children, who are in Guadalajara, California, and Colorado. Josefina concluded, "I have everything I need, but I am alone." Josefina endured hunger and homelessness, and the murder of her husband, to raise her children and live in Los Guajes. She misses her seven children but cannot imagine leaving the life she fought so hard to achieve. Josefina lives down the street from two sisters in their eighties who are in a similar situation. One sister explained that although she has eleven grandchildren, thirty-five great-grandchildren, and two great-great-grandchildren, there is nobody to take care of her because all of her offspring live in Guadalajara and the United States.

Distance and isolation have been taken up in cultural production as normative categories of experience. In an *El Tagüinchi* story etitled "El abuelo y la distancia" (The grandfather and distance), a child asks his wise grandparent, "What is distance?" The old man explains what it is literally—the measurement from one point to another—but then begins to describe distance in more metaphorical and ontological terms. Distance, he says, can separate one person from another, but "there are certain ways to overcome distance" by using the telephone, or even by looking at the same moon. The grandfather concludes: "Distance is relative like time or space; people can feel alone or distant with company, or together when they are alone." Then he asks the child, "What would you like to feel?" The child answers, "I would prefer to feel accompanied!"[76] In this story, distance is presented to the youth of Los Guajes as a feeling that can be internalized and normalized, as a condition that can be overcome by social and psychological bonds to other people and places.

Perhaps the best evidence supporting the criticisms of people who care for the elderly around Los Guajes is that the elderly themselves do not want to live in the asilo. Ramón Camacho notes: "The asilo is for all Guajeños, but those who live here don't have the desire to live in an old age home. They feel forgotten; it is not their culture." An albañil in his eighties who lives in Los Guajes offered a critique: "It is very good that there is an asilo, but why do they want it? Who is going to take a person from here to the asilo? Nobody—I think that nobody would."[77] Another woman in her seventies from a small pueblo to the north of Los Guajes who lives alone stated: "It is not necessary to have an asilo. People here are looked after, and the old ones are the ones who suffer. To go to an asilo is like being kicked out of the family, *castigado* [punished]. It is not proper."[78] It appears that although the old people of the village experience the effects of weakened familial networks, they view living in an institution as a stigma and as disrespectful of the elderly, so they resist it as an option for themselves. Given the political, financial, and logistical challenges the asilo faces, it will be difficult to convince them otherwise.

Despite the asilo's nonoperational status and many unresolved issues, Ramón Camacho still expressed optimism in 2008: "Here [in Los Guajes] I think the asilo will have a good outcome because there is a waiting list, and it will fill up. There are thirty people on the list; all of them live in Guadalajara or the United States, with two or three living here. For us it is a source of happiness that there are people who have lived outside Los Guajes for a long time and are still nostalgic for their land."[79] The asilo has a waiting list but lacks an organizational system to govern how the space will operate and who will benefit, as well as ongoing financial support from the municipal or state government. By 2012, Camacho did not want to discuss why the asilo was still abandoned or whether he believed there was still hope of reinvigorating the project. Camacho was so disheartened by the project's outcomes that he had given the keys to a woman in Los Guajes, who noted that "he won't even step inside" the asilo or "look at it," let alone discuss its future.

The failure rates of similar projects in nearby towns suggest that the difficulties of establishing new institutions go beyond immediate logistical constraints. In addition to the project in Los Guajes, the nearby pueblos of El Limón and Ejutla have new asilos. All three were built with 3×1 funds, have a courtyard plan, and at the time of this study were vacant and nonoperational.[80] El Limón's asilo was abandoned because of lack of funding for services and poor site selection. The asilo's location just outside the town's built fabric would further isolate its patrons and not allow them to participate in town life, even by watching activities taking place outside their window. Thus "nobody wanted to move there." Ejuta's asilo, in 2008, had not yet secured funding to provide full-time services, but the building was being used to prepare and serve meals. A need in all of these places has been identified, yet no consensus has been reached on what the solution is or how to implement it.

As with the cultural center in San Juan de Amula, state and federation representations of asilos have created a discourse that presents such large-scale projects in a favorable light. The 3×1 program directors in concert with the federation hold annual meetings in Jalisco to motivate municipal presidents and nascent HTAS to join remittance development. In 2007 the meeting in Degollado showcased several large-scale projects, including Los Guajes's asilo.[81] In 2007, before embarking on my field research, I interviewed the past president of the federation, Salvador García, to inquire about the impact of the 3×1 program on the ground. At that time he told me to go visit the asilo in Los Guajes, alongside the hospital in Ameca and the cultural center in San Juan, to get a better understanding of what the federation was capable of.[82] José Ochoa claims that the former governor of the state of Jalisco, Governor Acuña, came to Los Guajes in 2006 to see the asilo—a rare and unprecedented visit. Apparently the governor "didn't even stop in Juchitlán." Not only is the asilo represented in federation and 3×1 promotion materials, but it has increased the visibility and voice of Guajeños vis-à-vis the Mexican state.

* * *

This chapter has examined two different spatial practices—one set linked to migrant burials and another to migrant retirement. Together they represent migrants' attempts to fill gaping holes in the social safety net that for migrants and rural Mexicans is virtually nonexistent. These efforts have impacts on the spaces of rural communities.

Migrants' success in carrying out traslados and providing dignified burials in hometowns sharply contrasts to their failure to establish communal or cooperative retirement spaces in rural Mexico, and provides insights into the limitations of migrant remittances as a basis for social and spatial change. The outcomes of these projects show that while the state in Mexico, at both the federal and state levels, is invested in high-profile and symbolic efforts to assist migrants, it is falling woefully short of providing them even the most basic retirement and end-of-life support.[83]

Migrant burial practices and migrant retirement pose two very distinct sociospatial dilemmas for migrants, their families, and their communities. The traslado is a singular, immediate, and small-scale event. The finite nature of the traslado and its symbolic value within the Mexican diasporic community make it an arena in which the Mexican state is comfortable and indeed eager to participate. Conversely, the production of retirement or old age homes requires substantial, ongoing financial investments.

Remittance project implementation reveals challenges to migrants' efforts to address social needs through building despite enthusiasm, financial support, deep understanding of the local context, and willing local partners. In Los Guajes migrants could not control project costs and were forced to apply for funding through 3×1. Once the asilo became a 3×1 project, cabecera government engineers and officials replaced local project managers. The architectural plans were altered, and the people who were invested in the project felt displaced. Corruption and disorganization in the cabecera meant that funds were not provided as promised. Because of this, migrant sponsors are now in debt. Finally, and most detrimental, norteños did not anticipate the costs and complexity of running an institution, and the 3×1 takeover brought a lack of clarity about who was responsible for project maintenance and care. As a 3×1 project, the asilo has not addressed the needs of elderly nonmigrants, nor those "retired" migrants who can no longer work and wish to settle in their hometown.

While the future of migrant investment and 3×1 projects is unknown, unless the Mexican government creates a structure to provide services, ongoing maintenance, and logistical support to transborder migrants, many continue to focus on highly visible but ultimately symbolic projects. Building a true migrant asilo would require the Mexican government to expand its concept of social welfare, as well as increase investments in rural places and those dedicated to transborder migrants. While encouraging migrants to remit, the Mexican government has not taken responsibility for their well-being nor incorporated migrants into Mexico's public sphere. For the time being, ornate and expensive tombstones and capillas rather than old age homes dominate the remittance landscapes of aging and death. Reunification with family and homeland is possible in death, and almost half of Mexican consulate funding is being directed toward the realization of this migrant desire, while the living, as Gamio laments, "continue to go on unnoticed."

6 Migrant Metropolis

REMITTANCE URBANISM IN THE UNITED STATES

While the cultural landscapes of rural Mexican towns provide the primary site for the emergence of remittance space, remittance space itself spans the international boundary and exists in dynamic tension with "arrival cities"—the US "ethnic" enclaves and suburban settlements where migrants establish themselves. Just as understanding migration requires analyzing both "sending" and "receiving" places, as well as the exchange between them, fully grasping remittance space requires analyzing the environments both where money is spent and where it is earned. I use Chicago because, after Los Angeles, the second largest and most organized population of Jaliscienses lives in Chicago, from where they have financed hundreds of projects in Jalisco.[1] Chicago has always been an immigrant city. In 1890 primarily Germans, Irish, Poles, and Swedes made up over 50 percent of its population; today over one million immigrants from over one hundred countries live in the metropolitan region. Yet despite the multiplicity of immigrant groups, in 2010 Latinos made up more than 25 percent of Chicago's population. This is approximately equal to the percentage of the city's population that was German at the turn of the twentieth century.

Mexican migrants refer to Chicago as "Mexico's fifth-largest city," after Mexico City, Los Angeles, Guadalajara, and Monterrey.[2] Chicago is also the only US city where a Mexican state (Jalisco) owns a migrant meeting hall. Chicago's Mexican population dates back to the building of the railroads at the turn of the twentieth century but boomed after the 1960s. Coupled with the extent of urbanization that preexisted arrival, this demographic change—relatively recent compared to the long-established Mexican communities in Los Angeles and other cities in the American Southwest—has produced extensive change in

FIGURE 6.01. Western Union advertisement painted on overpass, Chicago. There are over 475 licensed community currency exchanges in the state of Illinois. Photograph by author.

the built environment that corresponds with the rise of remittance development.

Currently migrants in Chicago compete with those in Los Angeles for a central position in transborder migrant networks. However, more research needs to be done on Chicago to addresses a lacuna in academic scholarship, which has primarily focused on Latinos in the Southwest.[3] Oral and material histories are important ways to document the transformations occurring in recent decades due to a rise in Mexican migrant construction projects and spatial practices in Chicago.

By exploring the current moment of remittance space in Chicago, I outline directions for future multisited research. Historicizing these spaces shows how migrants are, and have been, integral to producing (not just inhabiting) the built environment of American cities for decades. I locate contemporary discourses on diaspora, migrant civil society, and the borderlands in the specific material and urban contexts of Chicago. My research shows that the relationship between remittance space in Mexico and that in the United States is not symmetrical. In Mexico, projects are intended to "improve" the hometown, demonstrate success, and renew attachments. In the United States, remittance space is geared toward forming physical and institutional infrastructures, social networks and solidarities that facilitate migration itself and support the attainment of both individual and shared goals. These distinctions can be understood in part through an analysis of departing versus arriving as extended social processes.

Arrival in a new social and spatial environment brings both real and perceived vulnerability, as well as opportunities to establish new forms of social solidarity. With few connections, especially for those who do not speak English and have limited financial resources, the arrival process forces *recién llegados*, or those migrants who have recently arrived, to seek out networks of mutual support—to connect them with employers, housing, and services. While migrants come from distinct places with divergent experiences, the choice to leave one's hometown is a shared choice to enter the spaces of migration. Migrants embark on a journey that involves adapting to new regulations and social norms, immersion in the English language, being outsiders, and potentially living "in the shadows" due to unauthorized entry. It is within this context that social and spatial systems of exchange and organization are vital aspects of migrants' urban spatial practices. Remittance space in the United States facilitates these exchanges and encounters.

Remittance space in US cities—related to the rural-urban continuum established in this book—assumes different forms and meanings from those found in rural Jalisco. In Mexico, territorially bounded pueblos provide a spatially contiguous unit of analysis for perceiving the material impacts of remittances. The activities of HTAS and remitters produce discrete public and private buildings in cohesive built fabrics that make the spaces of migration immediately visible. In the United States, migrants occupy complex and spatially fragmented environments where it is more difficult to identify the particular material conditions that result directly from the activities of migrants and distinguish them from similar forms or types. In the city, migrant and nonmigrant spaces overlap and influence one another. Making analysis of this environment more complex, the places that migrants inhabit and build reflect the extent to which they identify with their hometowns, the spaces of migration, the host city, or US society. Migrants express their desire (or lack thereof) for deeper connections to either American cities or Mexican hometowns through their engagement with urban and rural places in the United States. For some this engagement can result in changing "allegiances," or spaces of identification over time, in which the center of gravity of a migrant project may shift from rural Mexico to an American one rooted in the arrival city.

For these reasons, remittance space in US cities is less about building projects and more about social and spatial practices that construct migrants' sense of self and their place in the world. Subjectivities form, or re-form, as migrants navigate, create, and use the spaces of the American city within a spatial-temporal narrative in which past, present, and future are linked to geographical location. For many migrants, the US city provides the "present" to the migrant's aspirational future, while hometowns in Mexico provide the material and imaginary future context for realizing one's ambitions. For others, US cities are the places where they express the extent to which their hometown is actually a place associated with the past. The constant push and pull between the two is where migration and remitting as a way of life take shape. This chapter identifies three sociospatial moments in the process of arrival in US cities that define the contours of remittance space. In each example, migrants make critical decisions regarding their ties to hometowns, Mexican national and regional traditions, and host cities.

While HTA remittance dollars change landscapes in rural Mexico, the process of social organization produces new spaces in the American city of Chicago. I examine the creation of migrant solidarities through the development of HTA and federation meeting halls, namely, Casa Michoacán and Casa Jalisco. I then expand to the "migrant community" at large by investigating both the construction of Mexican sports arenas and event hosting. I conclude with a discussion of funeral homes and cemeteries involved in migrant burial practices. These three moments—solidarity, representation, and return—provide a "negative" of the remittance landscapes examined in previous chapters; the rural Mexican rodeo arena, cultural center, and old age home are associated with spatial practices that find expression in Chicago.

Rather than focusing on how migrants negotiate living in the shadows of American cities, I look at how migrants operate as agents of place-making, redefining what we think of as "the American city." Collecting information about what migrants build—be it actual buildings or transborder systems—allows us to see processes that are, to use Nicholas de Genova's term, "elusive" to the nation-state.[4] This empirical evidence complicates notions of placement/displacement, resident/stranger, and entrepreneur/parasite by refocusing our attention on the political economy and spatial practices of migrants rather than their imagined experiences or presumed roles in relation to a dominant and normative American society. Additionally, researching widely distributed, complex social and spatial systems in the United States that are produced by both documented and undocumented migrants challenges studies of Latinos as monolithic subjects. While "Latino" is a strong collective identity for some, regionally specific migrant streams and individual and families' complex immigration statuses complicate attempts to define a Latino urbanism, so much of which is hidden from plain view. In this chapter, the spaces examined begin to describe a remittance or migrant urbanism in which the US city itself structures and interfaces with the spaces of migration.

The Architecture of Migrant Civil Society

Since Mexican migrants in the United States began organizing into groups in the early twentieth century, they have needed meeting places to discuss shared concerns and coordinate activities. While little is known about early migrant meeting halls, a few examples suggest that they provided a focal point for the community, a space in which individuals formed new identities, and a platform for political organization oriented toward the places in which migrants lived.[5] For example, in the 1930s, Azteca Hall in the agricultural town of Brawley, California, was used to orient migrants in Brawley and help them manage local working and living conditions. Azteca Hall was the headquarters for Mexicans involved in the Club Deportivo Artes y Oficios (Young Men's Athletic Club), the Alianza Hispano-Americana, and Club Democrático. Beyond everyday uses, the hall became a meeting ground for workers during labor strikes in the 1930s and, as a result, a focal point for intimidation and raids by union busters. Other examples, such as Casa del Mexicano in Los Angeles, built in the 1930s, and Casa Aztlán in Chicago, initiated in the 1970s, are social and cultural centers and hubs of community life. The Mexican centers nurture "ethnic" traditions while providing tools for migrant incorporation into American cities, such as citizenship, job training, and language classes.

Today's *casas* are not modeled on turn-of-the-century Mexican social clubhouses. Rather than focusing on social and cultural activities and tools to assist immigrants in their transition into American cities, casas bring migrants' binational civic and political agendas into direct engagement with the host city. Casas also provide focal points for organizing, serving as spatial and institutional platforms for the definition of common ground: shared aspirations that define both individuals as "migrants" and migrants as a "public." As places where migrants meet, establish affiliations beyond their hometowns, engage in political activism, forge relationships with politicians in Mexico and the United States, and represent themselves, casas create new social, political, and economic possibilities for migrants. In this way they are more closely related to Chinese social and political clubhouses known as *huiguans* in nineteenth- and twentieth-century Chinatowns, where local activities were integrally bound up with the politics, economics, and social practices of mainland China.[6] Today's Mexican casas may also resemble the meeting places of Italian, Irish, and Polish migrants who maintained close ties to homelands at the turn of the twentieth century.

The term *casas* can refer to both migrant-initiated and managed meeting houses or cultural centers and Mexican government-run offices that attend to Mexican emigrant populations abroad. In some cases a casa may be comanaged by state officials and migrant groups. Casa Colima in Los Angeles and Casa Guanajuato in Chicago are examples of government-run offices that lend space to migrant groups (the state governments do not own the property; they rent and manage it). Casa Zacatecas (one in Los Angeles and the other in Chicago) are two examples of grassroots migrant headquarters fully owned and operated by migrant communities.[7] In doing their work, migrant-run casas supplement or replace services provided by the fifty Mexican consulates scattered throughout the country. While Chicago's consulate, in operation since 1884, aims to be "a house for all Mexicans," it struggles to meet the needs of its constituency. It serves an estimated three million Mexicans from the states of Illinois, Wisconsin, and Indiana.[8] Within this context, consular employees view migrant organizations as "intellectual Mexican capital in Chicago," whose federations and casas create a "reciprocal collaboration" with the consulate that "minimizes our work."[9]

In 2004 the Mexican consulate in Chicago expanded operations. It moved from the second story of a midsized commercial building on North Michigan Avenue in Chicago's downtown to its own building just west of downtown. Beyond relocation to a more accessible part of the city, the new consulate building was specifically designed to support the work of migrant clubs. Several meeting rooms named after Mexican presidents—Sala Juárez, Sala Madero, Sala Morelos, and Sala Hidalgo—were built for and are used by migrant clubs. The meeting rooms, which seat twenty to two hundred people, are equipped with digital projectors and large round meeting tables. While these rooms are frequently used, Alfonso Rosas Joule, a consular employee who works with HTAS, told me: "In this year, 2011, I have noticed an increase in independence—no, a maturity—in clubs and federations. Now that they have grown up and can walk alone, they have their re-unions in their communal casas."[10] Such casas have been desired in part because consular facilities do not allow alcohol, smoking, or loud music on the premises, and these prohibitions mean migrants can-not hold typical fundraising events there. Additionally, federations that use the consulate's facilities do not have their own street address, which may bolster a federation's legitimacy as a not-for-profit and help them acquire outside sources of funding.[11]

Migrant casas—which serve specific migrant groups according to their own needs rather than providing services for "all Mexicans" as part of a presumed national project—assume many forms and occupy a variety of spaces. San Luis Potosí's club has its meetings in a bank, the Oaxaca federation gathers in a migrant's home in Wisconsin, and Durango's federation often uses a room in a hospital where one of its members works. The location of meeting spaces depends on avail-ability and accessibility for club members. Clubs often formalize their meeting spaces incrementally, from backyards or basements to rent-ing offices to owning buildings. The migrants of Casa Michoacán—a model for other groups aspiring to have a casa of their own—once met in the basement of the federation president's house. Their his-tory illustrates the importance of identity and solidarity to the spa-tial program of the casa. "While we have many important activities [in the casa], educational, social, environmental, political, the main reason we built it is to make the migrants proud. We had meetings in the basement of churches, in my house crowded on milk crates. The casa is to give dignity to migrants who are perceived as poor and igno-rant."[12] Owning and maintaining a casa symbolizes a respected arrival in both the host city and home state at once.

Casa Michoacán: A Grassroots Home for Migrants

Casa Michoacán is located just south of downtown in the iconic Mexi-can neighborhood of Pilsen. A sanctified gathering spot for Michoa-canos, Casa Michoacán is just blocks away from several important institutional buildings providing services to the Mexican population. The National Museum of Mexican Art, Casa Aztlán (founded by Chi-canos in the 1970s and still offering language and citizenship classes), the Lozano Public Library, Chicago's first bilingual public schools, and several Spanish-liturgy Catholic churches complement Mexican res-taurants, grocery stores, and money transfer centers throughout the neighborhood. Leaders of the Federación de Clubes Michoacanos en Illinois (Federation of Michoacán in Illinois) chose to locate the build-ing within this dynamic space not only to position themselves at the center of Mexican Chicago but to further define Pilsen as the center of Mexican cultural and political life in Chicago. In 2004 the federation bought an unassuming two-story brick row building on Blue Island Avenue with its own funds and a one-time donation of $150,000 from the state government of Michoacán. The building was previously a storefront church and originally housed a turn-of-the-century print-ing press.

The Casa's explicitly binational agenda is represented in federa-tion charter documents. The Casa is intended to be a "center of opera-tions . . . to promote the complete participation of the migrant com-munity in the socio-political life of the communities where we are located." Those communities are understood to exist in both the United States and Mexico. In the United States, the Casa fights for migration reform, drivers' licenses for the undocumented, civil and labor rights, and protection of human rights. The Casa is also "establishing a perma-nent link between government officials and Michoacanos to advance the migrant agenda," which includes suffrage in Mexico, coordina-tion of binational forums, and promotion of 3×1 projects.[13] The Casa's

FIGURE 6.02. Casa Michoacán in Pilsen, Chicago. The Casa's facade has been remodeled; the wood siding is now cantera limestone tiles imported from Mexico. Photograph by author.

projects include collaboration with over thirty different HTAS, whose memberships range from twenty to one thousand families per club.

The finish materials and furnishings of the Casa do the important work of building a sense of place for Michoacanos in American cities through the materials, colors, and craft traditions of their hometowns. Artisanal pottery, metalwork, and textiles brought from Michoacán are on display, and the US and Mexican flags (donated by the Mexican consulate) stand side by side. Michoacano builders, carpenters, and painters donated their time to remodel the space, and ornamental woodwork of hand-carved pine from Tzintzuntzan, Michoacán, decorates the bookshelves. The wood brought from Michoacán is a part of an origin narrative; a federation member explained that because of bee pollination, this particular tree species grows only in Canada, the United States, Michoacán, and Mexico City. Similarly, the building's facade is covered in cantera stone, brought to Chicago from quarries in Mexico. The soft, easily carved limestone used throughout Mexico for the facades of churches and government buildings pub-

FIGURE 6.03. The cover of the annual publication of the Federación de Clubes Michoacanos en Illinois juxtaposes images of the basilica in Morelia, Mexico, and Chicago's skyline, symbolically linked by the flight of monarch butterflies.

licly announces the building as distinctly "Mexican." The project also makes use of less overt means to reference migrant origins, including landscape elements. The monarch butterflies whose migration paths connect Michoacán to the Midwest are a frequently referenced symbol for Mexican migrants. Down the street from Casa Michoacán, the federation built a small urban garden planted with milkweed to lure the butterflies en route from Michoacán to Canada. The federation also represents this narrative on the cover of its annual magazine: Chicago's skyline and Morelia's basilica are married by fluttering butterflies, symbolizing regional specificity, freedom of mobility, and interconnectedness.

The architectural plan of Casa Michoacán facilitates and promotes public engagement. Stepping through the door, one enters directly into a large open hall—a critical space for a fledgling democratic institution. This room, the most public space in the Casa, is used for federation and club meetings, posadas, dances, and meals, and as a gallery space for migrant and Michoacano art. Training and administrative work is conducted in the basement. A room equipped with over a dozen computers is used for binational education classes. The second floor combines living, semipublic, and administrative functions. Two upstairs offices house additional migrant organizations: NALACC (National Alliance of Latin American and Caribbean Communities), a transnational organization fighting for immigrant rights, and a Latino health institute. The third is an office for the 3×1 program. There is also an internal apartment with a communal kitchen, living room, and bedroom for visiting guests, and a communal library. These overlapping programs serve a range of individuals from government officials to activists, creating opportunities for networking and collaboration. Throughout the year, Casa Michoacán is buzzing with activity, migrants coordinating and innovating what they call "projects in a binational context."[14]

Even here Mexican officials and government funds play a significant, if minimal, role. The state of Michoacán pays the salary of one full-time employee running a state program called the Office for Attention to Migrants. This officer was selected by the government of Michoacán to work in Chicago because of her specialized knowledge of migration based on her experiences of daily life in an emigrant village in Mexico. Unlike the Mexican consulate, where migrants wait in long lines to be directed to another waiting area, Casa Michoacán provides immediate service to all Mexican migrants who call or come by, reinforcing its position as a community-based institution. Migrants come to the Casa to talk with the staff about their specific challenges in adapting to life in Chicago, including such matters as birth certificates, residency questions, or criminal charges.

Migrants from several Mexican states call Casa Michoacán a "house for everybody," due to both its institutional structure and its programming. Migrants own and manage the space, artists and activists use the space to perform and show art, and federation members use the space to hold meetings. Together, these functions have established Casa Michoacán as an important site for both services

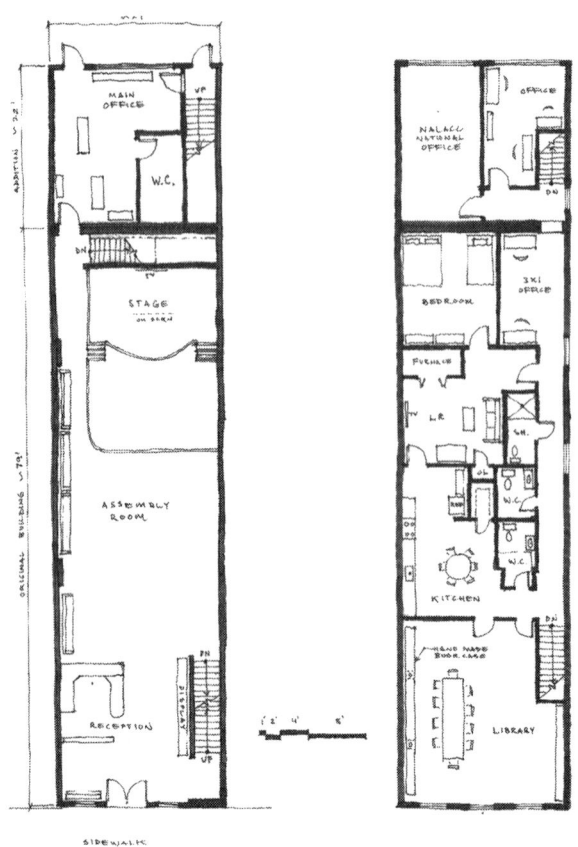
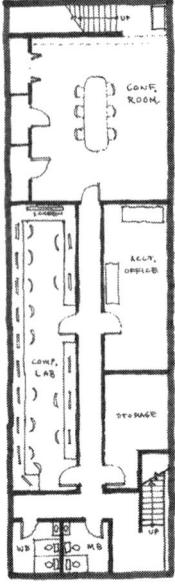

1st Level   2nd Level   Basement

FIGURE 6.04. Plan of Casa Michocán, Chicago. The compact layout of these three floors attests to the dense, layered program that has evolved over time and made maximum use of available space. The large area on the second floor set aside as a temporary residential apartment for visitors from Mexico and other US cities reflects the mobile nature of the federation's partners and transnational members. Drawn by Chesney Floyd.

and political activism. Referring to the mass migrant mobilizations against the Sensenbrenner Bill organized in 2006, migrant leader José Luis Gutiérrez asks, "Do you know what happened here? All the organizing for the protests of 2006. That is what happened here. That is what this place is capable of."[15] Rooted in the environmental and social fabric of Pilsen, Casa Michoacán deploys strategies of the civil rights era of protest movements, but in a binational context.

Buildings like Casa Michoacán change migrant discourses, structuring engagements between different migrant streams and their states of origin. Building "a place without borders" locates migrants in a permanent structure in the United States that foments remittance urbanism, a commingling of and engagement between disparate migration streams structured by the urban environment. For example, the federations that do not have their own spaces to hold meetings rent, borrow, or barter to use casas. The Federation of Durango president "feels good" about renting from Casa Michoacán because it is "supporting the migrant cause."[16] NALACC puts migrants from Latin America and the Caribbean into direct contact with one another. Mexican clubs now hold events at the United African Organization headquarters, an organization that also focuses on migrant rights. These interactions have practical, social, and political importance, contributing to the formation of migrant subjectivities and political consciousness. A member of NALACC and the Federation of Michoacán notes, "We realized we are transnational. We started using the term to incorporate Salvadorans and Guatemalans into our struggle."[17] The transnationalization of migrant activism occurred precisely through a heightened regional specificity as migrants began identifying as Michoacanos or Duranguenses rather than Mexicanos. Migrant buildings spatialize regional distinctions, and the new places that emerge create opportunities for disparate groups to engage around common goals.

As William Sites and Rebecca Vonderlack-Navarro argue, HTAS "scale out" and "scale up" as their activities require them to continually make political and institutional alliances with various levels of local and regional state governments.[18] For Casa Michoacán, "scaling out" occurred when the migrant-owned building required substantial maintenance and care in 2012. The federation was forced to make major renovations to secure a collapsing floor between the first story and the basement level. Due to the extent of these repairs, local city codes and requirements came into play (for example, accessible bathrooms were required), and Casa Michoacán was awarded a $100,000 grant from the state of Illinois for renovations (this is the second state grant in support of the building; the first was from the state of Michoacán). Rather than Michoacanos donating their time to remodel the space, as occurred during initial construction, the state grants required hiring state construction employees. By the end of the renovation, the project was $40,000 over budget. As owners of the building, the federation itself must assume this cost and raise funds to resolve the debt. As with all institutional buildings, once it was erected, a certain organizational flexibility was lost, and attention was (at least partially) refocused on the regional connections and responsibilities that a permanent structure creates. Acquiring a building resulted in new levels of engagement with the institutions and regulations of the host city.

Casa Jalisco: A Remittance Headquarters?

Casa Jalisco is an example of how increased government involvement in the production of casas can influence the level of formalization and daily activities of migrant federations. Built only five years after Casa Michoacán, Casa Jalisco is the result of a fundamentally different model of migrant organizing: its ownership, public facade, geographic siting, incorporation of trade, institutional alliances, and representational strategies together establish a more formal, business-oriented approach in partnership with Mexican state institutions.

According to Sergio Suárez, the president of the Federación de Clubes Jaliscienses del Medio Oeste (Federation of Jalisco in the Midwest) from 2007 to 2012, a state-sponsored Casa Jalisco for migrants was first promised by the governor of Jalisco, Alberto Cárdenas, who brought the PAN (Partido Acción Nacional) party to power in Jalisco in 1995.[19] Since the early 2000s, articles published in Mexican newspapers such as *El Norte*, *El Informador*, and *Mural*, alongside *La Opinión* in Los Angeles, reference the promises of several Mexican officials to build a center that would extend the resources of the Jalisco state government into US territory. Jorge Arana Arana, Jalisco's gubernatorial hopeful in 2000, imagined that the casa "would assist our people when faced with problems, above all with discrimination, transmission of documents, misinformation regarding prisons, all which our countrymen face."[20] Located in Los Angeles, such a casa would serve the estimated two million Jaliscienses in California at that time. In a 2002 interview for the Spanish-language Los Angeles newspaper *La Opinión*, Governor Francisco Ramírez Acuña promised to erect a Casa Jalisco that would link an entrepreneurial agenda with social activism. He imagined a casa that would display and sell Jalisco products, have a space for migrants to hold meetings, and serve as a shelter "where [Jaliscienses] without a specific place to go can find water, clothes, hot food, instead of finding shelter under a bridge or drain, which are places where they get initiated into drugs or contaminated with AIDS."[21] These statements explicitly outline social and political agendas to address the basic needs and protection of migrants, cultivating relationships through promises to provide critical support.

Beginning in 2009 and inaugurated in 2011, the first Casa Jalisco in the United States was not built in Los Angeles but in Chicago. Casa Jalisco in Chicago is the material manifestation of a migrant-state innovation intended to create a "Jalisco without borders."[22] The Casa was a five-million-dollar project paid for by taxpayers in Jalisco—and thus the premier example of a Mexican state-funded binational space.[23] Jalisco state employee José Luis Treviño explained, "Once Congress approved funds, Governor Emilio González finally made good on over ten years of promises."[24] Casa Jalisco is located in Melrose Park, a suburb of Chicago where thirty years ago the Latino population was allegedly only 10 percent; today it is 70 percent. The growing Mexican population in exurbs like Melrose Park, Cicero, and Aurora reflects the Latinization of Chicago's suburbs and exurbs more generally. This demographic shift is evident in the built fabric. The main street of Melrose Park, once marked by Italian shops and restaurants, is now peppered with MoneyGram stores, Mexican groceries, and dress shops selling gowns for quinceañeras.

Demographics alone, however, do not explain why Casa Jalisco—the state of Jalisco's biggest investment in its emigrant community in history—is in Melrose Park. Its location is an example of the importance of politically active, entrepreneurial individuals in defining hierarchical remittance space on both sides of the border. Sergio Suárez, a migrant from Jalisco who has lived in the United States for over thirty years, is deeply involved with the Federation of Jaliscienses in Chicago. His commitment to social organizations in both the United States and Mexico (he is the founder of Fundación Necahual, a civic organization in Mexico geared toward youth in poverty) explains his connection to and friendship with Jalisco's ex-governor Emilio González. Suárez lives in Melrose Park (his business and office are down the street from the Casa), and as a successful businessman, he also has connections with Ron Serpico, the mayor of Melrose Park, who helped facilitate the process of acquiring the Casa. The Village of Melrose Park's real-estate developer found the federation an abandoned bank building, which was remodeled to house migrant activities and Jalisco state programs. Suárez notes, "If the governor [of Jalisco] didn't trust me personally, this project never would have happened"—evidence of the fact that remittance space is defined not just by political action and entrepreneurial activities but also by individual connections.[25] Here personal trust was a prerequisite to government investment.

The materiality of the Casa reveals the project's stature. The building is a two-story prefabricated tilt-up concrete bank building built in 1967 (fig. 6.06). The gray concrete panels, separated by narrow vertical bands of tinted glass, create a fortified enclosure with a high degree of security and privacy. Tightly manicured shrubs and a sprawling parking lot surround the building. Treviño, a government employee deeply involved in the project, explains, "We didn't put a fence around the building because we want it to feel like home."[26] Despite this gesture, the building's stark concrete and glass exterior suitably represents the Mexican state. Upon entry, one is greeted by a suite of offices partitioned with floor-to-ceiling paneled glass. In 2011 six Mexican officials and support staff (including a secretary of education and secretary of culture), plus one full-time and three part-time nongovernmental migrant employees, worked at the Casa. The first floor also houses a trade gallery to promote Jalisco products such as tequila, regional candies, designer apparel, and a "Jalisco BlackBerry" or smartphone to an American audience. Behind the entry-area offices is a private room with a high-tech "smart board" for binational meetings and binational classes and a private office for the governor of Jalisco. The ground-floor corner office, labeled "Governor's Office," was envisioned as a room for Emilio Gonzáles to receive visitors during his brief visits to Chicago. Unlike the meeting hall at Casa Michoacán, the great hall used most frequently by migrant groups here is not visible upon entrance. Located on the second floor, it is outfitted with several expensive features—designer carpeting, a built-in wooden bar, artisanal ceramic vases, and state-of-the-art AV equipment—that create an elegant setting. The hall (approximately four times the size of Casa Michoacán's) allows migrants to hold forums, meetings, galas, fiestas, and fundraisers, and other migrant groups occasionally rent it for their annual events.

The public symbol of Casa Jalisco is a bronze replica of *La Minerva*, a statue in Guadalajara, which was donated by Governor Gonzáles to communicate the institutional identity of the Casa to a broader public. Located in front of the building, the statue carries Guadalajara's message of *justicia, sabiduría y fortaleza* (justice, knowledge, and strength) to Lake Street. Now (it is hoped) migrants can celebrate Las Chivas, Guadalajara's soccer team, by running circles around *La Minerva* in Melrose Park as Mexicans do in Guadalajara. Adjacent to the statue is an official government plaque—identical to the plaques on 3×1 projects throughout Mexico—that announces the government as the building's sponsor. In 2012 migrants from Jalisco's federations in Los Angeles, Seattle, and Las Vegas, as well as diplomats from Mexico, attended the inauguration of *La Minerva*. As diplomats and migrant activists were photographed in front of the statue, a local migrant reflected, "I think a part of this is that it gives migrants, it gives *us*, an opportunity to show our good side, and this is something to be proud of."[27] Too often migrant contributions to US urban landscapes are narrowly confined to the proliferation of Mexican restaurants and colorful commercial districts marked by large signage in Spanish and English. *La Minerva* represents migrants' local and long-distance civic engagements, presenting an "opportunity" to educate a broader public in Chicago about migrancy and Mexico more generally.

Jalisco's government builds political and cultural affiliations with migrants to maximize the potential of economic flows, a primary development strategy for Mexico. According to Treviño, the government is "most interested in the potential of the migrant entrepreneurs and the second generation. The second generation is an invaluable resource: they are working at Mac and IBM, and they want to connect with Jalisco." He told me that a group of migrants' children asked the secretary of culture—who is now accessible to them in Chicago

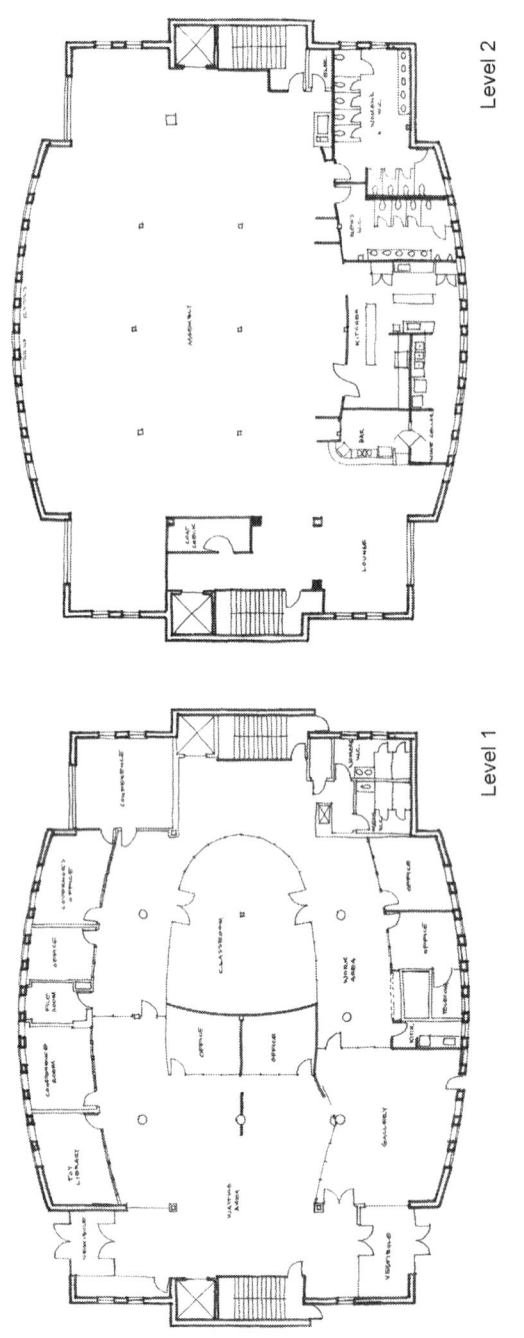

Level 1   Level 2

FIGURE 6.05. The floorplan of Casa Jalisco, Chicago, shows an institutional layout with a spatially defined program, formal space for public display in the first-floor gallery, and generously sized staff work areas. Arriving at the large assembly hall for public events requires leaving the main floor and ascending to the second floor. Drawn by Chesney Floyd.

FIGURE 6.06. Casa Jalisco on Lake Street in Chicago occupies a precast concrete building that once housed a bank. In the front of the building, surrounded by landscape plantings, is a replica of the *La Minerva* statue in Guadalajara, Mexico. Photograph by author.

through Casa Jalisco—"How can we love Mexico if we don't know it?" The answer, he said, was "You can't. You have to know it first. We have to bring Jalisco here for those that can't go there."[28] Jalisco's government is funding Jalisco's most reputable ballet and music troupes to perform at migrant events, in the hope that migrants and their children who stay connected with the culture will invest in Jalisco and that a "marca Jalisco" (Jalisco brand) will be born. Officials in Jalisco have learned that migrant HTAS and federations are powerful networking engines they can use to connect Jalisco products to migrant, Mexican American, and American markets. These networks can also bring human capital, knowledge, and training to Mexico. During an interview in Guadalajara with the director of the Office for the Attention of Jaliscienses Abroad (OJAFE), Gilberto Juárez González explained that one of the main goals of the office was to create export opportunities for all of Jalisco's products, which are in high demand in the diaspora. He illustrated the potential of this agenda anecdotally. On trips to Los Angeles he would go to restaurants owned by Jaliscienses and open the cupboards. "And what do you think I saw? Kraft cheese. We want to change that." Migrants need to be convinced to "buy Jalisco."[29] Tequila, jewelry, sweets, hand-sewn dresses, shoes, and other goods known as a part of the "nostalgia market" can be incorporated into Chicago's economy.[30]

While migrant activists likewise appear to prioritize Casa Jalisco as a center for economic development and trade, they view such development as a means toward social change. At a general assembly attended by migrant club presidents and participants, Suárez explained, "Social justice is never going to arrive if there is not economic development. This is our base here in the Federación de Jaliscienses, the base in business in order to help civil organizations with whatever cause they have."[31] Judith de la Mora, a principal activist in the federation, concurs: "Out of the three goals we have, business development is the most important. If you can develop businesses, you have more money; if you have more money, you can develop your country of origin there as well as here."[32] Although federation leaders publicly advocate for business development, most federation activities are focused on social and civic engagement. Out of 131 federation events and gatherings held in 2011, only three were focused on business development.[33] In keeping with the neoliberal ideal of empowerment through open markets, migrants in the Jalisco federation view economic advancement as a means toward social and civic engagement and political power. The Mexican government, however, is focused on boosting Mexican exports and fomenting trade as a goal in and of itself. What appear to be migrants' and the governments' complementary agendas have rather distinct long-term goals.

In 2011 Treviño argued: "Casa Jalisco is a win-win situation: migrants get government support and the government gets migrant investment and allegiance."[34] In part, this win-win situation is a reward for decades of remitting. According to Suárez, the government's five-million-dollar investment in the migrant diaspora is the least it could do: "This year we sent 2.8 billion dollars in remittances. They [the Jalisco state Congress] said, '[Five million is] a lot of money.' I said, 'Compared with what? Five million dollars? If we are keeping tabs, it is one-quarter of 1 percent of the amount we send annually. You only need to keep that money in the bank for three days to make enough money in interest for Casa Jalisco.'"[35] Meanwhile, Jalisco state's investment seeks to solidify its allegiance to migrants and affirm migrants' shared responsibility for their hometowns, deepening migrant investments in hometowns. Casas are also one way for the state to measure and influence the resources and political inclinations of its emigrants.

In addition to the migrant services it provides, Casa Jalisco is the result, in part, of an experimental land-acquisition process through which the state of Jalisco has purchased property in a foreign country. After years of research, Mexican state officials finally determined that the only way for a state-level foreign entity (Jalisco) to own property in another country outside of the consular system was through Jaltrade, a state agency whose mission is to foment international economic trade.[36] Jaltrade was forced to create Jaltrade USA, a nonprofit organization, to be able to pay Mexican functionaries to work in Chicago. In addition to the initial five-million-dollar investment and the functionaries' salaries, the building costs Jalisco taxpayers an estimated three hundred thousand dollars annually to operate and maintain.[37]

This model for a casa—whereby a state entity owns a building that is intended to be a meeting place and headquarters for a "grassroots" migrant organization—is beset by both logistical difficulties and internal tensions resulting from its hybrid mission. Just one year after the inauguration of the building, the functionaries returned to Mexico in acknowledgment that their work in Chicago was not as successful as intended. Judith de la Mora notes that Casa Jalisco "wasn't intended for every functionary to have an office here. . . . We at Fedejal know what people in the community want because they come and ask for it. Those in Jalisco, what do they know about what our people need here? So they put their own representatives that had to follow their orders and do what they thought people needed here . . . and it wasn't working out because they weren't getting the results."[38] The state's distance from migrant communities in the United States leads to misunderstandings and erroneous assumptions. Additionally, in 2012 Jaltrade drafted a written "landlord" and "tenancy" agreement that will require the federation to rent space from Jaltrade on a monthly basis (access to the open hall is to be granted upon written request). This agreement (which needs to be periodically renewed) raises anxieties about the Casa's future. If the government of Jalisco ceased financial support for Casa Jalisco entirely, the federation would most likely lose access to the building. In 2012 Jaltrade allowed the federation to use two offices, with potential for a third, while the remaining four offices, two conference rooms, classroom, gallery, and library stood closed, locked, and empty.

Despite internal complications, Casa Jalisco has been used by migrants in Melrose Park and throughout Illinois to build migrant unity, strengthen the organization, and represent regional Mexican identities to a broader American public through public performances. In 2007 the Federation of Jalisco began producing mobile cultural performances that are subsidized by the state of Jalisco. Jalisco *en* [in] Joliet, Jalisco en Cicero, and Jalisco en Aurora are names of events aimed at bringing Jalisco's most iconic cultural traditions to the mayors and public of Chicago suburbs. Suárez commented, "In Round Lake, the mayor was racist; he didn't want to have anything to do with the Hispanic community. We went, sat down, got them to lend the auditorium, and now he says, 'We have to do more of this.'" According to Suárez, Jalisco en "kills the stereotypes" that Mexicans are "narcotraffickers and illegals"; it strengthens ties between civic Mexican HTAS and local Illinois politicians, who will in turn support their organizational aspirations suburb by suburb. By 2012 Jalisco en was branded as "7N7" and taken to seven Chicago area cities in seven days.

In turn, Chicago officials are paying more attention to the specific characteristics of their migrant constituents. Melrose Park's mayor Ron Serpico has visited Jalisco over eight times and says that by now he is perceived as being very "Jalisciense" despite his Italian roots. In the upcoming election cycle, Serpico explained, he would be running against a Duranguense, and he was aware that he needed to break into "that community" to win. Thus migrant activities in Melrose Park have educated the mayor about regional Mexican and migrant identities, in effect "transnationalizing" him.[39]

The stately Casa Jalisco comes to life during festivals and fiestas, gatherings marked by amplified live music, an abundance of tequila, and regional dishes. At Casa Jalisco, local restaurateurs often donate Mexican sandwiches, pozole, carnitas, and refried beans to events. *Carreta de Oro Tequila*, produced in Sergio Suárez's hometown, Juanacatlán, is sold at the bar and sometimes dispensed for free. Mexican families with complex migration histories, young lovers, and solo entrepreneurs attend functions in formal attire and elegant dresses. There is an atmosphere of formality *and* familiarity during such community-building events. Reminiscent of discussions to "keep the tradition" of remitting to Mexico "alive" that take place during the inauguration of remittance-financed projects in Mexico, events in Chicago demonstrate the need to keep Casa Jalisco "open" and available for all migrants. The state government's short-term commitments create an atmosphere of uncertainty about the Casa's financial future. Migrant events are a chance to build solidarity as well as institute a local tradition in the face of possible change.

* * *

Currently, Casa Michoacán and Casa Jalisco present varying models for building binational space in American cities. While both federations are fighting to better the lives of migrants in the United States and Mexico, Casa Michoacán's activist rhetoric contrasts with Casa Jalisco's rhetoric of liberal development. The level of state involvement and scale of Casa Jalisco led a migrant leader from Durango's federation to comment: "Casa Jalisco is a different concept completely, . . . a megaproject. The government has contributed millions of dollars. . . . They are an arm of the state. To receive money for a down payment on a casa is one thing, but to be an arm of the state is another."[40] While the promotion of personal empowerment is intended to lift migrants out of poverty and give them voice, the Jalisco state government's ownership of Casa Jalisco and the economic agenda of Jaltrade influence migrant goals and threaten to weaken migrants' ability to organize grassroots civic networks. Even so, both casas symbolize a shift in the discursive potential of remitting as they further institutionalize what is a politics of redress, a correction of social injustices *in Mexico* by millions of individuals' voluntary remittances.

The explicitly political spaces of migrant casas are deeply embedded in an urban process. The president of Jalisco's migrant federation notes that in about 2006 the federation began to shift its attention from Mexico alone to Mexico and the United States.[41] In the process of acquiring a casa and working with other migrant groups throughout the city, many Jaliscienses realized that there was much local need and work to be done in Chicago's migrant community. As a by-product of its location, Casa Michoacán is increasingly invested in the activities of Pilsen, collaborating with migrant, Mexican, and Chicago institutions. The casas create a spatial center, a place of solidarity and visibility, a migrant place that had not existed before where new migrant identities take shape. It is an environment in which organizing and common purpose build solidarity and identification with a migrant public that transcends affiliations based on hometowns and familial networks. The casas also change how migrants dwell and operate in the American city. Far from being sequestered into traditional migrant enclaves, migrant communities are building networks across cities, states, and borders related to the values and practices important to and defined by migrants.

Migrant Infrastructure for an Emergent Public: The Mexican Rodeo

Jaripeos (bull-riding events) and charrerías (equestrian competitions) are Mexican sporting traditions that migrants brought to the Midwest during the second half of the twentieth century.[42] In the grassroots planning, construction, and use of these (mostly) informal venues, migrants transform their aspirations into built environments that support an emergent migrant public and build binational connections into the American landscape. My exploration here examines the historic development, spatial logic, and sociospatial meaning of migrant infrastructures for Mexican sports. Today a landscape composed of arenas, stables, performance venues, and ranches supports migrants' social, cultural, and psychological desires, crafting their own experiences in the American city and contributing to the vitality of remittance space.[43]

In the 1960s, when Mexican migrants first began practicing the charrería in Illinois, famous Mexican charros (horsemen) included Chicago in their US tours of what the Chicago Tribune called a "rodeo-circus-folk music horse show."[44] A charro named Antonio Aguilar performed the Chicago National Mexican Rodeo and Ballet of Horses in the International Amphitheatre in 1967. Even before that, the Federation of Charros from Mexico City had performed a charrería in the National Armory, a well-established performance venue for a public audience.[45] In the 1980s the Mexican charrería was again in Chicago's regional newspapers. In Chicago's Little Village neighborhood, the Midwest Regional Association of Charros helped construct a venue known as Garibaldi Plaza (named after Mexico City's Garibaldi Plaza) that included a ring, bullpens, and bleachers out of temporary building materials. Garibaldi Plaza is a dirt parking lot behind the Cook

County Courthouse, which is still at times converted into a temporary performance space. The *Tribune* reported: "The scene is exotic but the setting isn't. . . . Here 200 to 1,000 members of Chicago's Mexican community sit on battered wooden bleachers, belt down beers, munch tacos and watch the skills of about 25 horsemen as they try to harness wild bulls and bucking broncos with the deft turn of a lariat."[46]

During the same period, Mexican migrants began building their own arenas, buying bulls and horses, and accumulating the charro costumes and gear necessary to perform the charrería in small American towns—establishing core elements of traditional "rancho" lifestyles in the United States. According to several oral histories, in the 1960s migrants began organizing charrerías in Lowell, Indiana, using American-style rodeo arenas. Camerino Gonzáles—a veteran charro in the Chicago region—recalled attending charrería-like events in small arenas that were "sort of American rodeo style, not regulated like they are today," upon his arrival to Chicago in 1968.[47] According to Gonzáles, these early charros rented bulls from an African American cowboy who supplied animals for American rodeos.[48] In 1976 the Peña family, migrants from Jalisco who lived and worked in semi-rural Joliet, Illinois, attended one such charrería in Indiana. Inspired to build their own arena in Illinois, a partnership of four male family members bought land in Joliet at a time when the Mexican population could be "counted on one hand."[49] Using a book they carried with them from Mexico that spelled out the proper arena measurements, the men built a *lienzo*, a keyhole-shaped corral with a 60-meter tail and a circular terminus approximately 40 meters in diameter. When they were not working the railroad, factory, or construction jobs that were their full-time occupations, they sprinted on horseback into the circular central arena and practiced horse tricks. They named the arena La Herradura de Joliet (the Horseshoe of Joliet). The project converted ten acres of agricultural land into what anthropologist Kathleen Sands calls a "lienzo complex," composed of a specialized arena, a covered patio for eating and drinking, horse stables, parking spaces for trailers to maintain and move horses and feed, pens for bulls, and a dirt parking lot.[50]

Typical migrant-built horse stables in Chicago's suburbs—often adjacent to lienzos—are informal structures managed and maintained through a system of compadrazgo mapped onto migrant social

FIGURE 6.07. Rancho de los Charros, Joliet, Illinois. Note the proximity between the bulls, informally corralled by a metal fence, and the condominium developments beyond. Photograph by author.

networks. The compadrazgo system, characterized by social practices of bartering and borrowing and close-knit social and familial networks, is augmented by state-based migrant affinities and affiliations. According to ranch owners and users, migrant-run stables cost Mexican migrants less than half the price of keeping a horse on a "gringo" farm.[51] At some ranches, the stables are virtually free. Nicholas Flores built stables at his ranch, Rancho de los Charros, less than two miles from La Herradura de Joliet, in the 1990s, to provide boarding for horses through a barter system. Flores's stables consist of a doubled-loaded phalanx of wooden stalls on either side of a narrow dirt-floored passageway that houses approximately thirty horses. The stables were constructed using found materials: wooden crate scraps and shipping pallets nailed together form stable walls bearing the company stamps of their past lives. Beams fashioned from salvaged dimensional lumber support a low-slope plywood shed roof. Daylight streams in through gaps and irregularly sized, unglazed windows. A group of approximately thirty migrants from Flores's native state of Zacatecas make small donations for horse feed in return for stalls to board their horses. Each owner also cleans out his horse's stall and participates in events held at the ranch.[52] This arrangement makes participation accessible to migrants with limited resources. One such stable user, a migrant from Zacatecas who bought his horse in 2009, works the graveyard shift at a factory, allowing him to maintain his horse by day. Without Flores's stables, he says, "I could not have a horse."[53]

The lienzos in Joliet are located in what geographers refer to as an "urban fringe belt" region on the periphery of Chicago, characterized by relatively large land parcels.[54] Plenty of open space, access to freeways, open roads, and low population density facilitate this cultural endeavor. Over time, La Herradura has established a renowned reputation within the migrant community, and several migrants have purchased farmsteads and built Mexican-style lienzos in the region. The Peña lienzo now anchors what has become a hub for charrería in the Midwest, with an estimated ten lienzos built throughout Will County. This hub is a material manifestation of the networked spaces of migration; the constellation of lienzos allows distributed groups of migrants to create alliances, represent their identity to a multiregional migrant audience, and, importantly, stake claims to Illinois through practices originating in their home country. The cluster of ranchos permits migrants to choreograph highly specific uses of Joliet: using the stables at one ranch, migrants can clean and dress their horse, change into their formal attire, and parade on horseback through the suburban streets of Joliet to an event held at another ranch. This occurs in a city whose population is predominantly white; only 10 percent are foreign born, and of those most are from Mexico. For migrants who work long hours as laborers, riding a horse in cowboy gear or jeans and a charro hat rewrites the narrative of what it means to be a migrant in the American suburbs.

Migrant ranches in Joliet create unlikely proximities and build spatial difference in otherwise homogenous built environments. When Rancho de los Charros was built, the surrounding lots were sparsely populated. Since then, dense, highly manicured two-story condominium developments have sprung up next to Flores's lot lines. The living room and kitchen windows face Flores's lot, overlooking his wooden arena, the stables, and scattered, rusting trailers and tractor-trailer beds used to haul feed, animals, piles of dirt, and manure. Throughout the day, homeowners can watch as dozens of migrants come in and out of the property to walk, feed, and clean their horses.

On Sundays they witness people gather to eat typical Mexican dishes like *carnitas* and *bírria* (roasted pork and stewed goat), prepared and sold by Flores and his wife. This proximity, according to Flores, causes tensions and disruptions on his ranch. Neighbors do not hesitate to call the police and break up charrería events if they are bothered by the noise—an impediment to hosting the event that does not occur in rural Mexico. Now, Flores says, he does not play music.

The inward-looking lienzos in the Midwest are supported by complex binational systems. For example, for decades migrants have bought horses in Mexico and shipped them north, as well as exported horses from the United States to Mexico. An international (migrant-initiated) market "from below" enables today's migrants to not only practice charrería but also compete with the best charros in Mexico. According to Camerino Gonzáles, a premier charro and migrant from Jalisco, in the early 1990s two migrant brothers in the United States began buying American quarter horse foals, the preferred breed for charrería, and shipping them to ranchos (built with dollars) in Mexico to be trained. Whether selling the horses in Mexico or shipping them back to the United States, the brothers "made millions." In the 1990s shipping a horse between the United States and Mexico cost an estimated one thousand dollars. Today costs have almost doubled. Gonzáles notes, "Before we used to ship horses; now we ship people."[55] Rather than endure the risks involved in shipping live horses across international boundaries, skilled trainers are brought north to train the horses in states such as Illinois, California, and Texas. This movement north has resulted in what charros consider a "productive exchange," whereby Mexican and American equine experts share knowledge and innovate strategies that enhance the horses' performance.

The most prestigious charro organization in the world, the Federación Mexicana de Charrería, formally established in 1933 and located in Mexico City, is the center of gravity for this binational sport.[56] Just as any Mexican migrant can apply for the Mexican government's *matrícula* identification card, any migrant can pay one hundred dollars to become a formal member of the Federación Mexicana de Charrería. Many migrants who ride horses carry their membership identification card in their wallet daily (fig. 6.09). Due to the rising numbers of charros across the United States, the federation created a US chap-

FIGURE 6.08. Charros on Michigan Avenue, Chicago. Photo owned by Camerino Gonzáles, photographer unknown.

ter in 1991; however, annual competitions are always held in Mexico. And charro teams, of which there are approximately sixteen in the Midwest, compete with teams from other US cities to see which, if any, will attend the competition in Mexico.[57] Migrants take pride in purchasing charro gear, including ornate and expensive *trajes de gala*, or formal wear, from Mexico. Successful migrants send their children and nephews—second-generation American kids—to charrería schools in Mexico during vacation months to hone their techniques and bring specialized knowledge back to Chicago.

Participating in Mexico's national sport creates opportunities for new and controlled representations of migrants to a broader American public. Declared the national sport of Mexico, charros are publicly recognized as suitable replacements for the Mexican national army in public parades and processions. In Chicago it is not uncommon to see charros parading with the Mexican consul on Mexican Independence Day. During one such event, Camerino Gonzáles was personally invited "to accompany the consul in order to imitate soldiers, in our *traje de gala*."[58] A group of five charros, all migrants from various Mexican states, accompanied the consul in eighteen-pound suits adorned with gold and silver ornamentation to demonstrate the best of traditional Mexican equestrian culture to a broad American public.

In this context, migration provides pathways for Mexico's rural poor to participate not just in new economic mobility but in elements of traditional (and elite) Mexican culture as well. Raúl Muñoz's economic success in the United States allowed him to compete in the charrería at the national level. Muñoz, the late owner of Cuatro Caminos ranch in Joliet, came "illegally" to the United States as a poor seventeen-year-old from Guanajuato. In 1984 Muñoz built Illinois's second lienzo, later complemented by state-of-the-art stables and practice grounds. "I started to be a charro here. There I couldn't do it because I didn't have money. . . . I can do more in Mexico now than if I had always lived in Mexico. . . . I do charrería a lot at the national level—I go wherever they invite me."[59] According to Sands, "Elitist in Mexico, charrería is egalitarian in the United States."[60]

The vitality of charrería in the United States depends on the investments of successful migrant entrepreneurs who manage charro teams made up of young men and new migrants, and subsidize events. Camerino González came to the United States in 1968. He opened the restaurant Los Comales in 1973 and by the 1990s had built a regional franchise. González notes, "It would be more difficult to charrear if there weren't people with businesses. . . . I can do this because I have money from my business, but a person who works in a factory? No. The only thing he can do is buy his horse and maintain it."[61] As González's US business grew, so did his capacity to engage in building binational cultural infrastructures. For González, achieving the American dream was in part realized when in 1993 he was able to form his own team—in Mexico. Naming his team Arriara de Valle Grande after his grandfather, who was an *arriara*, or muleteer, in the "great valley" of Tonolá, González elected to base his team in Mexico to capitalize on the local knowledge of trainers and riders and more easily participate in national tournaments. His engagement with Mexican networks and systems in turn strengthens his position as an important charro in Chicago.

Migrant federations and HTAS also use events to fundraise for remittance-development projects. For several years an annual charrería has been the only moneymaking event that the Chicago Federación de Jaliscienses holds during its Semana Jalisco. This is true

FIGURE 6.09. Camerino Gonzáles with his bracero and charrería cards. Photograph by author.

across the United States; as Los Angeles's *La Opinion* reports, "Charreada could help to finish hundreds of projects in Jalisco."[62] In 2005 the president of the Los Angeles Jalisco Federation stated, "For each 25-dollar ticket, we achieve 100 dollars (due to government contributions through 3×1) for the causes of the municipalities that we represent."[63] In 2004 a grand charreada held in Los Angeles's oldest and more formal lienzo—Pico Rivera—raised $510,000, of which $205,000 was invested in 114 municipalities in Jalisco. Like other elements of migrant culture, charrería presents entrepreneurial opportunities that fuel remittance development.

A Poor Man's Sport: Undocumented and Famous

On the heels of the charrería, the sport of jaripeo (Mexican bareback bull riding) is blossoming in the Midwest. Whereas the charrería is a pedigreed and historically formalized Mexican sport whose main event is held in Mexico City, the jaripeo is an informal and unregulated activity conducted throughout Mexican villages, identified by a migrant from Guerrero as "of the poor, of us poor."[64] Unlike involvement in the charrería, participation in the jaripeo in Illinois does not typically elevate the status of migrants among Mexican nationals. Rather, participation in the jaripeo builds cultural infrastructures that serve as north-of-the-border spaces of representation for migrants "from below" as a direct extension of Mexico's rancho culture. In combination with other migrant forms of cultural expression, like the charrería, this rural ranching culture forms the basis of an emergent migrant public.

While the jaripeo has been possible in Illinois, Wisconsin, and Indiana since at least the 1970s and 1980s, when arenas built for charrerías could be used to perform jaripeos, an infrastructure built specifically for performing jaripeos has emerged as recently as the early 2000s. Upon arrival in Indiana in the 1990s, Miguel Muñoz, a "fourth-generation" cattle rancher from Guanajuato, began attending American rodeos; "I saw the American rodeo and thought, 'I want to have Mexican-style rodeos.'"[65] With limited English-language skills, Muñoz purchased his first bulls from American ranchers—breeding his *ganado*, or cattle, to bring jaripeo to Mexicans in Wisconsin. "I feel proud and happy to have realized a dream that didn't exist in this region."[66] Today there are at least eight migrant *ganaderos* in the Midwest, four formal venues used for jaripeos throughout the summer months, and several informal or temporary arenas in the region.[67]

The jaripeo affirms participants' rural roots, establishing a strong sense of identity after they have settled in an unfamiliar environment. Efraín Espinoza, a ganadero from Guerrero in Milwaukee said, "I was born with this"; the jaripeo is "a sport that raises one."[68] Muñoz echoes this sentiment, saying, "When I opened my eyes, when I was born, this [bulls and bullriding] is what I saw."[69] The reproduction of this childhood sport is about migrants coping with, and shaping, the spaces of migration (including limited movement) in the Midwest. "There are those that can't return due to migration. We bought the ranch to bring a bit of Mexico here, for our *compañeros* who migrate and for whom many years pass without seeing a pony or a burro or a horse." The moment of buying one's first bull, for Espinoza, is "the same as when you come here and want to buy your first car, and you save up for it. It is a sign of success."[70] As with the charrería, to be a ganadero in the Midwest is to realize migrant dreams in American places.

Producing the jaripeo in the United States requires the importation of brave young *jinetes* (bull riders) "direct from Mexico," as well as a circular arena and, of course, a bull. In Mexico jinetes do not follow the rules of the American rodeo (neither professional bull rider rodeos [PBR] nor independent rodeos). They do not wear safety vests, helmets, or wheeled spurs. Jinetes may ride for longer than eight seconds, and there are no restrictions on hand placement. Chicago event promoter Pedro Salazar explains: "There are no rules"; the jinete jumps on a bucking bull and hooks himself to its flesh with *ganchos*, or hooked spurs. The Mexican style is "more fierce" with "men flying, dizzy, and still they won't fall."[71] A famous jinete in the Chicago area, whose stage name is Rábano de Apango, or "Radish of Apango," is a twenty-nine-year-old father from Guerrero whose day job is delivering furniture. After approximately six years of bull riding in the United States, Rábano suffered his first major accident. A bull pinned him against the arena wall, breaking fifteen ribs and a clavicle, and puncturing one lung. Narrowly escaping death, Rábano was eager to get back on a bull in a year's time, and in the meantime continued to participate in events by coordinating and hiring other local jinetes.[72] For Rábano, who is undocumented, the jaripeo provides an opportunity to escape "the shadows" of American life and take center stage despite its obvious and very real dangers.

Whereas the jinete can be "imported" to the Midwest, the actual space of the Mexican jaripeo must be built from the ground up, adapted to the urban, rural, or fringe-urban setting of the United States. In Jalisco there are many ganaderos raising bulls for performances, and the region's dense network of pueblos and towns (most of which hold jaripeos) creates close proximities between bulls and performance venues year round. In the Midwest the few ganaderos with cattle trained and raised for the jaripeo are in high demand not only in Chicagoland but throughout cities spread across great distances. Since the early 2000s, the Muñoz family has taken the jaripeo on a wide-sweeping tour of American cities: "We were the first to take the Mexican-style jaripeo to St. Paul, Omaha, Columbus, Detroit, Cleveland. . . . We also went to Kansas, Denver, and Atlanta, but there we were not the first."[73] To bring the jaripeo to Omaha, Muñoz recalled, his family transported and cared for ten bulls with the hope that the long journey would not negatively affect their performance, and that the bulls would not get sick or become restless and overturn the moving trailers. "When we went to Omaha, Nebraska, during the event they announced, 'This man from

Wisconsin who came all this way to make this possible, blah blah,' and everybody applauded, and you feel very good. But then, when we leave on Highway 80, falling asleep on the road, fighting, and faced with all the risk ahead of us, we wonder if it is worth it."[74] With little financial gain, the family's reward for their efforts is the personal satisfaction of bringing a "genuinely Mexican" event to Mexicans occupying marginal positions in Midwest cities. The nascent grassroots infrastructure of the jaripeo requires migrants to assume substantial risk when transporting bulls across long distances. Further, ganaderos must keep their bulls healthy during six months of cold weather when the jaripeo season is over.

Jaripeo enthusiasts in Illinois must also navigate strict zoning regulations. Acquiring legal permission to build an event space requires knowledge of local county and city ordinances, submitting required documentation to local officials, acquiring numerous permits, posting a public petition outside the property, and personally informing neighbors up to 1.5 miles around the property. Because a large number of jaripeo participants are undocumented migrants, lack of knowledge regarding local regulations and lack of the resources required to negotiate them (such as fluency in English) are obstacles to rodeo registration.

Despite these challenges, the jaripeo infrastructure created by the hard work of migrants like Muñoz and Espinoza opens new possibilities for migrants. First, wealthy migrant entrepreneurs are beginning to enter, formalize, and expand the market. Pedro Salazar, the CEO of a dental implant company that is modeled on the American company he worked for in the 1980s, bought his horse and bull ranch in 2004. Today he is known among migrants for owning a team of bulls called Los Tsunamis, the fiercest in the Midwest, purchased at premium prices from the PBR association. His ranch also houses pedigreed stallions imported from Spain that perform traditional horse "dancing" at jaripeo events. Salazar puts on *espectáculos* that draw large crowds to see the jaripeo performed in a mobile rodeo arena in the parking lot of Toyota Park, a mega concert venue in Chicago. In 2012 he booked an indoor pavilion so he could hold a jaripeo in the winter. Salazar learns from carefully watching the PBR, as well as major bull-riding events in other countries, and wants to promote "Mexican-style jaripeos" that are "more like the American rodeos."[75] According to Salazar, formalization is required for commercial expansion. "As long as there are no rules, the jaripeo will not improve. There need to be rules. And it will be better for the bull riders and bulls. Then larger audiences will come, so that there is a real spectacle and more money. Everybody will win."[76] In a meeting at his ranch, Salazar asked Rábano, the young jinete, whether he knew how much money the PBR bull riders earned. "They make $500,000 while you guys make $200."[77] Salazar hopes "rules" will allow him to measure and quantify the worth of his bulls and the bull riders, formalizing and financializing the still "rustic" and wild jaripeo.

Promoters like Salazar recognize the jaripeo as the seed of a new industry with potential to move beyond the migrant community, an informal event on the cusp of crossing over to a broader audience. As a first step, Salazar has registered Mexico Promotions, a new business that aims to compete with the region's two other main Latino promoters of Latino events. These promoters are from Colombia and Cuba. Advertising his business as "100% Mexican," Salazar wants Mexicans to control the destiny of their events and reap profits from them. While Salazar aspires to turn the jaripeo into a financial boon, he currently loses money staging events.

As with the charrería, migrants are also using jaripeos to fundraise for remittance-development projects in Mexico. Gonzalo Rios, president of Doctor Miguel Ville Silva (an HTA named after the group's hometown in Michoacán), built his own rodeo arena over the course of two years out of wooden planks and railroad ties in Rochelle, a small town eighty miles west of Chicago. This investment was motivated by Rios's aspirations to build a school in his hometown. In part motivated by the knowledge that they are doing something positive for their pueblo, sometimes up to seven hundred people, he estimates, who drive to his events from all over the region are from his pueblo alone. The Rochelle arena is the only one in the region officially registered with its city. Unregistered arenas hold events that are broken up by the police when neighbors call to complain about the loud *banda* music that blasts for hours on end. Rios attributes his successful registration of the Rochelle arena to his club's affiliation with the Federation of Michoacanos in Chicago. Rios's club is politically organized; it has brought the mayor of their municipality in Michoacán to Rochelle and engaged with local city officials as representatives of the Mexican community. Rios notes, "I learned how to do this from Casa Michoacán, by going and listening and watching how things happen there." Rios believes that the project was approved because city and county officials want to "secure the Mexican vote."[78] Such connections between the arena and Casa Michoacán demonstrate the relational nature of remittance space in extended urban environments as migrants benefit from the growing political power of Latinos.

*   *   *

The production of both the charrería and jaripeo creates critical places for migrants in the Midwest that reproduce Mexican traditions in a foreign land, build binational networks into what is quickly becoming a migrant community, and innovate strategic uses of the built environment.

The arena supports events that, although they do not take place in Mexico, are in the *estilo del pueblo*. On weekends, migrants and their families will drive several hours to attend events "because they want freedom. The kids run around, people do what they want, you can drink. It's ranch style."[79] Events have no formal starting or ending time (people come and go throughout the day), people drink outside, women and men dress according to the latest Mexican fashions, attendees are Mexican migrants and their children, and they speak Spanish. Such an environment conjures the experience of home for Mexican migrants. José Roque enthuses: "I feel like I'm on a ranch. I like it from the bottom of my heart."[80] Events are a reclamation of ranchero sensibilities in the Midwest, providing migrants with a break from their personal ambivalence toward their status as migrants. Direct engagement with a performance provides a reprieve from the many tensions defining transborder life. According to Rios, the jaripeo was especially critical during the recession: "In 2008, when the economy went down, the jaripeo rose; people were trying to forget their problems." In Chicago it is important that migrants "have a place to go."[81]

Events contribute to the construction of a migrant subjectivity and solidarity despite regional and cultural difference among migrant groups. Advertisements for jaripeos and charrerías celebrate cross-state, cross-border alliances, using regional specificity and authen-

FIGURE 6.10. Poster advertisements for jaripeos in Chicago feature the places of origin and portrait photography of well-known regional bands from Mexico, as well as the featured bulls and riders.

ticity as a promotional tool. Breaking down the migrant population by skill set and state—"jinetes de Guerrero, banda de Morelos!"—these ads draw diverse crowds to events. "Authentic" jinetes who perform in the United States are often recent migrants trained in Mexico. It is rare that a second-generation Mexican American rides bulls with hooked spurs, although this may change. Bands hired "direct from Mexico" and migrant bands in the United States bring regional distinction to events. With advertisements in shops, on the radio, in newspapers, and sometimes on television, events address the specific regional histories of individuals (from Guerrero, from Michoacán, from Los Altos de Jalisco) to construct a migrant public, a group of individuals united in their celebration of a pueblo lifestyle. The sharing of distinct but complex identities and migration histories (eventgoers are from Wisconsin, Illinois, or Iowa *and* the Mexican states of Guanajuato, Michoacán, Guerrero, or Morelos) forms the basis for such a public. In this sense, the jaripeo creates a social platform not just for migrants but also for people who identify with migrants.

These informal spaces are sometimes clandestine. Camerino González estimates that more than 50 percent of charros are undocumented, which explains why "they don't know the laws" and why charrería is still not registered as an official sport in Springfield, Illinois, despite its recognition in Mexico. La Herradura in Joliet and La Esperanza in Rochelle are registered arenas, but others are not. In addition to the difficulty of acquiring permission for arenas, animal rights advocates have been increasingly vocal against the treatment of horses and bulls in both sports. Advocates have attended events, fined migrants, and even confiscated animals.[82] While the commingling of disparate migrant streams results in a dynamic event, the autonomy experienced in the pueblo is not achieved in the United States.

The proliferation of the charrería and jaripeo in Illinois marks the contours of a migrant version of the American dream. Instead of a suburban home, many migrants aspire to own what they call a *rancho*, or to become ganaderos. They buy American farmsteads in rural or urban-fringe regions to raise livestock, grow vegetables for their own consumption, sell modest amounts of agricultural products to a largely Mexican clientele, or build their own arenas. These decisions are critical choices about how migrants dwell in the United States and where they invest their money. Rather than remittance development or remittance homes in rural Mexico, they finance reproductions of the experience of rural Mexico in the United States. Such choices reflect an expansion of what is possible for migrants and how they navigate the process of migration itself.

The Migrant Way of Death

The casas and rodeo arenas both speak to how migrants modify the city to address the needs of a transborder way of life. A third way of negotiating the relationship of "here" and "there," place and identity, involves migrant burial practices and spaces of mourning. Funeral homes and cemeteries in Chicago address migrant connections to hometowns through both repatriations and rural-based burial practices.

The mobility that characterizes the migrant labor force today challenges the traditional place-based rituals of mourning and remembrance of the dead. In rural Mexico, mourning is often a communal process that takes place in the family's home. Community members gather all day and night to recite prayers and comfort the living. Processions transform the public spaces of the pueblo into sacred space. Remembering (as both a psychological state of mind and a sociospatial practice) is likewise a ritual rooted in time and place. While cultural rituals such as Día de Los Muertos are practiced in both the United States and Mexico, visiting a loved one's grave site takes place in a specific locality, forcing migrants to choose between two places that serve different purposes.

Migrants often choose to be buried in their Mexican hometowns for a variety of reasons. Electing to bury a family member in one's hometown is an important investment in communal hometown relationships and practices. The cemetery in one's pueblo, the land, is commonly spoken of as the place where migrants feel they "belong." And finally, it is the place where many believe they will be remembered. Funeral director Concepción Rodríguez lists the three phases of death: "First you have mourning, then one is remembered by family, and finally one is forgotten. . . . They do it [repatriate] to be remembered. They are afraid of being forgotten."[83] Upon deciding to repatriate, families experience immediate satisfaction; this choice does the hard work of maintaining the familial dream of one day returning home by affirming the pueblo as the center of gravity. Yet as migrants' families and investments grow in the United States, where one belongs, the center of gravity, and where one is more likely to be remembered become unclear.

Historicizing traslados in the urban context of Chicago reveals that it is a practice that has endured over time, regardless of specific immigration policies or economic recessions.[84] In fact, what funeral directors refer to as "ship outs" or "repatriations" have become not only increasingly common but also viable as funeral homes work with hospitals, consulates, airlines, HTAS, and families to increase consumer choice in this final decision. At the same time, however, even more migrants elect to be buried in Chicago, and the city's fragmented network of funeral homes, cemeteries, and churches has been transformed in response to migrants' rituals and customs. These critical choices—to return to one's hometown or to be buried in Chicago— reflect migrants' own perception of their place in the world. As both social and material infrastructures for the sprawling geographies of the labor force are built in American cities, impermanence is further institutionalized.

Catholic church death registers historicize and locate repatriations in Chicago's iconic Mexican neighborhoods, Pilsen and Little Village.[85] Adding specificity to the early days of this transborder practice, they record their deceased parishioners' names, closest family members, and places of burial. The populations of two parishes in these neighborhoods—St. Procopius in Pilsen and St. Agnes of Bohemia in Little Village—began shifting from largely Bohemian and Eastern European to Mexican in the 1960s and 1970s. A close examination of their registers provides insight into the details of traslados and provides evidence of how binational processes change local Chicago institutions.

The first Latino surnames in the St. Agnes death registers appear in 1971. By 1984 Latinos account for more than half of all deaths, and by 2001 they make up nearly all the surnames in annual registers. The first recorded "ship out" to Mexico is 1978. Between 1984 and 2000 the number of annual repatriations rose to between five and ten. From 2000 to 2008, they rose again to between eleven and twenty-one annually. This is still a minority of overall annual deaths, which averaged to sixty-two per year.[86] St. Procopius records also show a slow and steady shift from predominantly Eastern European to Mexican congregants over the course of thirty years; however, throughout this time few deceased members were shipped to Mexico. The first repatriation is recorded in 1987, with only one or two occurring each following year.

In Chicago, Mexicans have often characterized Little Village as an incoming immigrant/migrant neighborhood, whereas Pilsen is viewed as being a neighborhood of more established Mexican Americans. These characterizations are always in flux and often conjectural, and census records show that today the immigrant populations of Little Village and Pilsen are roughly equal. However, the fact that few families ship loved ones to Mexico at St. Procopius, while this trend is steadily increasing at St. Agnes, may indicate constituents' varying attitudes toward transborder social practices. Certain neighborhoods are characterized by what could be called a "migration index," or the extent to which a community is defined—at a particular time and place—by incoming and outgoing migrations. The St. Agnes and St. Procopius death records support this view of highly divergent socio-spatial practices despite demographic similarities. Demographers could measure the migration index of specific geographic regions by calculating rates of migrant mobility. Repatriations, triangulated in respect to other sources of information, may be another way to glean such information.

Handwritten notes throughout the death records provide fine-grained information about the familial relationships of the deceased, and occasionally the circumstances of death. St. Agnes's first recorded repatriation (to any country) in 1978 was a "divorced" forty-year-old man. This is the only mention of a congregant's marital status. Perhaps the Eastern European log keeper recorded this information to explain the repatriation of his body to Mexico. The records also identify the "closest living relative," who is most likely responsible for shipping the body, describing relationships that sometimes tell tragic stories. In 1992 a mother sends home a nineteen-year-old son who has been killed in a car accident; in 1993 a sister sends the body of her brother, a victim of AIDS; in 2008 a husband loses his wife just after she gives birth to a premature baby—he sends both bodies to Veracruz.[87] The incomplete pictures painted by the records raise many questions: Did the man who sent his twenty-four-year-old brother in 1990 have any remaining relatives in Chicago, or was the family in Mexico, leaving him to mourn alone? Who will visit the grave of the one-and-a-half-year-old baby sent by her parents to Mexico in 1994?

Over time, increasing the amount of geographic information re-corded, the place of burial changes from "shipped to Mexico" or simply "Mexico" to the state and even the pueblo to which the bodies are shipped. This demonstrates institutional change, as recordkeep-ers themselves were increasingly knowledgeable about the migration processes. By 2010 the states of Zacatecas, Jalisco, Puebla, Guanajuato, Querétaro, Durango, San Luis Potosí, Aguascalientes, Michoacán, and Veracruz had all been listed.[88] The regional specificity detailed in the records mirrors larger cultural shifts within the migrant community. Throughout the 1980s and 1990s, as the Mexican population of Chicago expanded, specific details about migrants' points of origin became more important.

Funeral homes owned and managed by Mexicans and other Latinos have created an urban infrastructure that specifically caters to migrants. Funeraria Caribe, one of Chicago's first Latino funeral homes, was started in the 1960s by an African American man and his Puerto Rican wife who were both active in the Latino community and perceived an unmet need.[89] Today Funeraria Caribe is one of Chicago's busiest "shippers." However, back in the 1970s and 1980s it was still common for Eastern European funeral homes to conduct Mexican repatriations. Marik Funeral Home and Noworul Home conducted St. Agnes's early repatriations and Mexican wakes. Throughout the 1990s and 2000s, funeral homes came to be increasingly owned by either Latino migrants or their second-generation children. In Little Village, a Mexican migrant who has been in the United States since childhood bought Marik Funeral Home and opened the Martínez Funeral Home, which sends approximately one hundred bodies to Mexico annually.[90] His knowledge of Mexican geography, customs, and language is a business asset. Some homes hire Mexicans to capture the Latino market. Concepción Rodríguez, a bilingual second-generation Mexican knowledgeable about traditional Mexican burial practices, has singlehandedly made Zephran Funeral Home's customer base (a Slovenian American–owned home) 60 percent Latino.[91] In 2011 all five Chicago funeral homes listed in the Mexican consulate's manual for migrants as recommended places for both repatriations and local burials are owned or managed by Latinos.[92]

Despite the increasing popularity of traslados, several funeral homes that conduct repatriations are in need of maintenance and repair. Popular Latino homes such as Funeraria Caribe, Funeraria de la Torre, and Vasquez Funeral Home keep costs at a minimum in an attempt to cater to the socioeconomic status of their clientele. The exteriors of their unadorned, run-down buildings lack fresh paint, marquee-style signs have dropped letters, and modestly furnished interiors are renovated infrequently. Such homes are permanent built-environment features catering to the migrant poor. Caribe's funeral director notes that once migrants have climbed the socioeconomic ladder, they seek homes with more amenities. However, the consistent flow of incoming migrants has maintained her business for several decades. In part, these funeral homes (the majority of Caribe's business is "ship outs") are products of local disinvestment, as a portion of their clientele's funerary expenses are spent in Mexico.

As Mexican migrants have moved into smaller cities and towns throughout the Midwest, white- and black-owned funeral homes have assumed the practice of traslados and migrant funerals as well. Casimir Pulaski, owner of Lakeview Funeral Home and Crematory in Laporte, Indiana, started providing migrant repatriation services in 2007. Since Chicago's Mexican consulate is responsible for a large geographic region, when accidents or tragedies occur throughout the Midwest the consulate will contact nearby funeral homes to facilitate burials abroad. For example, the consulate contacted Pulaski to arrange shipping the bodies of four migrant restaurant workers who died in a house fire in Indiana. These men did not have family in town to make such arrangements for them. Pulaski struggles to understand this practice: "My parents came from Poland, but they don't want to be flown back. If they came here, pay taxes here, they should be buried here. If they want to be buried in Mexico, why didn't they stay in Mexico?"[93] As Pulaski compared Mexican migrants' choices with those of his family, he considered the complexities migrants face: "The flipside, perhaps, is that not everybody was able to come here." For migrants, Mexican burials might be the only way to "reunite" with family in Mexico.

Pulaski also struggles to understand traslados because—as he views it—they incur costs many migrants cannot afford. The complexity of transnational funerals (which may involve a viewing in Chicago, shipment, and second viewing in Mexico) makes it difficult for migrants to evaluate cost with accuracy. If a body is shipped, migrants who belong to federations get discounts from certain funeral homes and certain "sponsor" airlines. Without such discounts, the cost of shipping from Chicago starts as low as $3,600 but can be several thousands more, especially from smaller towns like Laporte. In Chicago, families who qualify for Catholic "charity burials" keep funeral costs below $2,600.[94] Many poor migrant families that choose to be buried in Chicago take advantage of this program. This can be compared to standard funerals starting at around $6,000. While the initial cost to ship to Mexico might appear to be lower than that of a local funeral, it is often more expensive due to local wakes, expensive coffins, costs in Mexico, and transportation costs for the family to travel to Mexico for the funeral.

For both repatriated deceased migrants and those buried in Chicago, families hold wakes in Chicago that assert migrants' cultural practices associated with mourning in Mexico. Most notably, the funeral service and time with the deceased is extended. Father Alvaro Nova, a Colombian migrant who was hired to direct a Milwaukee funeral home that opened in the early 2000s to capture the Latino market, describes what he calls "Latino funeral culture." "The Anglo funeral is . . . more strict with hours; they come and go, whereas we accompany the person longer. We do not eat and talk and socialize among family. It is less of a social event and more of a spiritual one."[95] Several funeral directors throughout Chicago added to these distinctions: "The focus in the Mexican funeral is on the *difunto* [the deceased]," not on the family. All persons in attendance are gathered in the *capilla* to pray. The viewing takes four to six hours as opposed to the standard two to three. Anglos families are "in and out," whereas "we [Latinos] have to set aside a whole day."[96] A four-to-six-hour viewing in Illinois can be compared to the twenty-four-hour viewings common in migrant hometowns.

Chicago funeral directors adjust to migrant viewings by incorporating imagery and symbols of loss, separation, and nostalgia, as well as "journey" and place, into their services. Music is often played either during wakes or at graveside. Director Concepción Rodríguez plays songs such as "El amigo que se fue" by Intocable, which speaks of both "a friend that went away" due to death and the painful absence of loved ones who are far away. During viewings, Rodríguez has seen several migrant families place objects in the coffin that represent the deceased's migrant journey. One particularly poignant example was a family from Guanajuato who brought little bags of dirt to the viewing of a young man. The dirt had been collected when he initially crossed the US-Mexico border with his brothers; they had "carried this little piece of Mexico" around with them ever since.[97] Sprinkling his corpse with his native soil, the family closed the casket on his aspirations for a new and different life in a foreign land.

When rural migrants elect to be buried in Chicago, they often bring rural funeral rituals to the cemetery. As in Mexico, after the viewing the family goes to the grave site and waits—sometimes for hours and accompanied by mariachis—until the coffin is not only lowered into the ground but completely covered with dirt. An employee at Catholic Cemeteries notes that when a "Latino death" is scheduled, the cemetery arranges to have a tractor and operator present to completely cover the coffin with dirt on the spot.[98]

Despite a clear separation between public space and spaces of mourning in Chicago, migrant funerals sometimes traverse the two. In rural Mexico, public processions are an important moment for the whole community to recognize and pray for the dead. Family members carry the deceased from their home, where the viewing is held, to the cemetery as extended family, friends, and community follow on foot singing and praying. Most Latino funeral homes in Chicago are in densely populated neighborhoods, on busy thoroughfares. Chicago cemeteries tend to be far from where migrants live, as their pattern of development has historically marked the edges of a growing metropolis. However, some families carry the coffin from the wake or chapel to the grave site, even if it is a mile away, allowing the family to practice its customary mourning march. Families have also followed hearses to the cemetery on foot rather than in a motorcade.

Unlike the early German, Polish, Lithuanian, and Slovenian immigrants in Chicago, Latinos do not have their own cemetery. After almost a century of Mexican burials in Chicago, Catholic Cemeteries responded to its growing Latino clientele by building Chicago's first Our Lady of Guadalupe shrine at Maryhill Cemetery in 1977. Between 1991 and 2002, three more shrines to Mexican saints were built. In the late 1990s, cemetery planners designed new tombstones with the Virgin of Guadalupe's image etched on the markers. The epitaphs are now frequently in Spanish, indicating Latino burial sections in multiethnic cemeteries. All of Catholic Cemeteries' informational pamphlets were translated into Spanish in 1998, as was its website in 2007.[99] The translations of Catholic Cemeteries' institutional materials from English to Polish and now Spanish represent Latinos' central role in Chicago's Catholic institutions and the city itself. However, Latinos have not had enough resources or political power to buy and build the kinds of ornate cemeteries and burial markers common throughout Mexican towns.

Migrants can now choose whether they want to be buried in their hometown or in the United States. This newfound choice reflects the difficult decisions they live with daily regarding where they want to invest their time and money. Migrants who repatriate in death return to a place they identify with, to a pueblo that performs dignified funerary rituals, and often to a cemetery marked with a monumental remittance tombstone.

* * *

None of the spaces examined in this chapter could exist without related spatial processes occurring simultaneously in Mexico. Chicago's remittance space reveals the mutually constitutive formation of rural spaces and migrant urbanism in Mexican and American cities. Migrant organizing, ranchero sports, and funeral customs are three practices shaping American cities. Meanwhile, the characteristics of American urban environments influence how migrants build, what they build, and their spatial practices. Taken together, these examples tell a story about a migrant population in Chicago that is increasingly organized to sponsor projects (that support the initial goals of migration) on both sides of the border.

In Chicago, casas are evidence of migrants' initiative and collective strength. The buildings affirm their actions and strengthen relationships among migrants not only from one pueblo but also from across their state, across Mexican states, and even increasingly across Latin American countries. Migrant federations do not have meeting halls in rural Mexico. When in their Mexican hometowns, migrants use homes, public plazas, or the *casa ejidal* to convene. However, the cultural center built in San Juan de Amula by a migrant HTA with the help of the 3×1 program is in many ways an extension of the logic motivating the construction of casas in Chicago. Both buildings were intended to be places by migrants and for migrants, and both hold quinceañeras and weddings. However, they serve different purposes: whereas casas in the United States strengthen migrants' social and political agendas, the casa de cultura creates a space for the realization and fruits of that struggle. The buildings announce migrants' presence in their pueblos as well as in host cities, marking out a new migrant political, cultural, and economic project with a foot placed firmly on each side of the border.

Migrants' grassroots efforts to build charrería and jaripeo arenas transform their relationships with both the American city and the Mexican hometown through the representation and enactment of uniquely Mexican cultural practices. The display of strength and skill allows migrants to reproduce forms of ranchero masculinity in the United States. Young jinetes, who learned to be bullriders in Mexico, perform their socioeconomic position within Mexican society at great distances, while migrant charros who may not have had access to cha-rrería in Mexico achieve a new status in the United States. These dis-tinctions help clarify the kinds of decisions migrants are making in remittance space and what they mean. In many ways, the two sports arenas (in Mexico and in the United States) function as two imperfect halves. Mexican arenas in rural Jalisco, such as the Lagunillas rodeo, lack continuous funding and ample audience but have "freedom" and "autonomy," whereas US arenas benefit from a robust migrant public but run into both legal and social constraints.

Finally, the landscapes of death in the United States are slowly becoming places that foster migrant dignity, respect, and tradition, which might involve repatriations to hometowns. What takes place in Chicago is directly linked to what is or is not occurring in Mexico. Wakes are sometimes performed twice, but the body is buried only once. Shipping bodies home allows pueblos and small towns to con-tinue to hold on to their emigrants, just as it allows migrants to hold on to the dream of return or demonstrate their allegiance. The rise in traslados is coinciding with an absolute decrease in Mexico's rural population. It remains to be seen how long this practice will continue—especially considering the effort required to support it. As these changes are institutionalized in the urban fabric of US cities and migrants increasingly have "consumer choice" regarding where they want to be buried, the inequities that make this choice necessary in the first place recede further into the distance. Indeed, the rise of traslados is evidence of the normalization of unrealistic expectations hoisted onto the shoulders of migrants themselves.

Like the projects in Mexico, all three moments in the United States are defined at first by ad hoc and informal processes but then evolve to take on the characteristics of formal institutions. Informal meeting places in migrant houses lead to binational building projects; rustic rural rodeos become commercial opportunities; isolated traslados give rise to Latino funeral homes. This transition coheres with a new level of organization and planning that renders projects and practices visible to a broader Latino and even American public. Such spaces may attract Mexican government funding, government and corporate sponsorship, broader initiatives and ample personnel, the building of more permanent institutions, and the commencement of migrant political affiliations with US state officials and institutions. *Remittance urbanism* signifies the process by which migrant grassroots activities engage with the production of urban space more generally.

Migrant sociospatial practices underpinning American urbanism have different effects on American urban environments when compared to earlier migration streams. For many Mexican migrants, the US city is not a site of assimilation but of the formation of increasingly distinctive migrant subjectivities defined by life simultaneously invested in multiple locations. This is different from a diasporic longing for a homeland underpinning the constitution of ethnic enclaves, or the "hybrid urbanisms" resulting from the spatialization of hybrid peoples and cultures.[100] Daily transborder life results in urban environments that are geographically distributed products of migrant networks, pervasive spaces that are largely invisible to the nonmigrant population but fundamentally define urbanism in the United States. These spaces help define remittance urbanism as a both/and: both belonging to the American city through the formation of long-distance networks and belonging to a hometown at a distance. They result from migrants' cumulative and continued assertion over the conditions of their lives in the United States and the lives of those in hometowns in Mexico. In a sense, remittance space complicates notions of the city as a coherent, tangible, objective thing. Remittance space shows cities in dynamic exchange with narratives and distant places, informed by and informing new migrant practices and allegiances in multiple localities.

Conclusion: Rethinking Migration and Place

Carlos García built Hacienda Tecalitlan on Ashland Avenue in Chicago in 1995. Investing a fortune made as a businessman in the United States, García imagined a restaurant that would transport its patrons to colonial Guadalajara.[1] To create a haciendalike dining room, García imported Mexican furniture, finishes, and building materials and brought a Mexican architect from Jalisco to analyze the site and create a design. The design of the project prominently features the use of cantera stone—a generic name for various types of soft limestone used as cladding or structural masonry for many of Mexico's most famous cathedrals, government buildings, and haciendas. Until 2012, when the Federation of Michoacán used cantera to cover the facade of Casa Michoacán, Hacienda Tecalitlan was the only building to prominently feature the stone in Chicago.

The limestone for García's hacienda was quarried and carved in Mexico, then shipped in pieces to the Midwest. According to one of García's partners involved in the building project, it took two years for stonemasons to excavate, sculpt, and transport the vast quantities of material needed for the project. A friend of García's, an importer of Mexican produce to Chicago, used his fleet of trucks to transport columns, arches, and tiles, along with leather chairs and tables, doors, and windows from Degollado, Jalisco. As the stone pieces and other materials arrived in Chicago, Mexican artisans and stonemasons assembled them following the architect's plans. Hand-cut lintels span the window openings, while the custom wooden doors replicate the appearance and proportions of traditional hacienda facades. The interior could be a stage set for a *telenovela* based in sixteenth- or seventeenth-century colonial Mexico: an expansive courtyard paved with Spanish tiles and anchored by a central fountain made out of ornately carved cantera is surrounded by a stone colonnade and second-

FIGURE 7.01. A cognitive map of San Juan de Amula, based on one woman's knowledge about the sources of funding used to build locals' homes—remittances sent by migrants, remittances combined with pesos, or only pesos. Drawn by Chesney Floyd.

FIGURE 7.02. Hand-carved cantera stone columns, an ornate fountain, and decorative archway trims give the interior courtyard of Hacienda Tecalitlan in Chicago the feel of a sixteenth-century Spanish hacienda. Photograph by Nina Kuna.

story balcony on four sides. The design, materials and detailing brings the iconic interior patio of Mexico's colonial past to Chicago.

Such a setting provided an appropriate site for migrant organizing—a grand and elegant space that evokes the architecture of both colonial and contemporary Mexican authority. Sergio Suárez, an activist in the Jalisco federation, told me, "I installed the air conditioner and ventilation system in the restaurant. I did this about fifteen years ago. I was part of building this place, and other founders of the federation too because we knew we would have events there. . . . There [at Hacienda Tecalitlan], in the building, began the history of the federation."[2] A friend of García, Suárez explained that just as Jalisco HTAS in Chicago were gathering strength, the restaurant was completed. With "our tables reserved in advance, because it was a place of glamour," and with a sense of excitement and possibility, key migrant activists began discussions about consolidating HTAS into a more unified migrant federation. They imagined the Hacienda as a future site for events and meetings. "We wanted to use the name Casa Jalisco. That was when we knew for the first time that the governor, Alberto Cárdenas, was interested in migrants."[3] In the entry vestibule of the restaurant, a plaque donated by Cárdenas (identical to official plaques that grace many 3×1 projects in Mexico) hangs on the wall. On the opposite wall hangs a framed letter from Chicago's ex-mayor Richard M. Daley, thanking García for "the exceptional hospitality of your restaurant," which he notes is a "beautiful re-creation of a hacienda." Both the plaque and the letter demonstrate García's extensive political connections in both Mexico and the United States.

Like impressive remittance homes that are abandoned in Jalisco, the Hacienda is a ruin and a monument to the complexities migrants face. In 2007, for reasons unknown, García fled the country and abandoned his restaurant. In 2011 I attended an auction for a bank-owned foreclosure of the property. Chicago investors, developers, and financiers made opening bids. The Hacienda, allegedly worth four million dollars, sold for $750,000 dollars to a doctor who planned to use the space for a private medical practice. Auctioneers did not know what to make of the Hacienda, and most believed it was a relic—an old, run-down building that had fallen into disrepair. They did not realize that the stone had been imported and assembled in the 1990s to construct a vision of another place and time. Within the Mexican community, Suárez was not the only one who was "sad to hear that the bank owns it."[4] Migrants I spoke to throughout Chicago expressed sorrow at the loss of a building with which they identified—a place that honored their journeys and accomplishments, a place designed for them, where they could gather, enjoy themselves, and plan for the future. The Hacienda auction was an anticlimactic end to an esteemed institution, less the symbol of permanence migrants had hoped for (and built) and more an emblem of uncertainty in a world of constant change. Nonetheless, the cantera monument is material evidence of migrant "worlding," of the possibilities of remittance space as material practice.[5]

While the Hacienda does not cohere neatly with the remittance projects explored in this book—it was not born out of migrant networks "from below," nor did it attempt to be representative of such groups—it shows the importance of comparing different projects that utilize extensive migrant networks to plan, finance, and construct new buildings, infrastructures, or other cultural projects. The Hacienda is a product of migration as a way of life, as well as a migrant space of representation. Like the remittance houses, casas, rodeo arenas, asilos, and funeral homes, it opens sociospatial possibilities while being permeated by internal contradictions, risks, and instability. The Hacienda project illustrates that remittance space is more than a collection of individual aspirations and isolated projects. Remittance space unfolds in dynamic exchange between the material environment and social worlds that span international boundaries.

* * *

From remittance-funded projects to remittance urbanism, this book documents a social-spatial continuum between the material environments of rural Mexico and urban United States that reframes how we think about both migration and places. In many ways, the findings from this study extend globalization theories that spatialize flows of global and transnational capital, identifying the restructured relationships between urban environments. This research documents how remittance capital from below, sent and spent strategically by grassroots networks, makes visible connections between places in an era of globalization and mass migration. Such capital from below—as it accumulates and is deployed—repositions the migrant as a global agent, a transborder author of environmental change. Studying what migrants build clarifies migrants' ingenuity as well as the consequences and risks of such actions.

Focusing on the act of remitting foregrounds the connection between social life and personal desires, on the one hand, and material transformation of the built environment in the context of migration on the other. The current definition of *remittance*—according to the *Oxford English Dictionary*—is "a sum of money or (formerly) a quantity of an item transferred from one place or person to another . . ."[6] It is the sociospatial implications of this transfer that are of interest, one of which is captured by another, less common definition of the verb *remit*: "to postpone, put off, defer."[7] Remitting is simultaneously an action and a postponement. Depending on the situations of individual migrants, this deferment can result in a range of different migrant attitudes toward—and project outcomes in—their hometowns. For some migrants distance and deferment lead to idealization of the hometown; they become boosters and invest considerable time and money into building the pueblo as they imagine it should be. For others, unforeseen events intervene, or they begin to identify with and invest in their immediate surroundings, sometimes abandoning "dream homes" in Mexico. In these cases, as with the Hacienda Tecalitlan and self-built jaripeo arenas, migrants attempt to bring the dream north.

Regardless of the particular orientation of a given migrant, to remit is to act out one's relationships with two places bound in a single, continuous life-world. In this relation of different places through the transfer of money, Mexican landscapes usually provide the site for migrant-initiated social and spatial transformation; they also act as places of memory and identity. In this equation, the American city is the environment of accumulation, the site for the production of an evolving remittance urbanism that includes networks, environments, and institutional resources serving a transborder public. The projects that an individual or a group realizes through remittances tell a story about the relationship between these two distinct yet mutually constitutive worlds, the accumulatory and the aspirational. Over time the distinction between the two blurs, inevitably sublimated in the everyday lives of the persons who make these spaces possible through their transactions, movements, and desires.

Today the migrant has become a permanent feature of an evolving global economy. Such individuals provide essential labor for the US economy and now essential resources for Mexican society. The state, global banks, and NGOs are eager to assist in rural remittance development, to help put little towns like Vista Hermosa "on the map" by contributing to state-of-the-art buildings and infrastructure. While the Mexican and US governments facilitate the production of remittance space, both fail to fully acknowledge the social and psychological costs sustained by migrants producing it. Mining the sociospatial logic and materiality of remittance space contributes to a material history of place as increasingly defined by a flexible and mobile transborder labor force. Normalizing distance between close friends and loved ones leaves migrants to negotiate the longing, loss, and ambivalence that displacement produces. State policies institutionalize distance as the way up and out for rural Mexicans, at migrants' own expense. By the time the cost of remittance space is understood by one group of migrants and their communities, another group of club members invests in new projects, and another generation of youth has been inspired to embark on the journey north. As more migrants leave to play their parts in a global economy thirsty for cheap and flexible labor, they entangle their mostly poor rural pueblos in systems of social and spatial production that will fundamentally alter not only their homes but also the cities they arrive in. Migrant hometowns are today the distant hinterlands of American cities (fig. 7.01).

Rural-Urban Remittance Space

When these ideas are placed in specific geographic contexts—the remittance landscape of Jalisco and migrant Chicago—several recurring conditions and qualities of remittance space emerge. Perhaps most fundamental is the persistent gap between initial migrant aspirations and ultimate project outcomes, a result of the many unforeseen challenges migrants face both in carrying out projects and in managing their everyday lives. This gap between imagination and reality can lead to incomplete or abandoned projects or to a host of unintended consequences of "successful" ones. With remittance homes, for example, the effects of long-distance building are evident in the built fabric of small towns in Mexico. Abandoned and partially finished homes are common, the material manifestations of complex individual situations as migrants start new families, achieve financial success or ruin in the North, or encounter legal issues that prevent return to the hometown. For public projects financed by migrant groups, however, outcomes are even more uncertain due to the inconsistent and often internally fraught involvement of a wider array of public and private institutions, the complexity of project programs, and generally larger-scale works.

Most difficult for migrants to plan for are the economic, political, social, or institutional webs in which they find their projects snared. Migrants investing in Lagunillas's remittance rodeo did not anticipate how the rise of remittance rodeos throughout the region would affect their plans. Rather than providing economic engines, rodeo building has now implicated norteños in what appears to be a race to the bottom in a regional competition between towns for a fickle flow of remittance capital and audience dollars. In San Juan, migrants' desires and personal sacrifices to build an impressive and modern community center created new lines of social tension instead of civic pride.

The project challenged the sociospatial logic of the town's center (and communal life), and different members of the "emigrant community" were left to fight for, and represent, their way of life within a changing milieu. Finally, those who planned the Los Guajes asilo, designed to take care of the elderly in the context of migration, never articulated a clear definition of who constituted the elderly or how they would be cared for. In the absence of a clear plan for managing this new institution, competing visions and opinions regarding the project (combined with lack of funding) explain why the completed building has been locked and empty since 2007.

Once built, the projects do more to expose the complexities of contemporary life for migrant communities than to solve them. The envisioning and execution of projects in Mexico must contend with migrants' geographic distance from their place of investment—the place where dreams can become reality. In the process of building at a distance, migrants learn the hard way a lesson that even professional planners and architects often struggle to understand: building projects, no matter how handsome, reveal the limitations of physical infrastructure to bring about social change in the absence of larger institutional, social, and spatial transformations.

Taken together, these examples raise important questions about the responsibilities of nation-states to their transborder migrants, their expatriated citizens. The tensions evident in these projects are direct outcomes of migrants' initial visions realized on a large scale due to the financial support of the 3×1 program; given this, what are and should be the responsibilities of the Mexican state vis-à-vis its emigrants? This question points to a second broad theme that emerges in remittance space: the dialectic between grassroots organization and action, on the one hand, and the channeling of migrant money and motivation by formal institutions on the other. Migrants and the state have different goals, yet those differences are often subsumed under the rubric of "remittance development." Within remittance development, formal-informal "partnerships" tout an equal footing between migrants and politicians where there actually is none. Migrants' power comes from an accumulation of primarily individual actions (nascent power rising from the formation of federations of HTAS), whereas the state has cohesive institutional entities crafting the structure of the remittance discourse at large.

From the perspective of national policy, the Mexican state is committed to a unidirectional push toward remittance development and a robust remittance economy. Remittance development is one of the ways—alongside programs such as Oportunidades—that the state addresses rural poverty and endemic migration. More important, remittances are now viewed as an integral part of the Mexican economy. The rising number of HTAS attests to a growing desire to collectively remit to hometowns; however, the migrants spearheading projects funneled through state programs take on new responsibilities without adequate support to manage and maintain complex projects. By relying on entrepreneurial individuals as economic engines in rural Mexico, the state harnesses migration itself as an entrepreneurial project. This institutionalization of remittance development "from above" presents significant personal and financial risks for migrants.

The 3×1 program also influences what, and how, migrants build by funneling their dollars toward basic infrastructure as opposed to more socially and culturally visible projects. Migrants still often start negotiations with either federation leaders (who report to the state) or politicians themselves, by explaining their desire for projects that one can see and appreciate—building projects that literally and symbolically stand in for migrants themselves, filling the voids left by absent sons and daughters. Building a sports arena and remodeling a church are actions that hold meaning for migrant communities that extend beyond the stated goals of 3×1 to address endemic poverty and support marginalized communities.

In addition to funneling migrant money toward infrastructure, the formalization of remittance development from below is structuring how migrants approach development. Institutional support opens roads for migrants by increasing the scale and speed of long-distance building projects. Suárez notes, "3×1 is a way to grow what we already want to do in our pueblo."[8] Private businesses are also changing how migrants finance projects. Construmex was another program that allowed migrants to expand their reach by buying cement in the United States that would be remitted to hometowns instead of cash. This system provided formal insurance against misuse of remittance funds by family or friends. Cemex, Construmex's parent company, is currently organizing meetings with migrants to discuss supporting their development projects without the involvement of the middleman—

the state. Such collaboration is a pioneering effort to form a public-private transborder partnership both from below and from above. The 3×1 program, Construmex and Cemex, alongside global institutions such as the Inter-American Development Bank, present exciting possibilities for migrants who have witnessed (as in Lagunillas, Magdalena, and all across Mexico) painfully slow and incremental road building and other projects. Migrants have also struggled with accountability—as was clear in San Juan's projects in the 1970s and 1980s—and welcome formal partners that will track how money is spent. As available resources increase, the scope of migrants' ambitions expands. HTA member Luis Frausto expresses a broad vision: "We need to build a big project, a state project, like a Disneyland or park, to bring tourism and create employment."[9]

Analysis of the state's involvement in large-scale remittance development sheds light on tensions between formal and informal partnerships that would apply to projects beyond the 3×1 program. First, support for building projects in rural places must address age-old tensions between pueblos and cabeceras. A legacy of disinvestment, corruption, and just plain envy between cabeceras and their dependent localities has resulted in relationships that lack trust, accountability, and common goals. In Lagunillas, the relationship between ejidatarios and municipal officials is so fraught that the ejidatarios do not want the state to formally own the project. Officials' promises to give locals control have done nothing to assuage their fears. In San Juan de Amula, municipal officials allegedly did not pay the municipality's full share of project costs, saddling migrants with unexpected debts. Both migrants and academic researchers evaluating the 3×1 program throughout Mexico have reported these kinds of conflicts and abuses.[10]

Additionally, formalizing building processes (demanding receipts, keeping timelines, employing supervisors to inspect progress) should not happen in the absence of long-term project planning.[11] Operating and maintaining nascent institutions is complex—and even more so in the context of emigrant communities. This contributes to the state's interest in focusing on basic infrastructure. However, whether supported by 3×1 or not, migrants will continue to desire and fund more ambitious projects. Planning and oversight are needed to prepare migrants for the sociospatial implications of their endeavors.

These lessons pose important questions for policy makers. What are the goals of remittance development? Is this remittance-development model based on a stable enough set of conditions to realize long-term economic or social development in rural Mexico? What are the regional impacts of alliances with migrants and the impacts on migrants themselves? Perhaps continued migration and continued remitting are viewed as one way to transform Jalisco's rural Mexican pueblos into what are called "magic pueblos" (well-preserved traditional pueblos that are magnets for tourism). If the state is supporting the transformation of rural zones into idealized repositories of "authentic" Mexican culture, what are the implications for migrants and their communities?

While these discoveries address development policy, the larger purpose of this book is not to outline the successes or failures of the 3×1 program or prescribe a policy fix. A book analyzing 3×1 would undoubtedly include a wide range of project types in multiple locations, with a focus on basic infrastructure. Rather, these findings cohere with a framework for development and planning research that Ananya Roy calls "slow learning," where the global and macro forces propelling development are momentarily punctured and interrogated.[12] This historical and ethnographic approach to the products of 3×1 treats each project—no matter how distinctive—as critical to an understanding of how the logic, mechanisms, and discourses that motor these developments work. Remittance development is a fundamentally complex social process that begins with individual aspirations but quickly engages institutions at many scales, as well as clashing social worlds. The dialectic between migrant intentions and state agendas can be grasped only when one views how each initiative interfaces with material situations.

Finally, the material culture of remittance space illuminates migrants' own role in the production of new migrant subjectivities; in migrants' journeys to change the circumstances of their lives, they are subject to transformation themselves. Shifting between two distinct sociospatial systems, from the rural hometown to the foreign city, migrants' understandings of social hierarchy, gender, class, family, and community change. For example, the organizational potential of migrant federations and their casas contributes to the rise of pan-migrant solidarities. In US cities, migrants assume new cosmopolitan identities that reflect their increasingly complex relationship with historic allegiances to hometown or nation. Migrants create links to Mexican networks and economies—and perform Mexican identities—by practicing traditional jaripeos and charrerías. Public remittance projects in migrants' hometowns can result in their assertion of political authority and power, not just as sons and daughters of the community but as representatives of a new cosmopolitan migrant class. Indeed, migrants are not just workers, fathers, or daughters but also makers of highly representational spaces that influence how they understand themselves and the world around them, as well as how they are understood by a broader public.

Material culture is an important way in which identities are constituted and represented. In 1926 Manuel Gamio, in his study of return migration, documented what migrants carried across the border. Mowers, sewing machines, and overalls changed not only production in sending areas but also self-representation, as certain items—for example, the wrist watch—became identifiers of a life operating on multiple scales. Today the material culture of migration in Mexico has proliferated from "lazy susan" spice racks purchased at Pottery Barn (commonly found in remittance kitchens) to the layout of residential homes and to the ornamentation of town plazas.

The production of new forms of migrant identity and culture results in part from migrants' ambivalence about their roles in the globalization and transformation of their hometowns. For example, migrants want to preserve the pueblo of their childhood, but they also want to improve it; they are motivated by a vision of a tranquil, pastoral life that is the same as it was but better, cleaner, and more modern. According to historian José Refugio de la Torre Curiel, "Migrants want elegant vacation spots, places of luxury that will also feel like home to them."[13] This desire invites a paradox of preservation and development, a paradox evident in the exodus of migrants who, by leaving in order to preserve their hometowns, inevitably change them. Rural Mexico continues to be drained of its constituents. Perhaps no amount of investment or planning can fully counter the effects of this loss.[14]

These findings raise questions for migrants as well. How does dividing one's attention and investment between multiple places affect individual and family life over time? Do migrants achieve successful outcomes for themselves and their pueblos through remitting, and is remittance development a viable model for the long-term health of communities? What are the consequences of the new alliances that migrants form to complete their projects?

Remittance Urbanism and New Directions for Future Research

Examining remittance urbanism—defined as the influence that migration and remitting as a way of life have on material culture and the organization, infrastructure, and experience of the city—sheds new light on the remittance landscapes of rural Jalisco. This work has identified several questions for future research.

In remittance space, individuals motivate entrepreneurial and civic development; as a result, its material expression is often highly varied and idiosyncratic. Instead of a monolithic group, this study shows that migrants employ diverse strategies to achieve specific individual goals through communal means. Contextualized ethnographic data is necessary to clarify Latinos and migrants' role in the creation of places and society. The "look and feel" of the remittance landscape is influenced by where migrants send money from in the United States, just as remittance urbanism is influenced by where migrants originate in Mexico. For these reasons, comparative studies will be required to determine the effects of migration patterns, specific institutional partnerships, and environmental contexts on the material cultural of remitting. The rural–urban (Jalisco–Chicago) examples here are only one aspect of this phenomenon. Such further work requires the expertise of historians, city planners, architectural historians, and sociologists to add archival quantitative material, and policy-oriented analysis of how these spaces operate and what they mean. I outline three frames for additional research below.

First, how do different migration streams affect remittance space in Mexico and the United States? Do urban–urban, urban–rural, or rural–rural streams produce forms of material culture that are different from the rural-to-urban (or suburban) flows documented here? For example, migrant activists in Chicago and Los Angeles have identified some of the difficulties migrants face in rural American towns when trying to organize, due to the absence of dense, spatially overlapping migrant networks, as well as arrival and organizing infrastructures common in urban areas. Similarly, urban migrants from Guadalajara and Mexico City have expressed the difficulty of forming and maintaining HTAS in the United States in part because urban Mexicans do not generally have the tight place-based networks of their rural counterparts. Their remittance projects have less of an immediately visible impact on the urban fabric. They also arrive in the United States with different skills and expectations. Despite these challenges, migrants from Mexican cities and in rural American towns are remitting and organizing. The question becomes, what is the influence of disparate points of departure and points of arrival on the formation of remittance space? In terms of material culture, how does migration to particular US cities—Atlanta versus Seattle versus Chicago—influence migrants' envisioning and execution of building projects in Mexico? Finally, comparing internal migration streams across time, such as Chinese remitting and building practices at the turn of the twentieth century to the Mexican cases discussed here, will reveal what—if anything—is unique about the production of Mexican remittance space. All of these questions address the relationship between migration patterns and the material spaces they produce.

A second approach is to reexamine the nature and goal of remitting itself vis-à-vis the landscapes that are produced. In addition to the personal investments in domestic projects and group investments in communal projects examined in this book, migrants are investing in other ways. Two examples are investments in remittance-funded businesses and individual funding of public projects. Migrant businesses range from private, informal endeavors to collective enterprises.[15] The material culture of migrant businesses makes a dramatic imprint on the social and spatial environments of small Mexican towns. For example, the names of small migrant owned businesses reveal the migration narratives of their owners. On a rural road in southern Jalisco, a corner store or bodega called EL 7 ELEVEN appropriates the ubiquitous American franchise. Stores in the towns of Autlán and El Grullo are called California Beach and Forever New York. Sometimes businesses started by nonmigrants use naming to strategically connect their business with migration flows.

Beyond naming, migrants are also bringing American business culture, products, and services to Mexican villages and towns. A migrant from Berkeley who worked in a café selling pizza, sandwiches, and

FIGURE 7.03. Hand-painted signage and beer advertisements on the El 7 Eleven bodega address passersby on a country road surrounded by sugarcane and corn fields. Photograph by author.

FIGURE 7.04. The Beverly Hills Autobaño imports a new program, business model, and building type—the open-air hand car wash—from Southern California. The blue concrete columns, extended roof, and tapered parapet wall suggest the highway vernacular of American gas stations, built here with concrete block. Photograph by author.

burgers opened his own burger and pizza joint in Guanajuato upon his return. Burgers and pizza are common in Mexico but still unusual in small villages and pueblos. His shop is not the product of generic top-down "globalization" but of the entrepreneurial opportunism of remittance space "from below." An examination of these sites will begin to reveal the extent to which migrants carry specific impressions and spatial knowledge from Los Angeles, Chicago, or St. Louis that are subsequently expressed in the built environment of their hometowns. The materiality of remittance businesses will further refine ideas about how remittance flows bring noncapital transfers, such as culture and "aesthetics," to Mexico, changing the way building happens in rural places. These investigations will also contribute to a better understanding of how the competing influences of globalization, modernization, and migration influence the history and production of the built environment in Mexico.

Finally, through oral histories this book shows that migrant leaders who came to the United States before 1986 and subsequently acquired US residency or citizenship occupy central positions in the development of remittance space and binational infrastructures. But what other historic frames have greatly influenced remittance space? Specifically, how have technology and big-box retail influenced what migrants envision and build? How has—perhaps indirectly—the history of US "civil society" influenced the spaces of rural Mexico? Time is a critical component of the formation of remittance space. Precisely how specific historical conditions delimit or frame what is possible for migrants warrants further analysis. Such a lens will also situate the continued formalization of these processes as larger companies like Western Union and Cemex come to view migrants as potential collaborators, influencing both what is possible and what is probable.

* * *

This book tracks the development of remittance space in one specific region of Jalisco, from the first remittance house built during the Bracero program to contemporary migrant projects under way in the United States. As migration from Mexico to the United States increased throughout the 1980s, 1990s, and 2000s and become more regionally varied, remittance-financed projects expanded, accumulated, and diversified. The examples presented here show primarily how this process has played out in rural Mexican environments but leave us with complex questions about urban areas as well.

Namely, how does viewing Mexican pueblos as distant hinterlands of American cities change the way we see and understand American cities? Beyond the flows of capital and information, the movement of ideas, people, and objects, as well as the spatial practices of migrants, reveals that "places" may be formed simultaneously of codependent but geographically distinct locations. Remittance space is not about observing how flows or transborder influences manifest in place—rather, it is about observing the mutually constitutive coevolution of places. The rural towns of Jalisco are becoming extensions of, and are in dynamic exchange with, American cities. This then raises further questions: To what extent is the American metropolis predicated on the rapid transformation of sending communities throughout the world? What are the implications of this fragmented urbanism?

I began this story with a reproduction of the Statue of Liberty, carved from cantera stone and placed in the central courtyard of a migrant's remittance house. I end it with the elegant grotto of the Hacienda Tecalitlan, built with the same Mexican stone, on Ashland Avenue in Chicago (fig. 7.02). Both images are personal, idiosyncratic, and emblematic of the triumphs and ambivalence, risks, and rewards of remittance space. When we juxtapose the two, it is clear that we must examine the history of the built environment in a broad context in which we acknowledge the presence of "distant" places, cultures, and times in our immediate surroundings. Remittance spaces also reveal the unstable, layered nature of places in the context of extended and multiple environmental affiliations. The transactions of individual migrants provide a portal through which we can understand these processes, a view not (yet) obscured by corporate representations, policy discourse, or extensive capital investment. It is still possible to see the individual aspirations and actions shaping twenty-first-century cities and pueblos.

This book is only the beginning of a conversation about remittance space. Migrants themselves have spearheaded its production, and their continued exertions will shape its future. As the unbundled energy of their instinct and desire to build a better future collides with macro policies and financial incentives, migrants are faced with the challenge of spanning worlds—here and there, past and future, preserving what is most important by building it anew and making a coherent narrative out of fragments.

Notes

PROLOGUE

1. My initial answers to these questions can be found in Sarah Lynn Lopez, "The Remittance House: On the Cultural Landscapes of Mexican Migrancy" (master's thesis, University of California, Berkeley, 2006).

INTRODUCTION

The epigraph to this chapter is from Antonio Rodríguez, interview by author, California, August 2008.

1. This use of the term is not to be confused with its application to northern Mexicans from the states of Sonora and Chihuahua.

2. Through this book I use pseudonyms for the individual migrants interviewed, unless they specifically requested that I use their real names. I use real names for public figures.

3. Daniel Gutiérrez, informal conversation with author, Jalisco, Mexico, March 2008.

4. For up-to-date information on remittance flows, see the World Bank blog: http://blogs.worldbank.org/peoplemove/worldwide-remittance-flows-updated -to-483-billion-for-2011. Also see Migration Policy Institute, "Global Remittances Guide," 2010, www.migrationinformation.org/datahub/remittances.cfm. Note that more than three-quarters of these monies were sent to developing countries. Also note that these data capture only remittances sent through formal channels, such as banks and money transfer services.

5. For a comprehensive overview of these debates, see Dovelyn Rannveig Agunias, *Remittances and Development—Trends, Impacts, and Policy Options: A Review of the Literature* (Washington, DC: Migration Policy Institute, 2006), www.migra tionpolicy.org/pubs/mig_dev_lit_review_091406.pdf.

6. See Caglar Ozden and Maurice Schiff, eds., *International Migration, Remittances, and the Brain Drain* (Washington, DC: World Bank, October 2005).

7. In the early 2000s remittances were only 3 percent of Mexico's GDP, compared to 10 percent of the GDP of the Philippines. See Dilip Ratha, "Workers' Remittances: An Important and Stable Source of External Development Finance," in World Bank, *Global Development Finance 2003: Striving for Stability in Development Finance* (Washington, DC: World Bank, April 2003), 157–59. For current

information on remittance flows, see both Banco de México and the World Bank to compare how flows are measured.

8. Roberto Suro, "A Survey of Remittance Senders and Receivers," in *Beyond Small Change: Making Migrant Remittances Count*, ed. Donald F. Terry and Steven R. Wilson (Washington, DC: Inter-American Development Bank, 2005), 23.

9. See Banco de México for up-to-date information on how flows are measured by state: http://www.banxico.org.mx/.

10. Raúl Delgado-Wise and Luis Eduardo Guarnizo, "Migration and Development: Lessons from the Mexican Experience," *Migration Information Source*, February 2007, www.migrationinformation.org/Feature/display.cfm?id=581, and Encuesta Nacional de Inclusión Financiera 2012 (INEGI's national household survey), www3.inegi.org.mx/rnm/index.php/catalog/53.

11. Agunias, *Remittances and Development*, 10–11.

12. Sergio Bendixen and Erin Onge, "Remittances from the United States and Japan to Latin America: An In-Depth Look Using Public Opinion Research," in *Beyond Small Change*, ed. Terry and Wilson, 48.

13. For ethnographic accounts of migration between home and host places, see Peggy Levitt, *The Transnational Villagers* (Berkeley: University of California Press, 2001); Robert Courtney Smith, *Mexican New York: Transnational Lives of New Migrants* (Berkeley: University of California Press, 2005); and Jeffery Cohen, *The Culture of Migration in Southern Mexico* (Austin: University of Texas Press, 2004). Michael Peter Smith and Matt Bakker's book *Citizenship across Borders: The Political Transnationalism of El Migrante* (Ithaca, NY: Cornell University Press, 2007) addresses larger structural transformations.

14. See SEDESOL for current information on government spending; http://www.sedesol.gob.mx/es/SEDESOL/Programa_3x1_para_Migrantes. In 2009 the *Cuarto informe trimestral de SEDESOL* reported that the federal government spent 530.3 million pesos. This is the budget for the federal and state portions of the program; the municipal governments and migrants contributed an amount at least equal to this.

15. Ananya Roy theorizes the incorporation of the poor into development discourses as "millennial development." See Ananya Roy, *Poverty Capital: The Making of Development* (New York: Routledge, 2010).

16. While the relationship between architecture and remittances has received scant attention, a few studies on migrant home-building practices have emerged. A review of the literature on this subject is given in chapter 2. For an important work on the relationship between architecture and migration, see Stephen Cairns, ed., *Drifting: Architecture and Migrancy* (London: Routledge, 2004).

17. For decades Anthony D. King has been researching and writing about the material culture of transregional flows of capital and the spaces produced by colonialism, postcolonialism, and globalization. This work has found much inspiration in his multisited study of the migration of a building type. See *The Bungalow: The Production of Global Culture* (London: Routledge and Kegan Paul, 1984).

Also see King, *The Spaces of Global Cultures: Architecture, Urbanism, Identity* (London: Routledge, 2004).

18. See Nina Glick-Schiller and George Fouron, *George Woke Up Laughing: Long Distance Nationalism and the Search for Home* (Durham, NC: Duke University Press: 2001); and Peggy Levitt, "Social Remittances: Migration Driven Local-Level Forms of Cultural Diffusion," *International Migration Review* 32, no. 4 (1998).

19. "Cash Returns to Europe: Immigrants Send Millions Back to Homes," *New York Times*, February 18, 1906.

20. For a comprehensive immigration history that addresses migrant ties to homelands, see Donna Gabaccia, *Foreign Relations: American Immigration in a Global Perspective* (Princeton, NJ: Princeton University Press, 2012). See especially chap. 2.

21. See Madeline Y. Hsu, *Dreaming of Gold, Dreaming of Home: Transnationalism and Migration between the United States and South China, 1882–1943* (Stanford, CA: Stanford University Press, 2000); and Yong Chen, *Chinese San Francisco, 1850–1943: A Trans-Pacific Community* (Stanford, CA: Stanford University Press, 2000). David Fitzgerald reveals that collective remittances have been used for various projects in Jalisco since at least the 1940s. See *A Nation of Emigrants: How Mexico Manages Its Migration* (Berkeley: University of California Press, 2009).

22. While the built environment was not her focus, Hsu's *Dreaming of Gold* does discuss a migrant entrepreneur's remittance-financed project (a railroad) in China. See chap. 6. This is true for the twentieth and twenty-first centuries as well.

23. Jonathan Fox and Xóchitl Bada, "Migrant Organization and Hometown Impacts in Rural Mexico," *Journal of Agrarian Change* 8, nos. 2–3 (April-July 2008): 435–61.

24. For examples see Katharyne Mitchell, *Crossing the Neoliberal Line: Pacific Rim Migration and the Metropolis* (Philadelphia: Temple University Press, 2004), and Kris Olds, *Globalization and Urban Change: Capital, Culture and Pacific Rim Megaprojects* (Oxford: Oxford University Press, 2001). For elaborations on transnationalism "from below," see Luis Eduardo Guarnizo and Michael Peter Smith, eds., *Transnationalism from Below*, Comparative Urban and Community Research (Piscataway, NJ: Transaction, 1998).

25. Arijit Sen refers to migrant urban practices as "embodied placemaking." See "Transcultural Placemaking: Intertwined Spaces of Sacred and Secular on Devon Street, Chicago," in *Transcultural Cities: Border-Crossing and Placemaking*, ed. Jeff Hou, 19–33 (New York: Routledge, 2012), and Arijit Sen and Lisa Silverman, eds., *Making Place: Space and Emodiment in the City* (Bloomington: Indiana University Press, 2013).

26. Roger Waldinger and David Fitzgerald, "Transnationalism in Question," *American Journal of Sociology* 109, no. 5 (2004): 1178. Available at http://works .bepress.com/roger_waldinger/25.

27. Lynn Stephen, *Transborder Lives: Indigenous Oaxacans in Mexico, California, and Oregon* (Durham, NC: Duke University Press, 2007).

28. Reliable quantitative statistics on how many Mexican migrants (both documented and undocumented) maintain strong ties to home do not exist. According to Agunias, *Remittances and Development*, just below 50 percent of undocumented migrants remit. This is an indicator that the number of migrants with strong ties to hometowns is significant.

29. While US-Mexico migration can be traced back to this time, other migration corridors have older antecedents. For example, see Hsu, *Dreaming of Home, Dreaming of Gold*.

30. In the 1920s, Paul S. Taylor recorded the wage rates of several participants in his study on Mexican labor in the United States. His findings illustrate a wide range of potential earnings. For example, in 1929 one man received 35 and 40 cents per hour working on the railroad, whereas coal-mining, steel, or car manufacturing wages were in some cases as high as $6, $7, or even $9 per day (12, 14, and 18 pesos). See Paul Schuster Taylor, *A Spanish-Mexican Peasant Community: Arandas in Jalisco, Mexico* (Berkeley: University of California Press, 1933), 25. Yet Taylor also claims that even as early as the 1930s people were migrating north "not from economic necessity, but to *aventurar* in the United States" (ibid., 40).

31. The Social Science Research Council was then a privately funded organization whose mission was to study the scientific aspects of human migration.

32. Gamio's work has been extensively published. See Manuel Gamio, *Mexican Immigration to the United States: A Study of Human Migration and Adjustment* (Chicago: University of Chicago Press, 1930), and "Notes Gathered for His Book, Mexican Migration to the United States, and Related Material, 1926–1928," Bancroft Library, University of California, Berkeley.

33. Paul S. Taylor continued studying Mexican migration as one of his lifelong interests. The Bancroft Library has an extensive collection of field notes, correspondence, interviews, and more. For a portrait of Mexican modernity in the 1930s, see Taylor's *Spanish-Mexican Peasant Community*. For a more general discussion of migration, see his *Mexican Labor in the United States*, 3 vols. (Berkeley: University of California Press, 1928–34).

34. While these were the first studies to analyze what migrants brought with them across the US-Mexico boundary, thus leaving open the question of when these practices began, the Gamio and Taylor manuscripts document emergent changes, suggesting the relative newness of the practice of remitting objects alongside dollars in the 1920s and 1930s.

35. "Immigrants Send Less Money Home," *New York Times*, July 3, 1930.

36. Taylor, *Spanish-Mexican Peasant Community*, 57.

37. According to Taylor, customary local dress included the palm sombrero, the cotton *camisa* and *calzones* (cotton shirt and trousers), and *guaraches*. On Sundays the returned emigrants, both in town and from the ranches, sometimes wore tailored or ready-made suits and the hats and shoes that they had brought back from the United States. Ibid., 56.

38. Aside from road building, Taylor notes that overall factories were built in response to the demand for overalls. This spatial change was most likely an iso-

lated occurrence. It does, however, suggest that the built environment of Mexico was responding to migration in several ways.

39. Gamio, *Mexican Immigration*, 68.

40. An album of Gamio's photographs, *Fotografías diversas correspondientes a la colonia Acambaro*, is available at the Bancroft Library, UC Berkeley.

41. Taylor, *Spanish-Mexican Peasant Community*, 63.

42. Ibid., 58. This comment can be contrasted to another of Taylor's anecdotes: "I talked with repatriates—one of them from Mason City, Iowa. He had returned with savings of $3,000 and was living in ease on his father's ranch with part of his savings out at interest of one and one-half per cent per month." See Paul Taylor, "Vignettes from Old Mexico," *University of California Chronicle*, April 1932, 128.

43. Taylor, *Spanish-Mexican Peasant Community*, 63.

44. Ibid.

45. Gamio, *Mexican Immigration*, 42.

46. Taylor, *Spanish-Mexican Peasant Community*, 54. In Gamio's study, an interviewee expresses the opposite sentiment: "I would rather cut my throat before changing my Mexican nationality. I prefer to lose with Mexico than to win with the United States. My country is before everything else and although it has been many years since I have gone back I am only waiting until conditions get better, until there is absolute peace before I go back. I haven't lost hope of spending my last days in my own country." See Gamio, "Notes Gathered."

47. Taylor, *Spanish-Mexican Peasant Community*, 52.

48. Taylor, "Vignettes from Old Mexico."

49. Paul Taylor, "Perspectives on Mexican-Americans," unpublished essay, 6, in Paul S. Taylor Papers, Bancroft Library, University of California, Berkeley.

50. Guadalupe Gómez is the cofounder of the Federación de Zacatecanos. He is quoted in Gaspar Rivera-Salgado, "Mexican Migrant Organizations," chap. 2 of *Invisible No More: Mexican Migrant Civic Participation in the United States*, ed. Xóchitl Bada, Jonathan Fox, and Andrew Selee (Washington, DC: Woodrow Wilson International Center for Scholars, 2006), 5.

51. As governments and institutions attempt to channel flows of capital, their actions sometimes subject migrants to predatory tactics and strategies. In 2000 a class-action suit was filed against Western Union, the largest and oldest wire transfer company, as well as several other companies, not only for charging exorbitant transaction fees ($30 for sending $300) but for failing to disclose a foreign exchange markup—the difference between the exchange rate used to convert dollars to pesos and the bank rate—to remitters. The companies settled the lawsuit for some $375,000 and agreed to give coupons to remitters who had made transactions between 1993 and 1999. Migrant lawyers, however, do not expect that remitters will redeem the coupons. See "Mexico: Agriculture, Remittances, Social Security," *Migration News* 10, no. 1 (2003), http://migration.ucdavis.edu/mn/more.php?id=23_0_2_0.

52. Most notably, Western Union and MoneyGram control wire transactions.

However, scores of small local businesses in small and large towns across Mexico are making a living off the remittance business.

53. Miguel López Covas, interview by author, Michoacán, Mexico, August 2008. All interviews from Mexicans and migrants took place in Spanish and have been translated by the author.

54. US Government Accountability Office, "Illegal Immigration: Border-Crossing Deaths Have Doubled since 1995; Border Patrol's Efforts to Prevent Deaths Have Not Been Fully Evaluated," report, August 2006, GAO-06-770, www.gao.gov/new.items/d06770.pdf.

55. Jorge Reyes, interview by author, California, November 2008.

56. Juan Zamora, informal conversation with author, Jalisco, Mexico, June 2008.

57. Juan Zamora, interview by author, Jalisco, Mexico, June 2008.

58. Electrician, informal conversation with author, Jalisco, Mexico, March 2008.

59. Javier and Ruby Villaseñor, interview by author, Jalisco, Mexico, 2007.

60. Miguel López Covas, interview by author, Michoacán, Mexico, August 2008.

61. See David Harvey, *Spaces of Hope* (Berkeley: University of California Press, 2000).

62. Javier and Ruby Villaseñor, interview by author, California, May 2007.

63. Daniel Gutiérrez, informal conversation with author, Jalisco, Mexico, March 2008.

64. Javier and Ruby Villaseñor, interview by author, California, May 2007.

65. Daniel Gutiérrez, interview by author, Jalisco, Mexico, April 2008.

66. Henri Lefebvre, *The Production of Space* (Oxford: Blackwell, 1991).

67. Miguel López Covas, informal conversation with author, Michoacán, Mexico, July 2008.

68. In small towns, remittances have funded projects that refer to the United States on all scales. From replicas of the Statue of Liberty in personal homes to supermarkets built in "the style of the US" where shoppers use carts and pay at checkouts rather than the typical storefront model, these material expressions suggest, but do not provide evidence of, migrant success in the United States.

69. Raul Robles, interview by author, Jalisco, Mexico, April 2007.

70. Héctor Alarcón, interview by author, California, August 2007.

71. José Ochoa, interview by author, Jalisco, Mexico, December 2007.

72. Josefina Hernández, interview by author, California, April 2007.

73. "Remittance development" is more explicitly dealt with in chapter 3.

CHAPTER ONE

1. Remittance houses need not be associated only with migration across international boundaries. Throughout the first half of the twentieth century, African Americans sent money from large US cities in the North and West to their families in the Deep South to build their dream houses.

2. "Immigrants Rehabilitate Europe with Our Money," *New York Times Magazine*, September 21, 1913, 7.

3. For information about remittance flows in several countries, see Jason DeParle, "A Good Provider Is One Who Leaves," *New York Times*, April 22, 2007. For scholarly work that addresses migrant housing in Portugal, see Roselyne de Villanova, Carolina Leite, and Isabel Raposo, *Casas de sonhos: Emigrantes constru-tores no Norte de Portugal* [Dream houses: Emigrants building in northern Portugal] (Lisbon: Edições Salamandra, 1994), also published in French. More recent examples have emerged from African migration streams. For example, see Lothar Smith and Valentina Mazzucato, "Constructing Homes, Building Relationships: Migrant Investments in Houses," *Journal of Economic and Social Geography* 100, no. 5 (November 20, 2009): 662–73.

4. I confirmed the existence of remittance houses in Jalisco, Michoacán, and Guanajuato. Catherine Rose Ettinger and Salvador García Espinos at the Universidad Michoacana de San Nicolás de Hidalgo are studying the impact of remittances on housing in Michoacán. See also Álavaro Sánchez Crispín and Salvador García Espinosa, "Impacto de las remesas sobre el recurso turístico de la imagen urbana en localidades de la Sierra Purhépecha y ribera del lago de Pátzcuaro, México," *Boletín del Instituto de Geografía*, no. 65 (2008): 102–17.

5. For scholarship on the Mexican remittance house, see anthropologist Peri Fletcher, *La Casa de Mis Sueños: Dreams of Home in a Transnational Migrant Community* (Boulder, CO: Westview, 1999); Catherine R. Ettinger, *La transformación de la vivienda vernácula en Michoacán: Materialidad, espacio y representación* (Morelia, Michoacán: Consejo Nacional de Ciencia y Tecnología, 2010); and Julia Pauli, "A House of One's Own! Gender, Migration, and Residence," *American Ethnologist* 35, no. 1 (2008): 171–87.

6. My method of spatial analysis builds on that of Bill Hillier and Julienne Hanson, *The Social Logic of Space* (Cambridge: Cambridge University Press, 1989), especially chaps. 1 and 5.

7. Ibid.

8. The material implications of migrant disinvestment in American immigrant neighborhoods linked to the remittance house have yet to be studied.

9. For a discussion of early migration to the western states of Mexico, see Douglas Massey et al., *Return to Aztlan: The Social Process of International Migration from Western Mexico* (Berkeley: University of California Press, 1990).

10. See Instituto Nacional de Estadística y Geografía (INEGI), Mexico's national geographic institute, for more information about rural demographics and migration trends at www.inegi.org.mx. Also note that some migrant remitting communities in Jalisco, especially in the region of Los Altos, date back further than San Miguel, while others are more recent.

11. For an earlier version of this chapter, see Sarah Lynn Lopez, "The Remittance House: Architecture of Migration," *Buildings and Landscapes: Journal of the Vernacular Architecture Forum* 17, no. 2 (Fall 2010): 33–52.

12. Here I am limiting myself to remittance capital "from below" as well as informal capital flows.

13. It is important to note that the courtyard house type and its variations extend throughout the Southwest. See Chris Wilson, "When a Room Is the Hall: The Houses of West Las Vegas, New Mexico," in *Images of an American Land: Vernacular Architecture in the Western United States*, ed. Thomas Carter, 113–28 (Albuquerque: University of New Mexico Press, 1997).

14. Jorge Martínez, interview by author, Jalisco, Mexico, July 2007. Also see Mariana Yampolsky, *The Traditional Architecture of Mexico* (London: Thames and Hudson, 1993).

15. For a basic history of Mexico, see Enrique Krauze, *The Biography of Power: A History of Modern Mexico, 1810–1996* (New York: HarperCollins, 1997).

16. The term *norteño* is used in this region to connote a migrant, somebody from the pueblo who goes north. It is not used to refer to an American from the North, who would be called an *americano*.

17. A national study estimates that 11.4 percent of remittances are used for buying land or homes, remodeling homes, or buying cars. See Encuesta Nacional de Inclusión Financiera 2012, www3.inegi.org.mx/rnm/index.php/catalog/53. However, these figures dramatically contradict the findings of Álvaro Sánchez Crispin and Salvador García Espinosa in Michoacán, where a higher percentage of remittances are used for home construction. In my case studies, more than 11.4 percent of family remittances was spent on the construction industry.

18. See Fletcher, *La Casa*, for a discussion of women's use of the interior of new houses.

19. Hugo Galindo, interview by author, Jalisco, Mexico, March 2008.

20. See Paul Groth, "Lot, Yard, and Garden: American Distinctions," *Landscape* 30, no. 3 (1990): 29–35, for a historical genealogy of the terms *lot*, *yard*, and *garden*.

21. Tonio Ortiz, interview by author, Jalisco, Mexico, October 2007.

22. Gustavo Chávez, interview by author, Jalisco, Mexico, January 2008.

23. Rodolfo Sahagún Morales, interview by author, Jalisco, Mexico, January 2008.

24. José López, interview by author, Jalisco, March 2008.

25. In rural Jalisco, the Bracero era in the mid-twentieth century is one indicator of changes in the amounts and influence of remittances on local economies. Further research needs to be done on how a history of remitting influenced the construction industry. In general terms, the rise of the architect and the professionalization of the albañil is a post-Bracero phenomenon.

26. Hugo Galindo, interview by author, Jalisco, Mexico, April 2008.

27. José López, interview by author, Jalisco, Mexico, December 2007.

28. Barba family, interview by author, Jalisco, Mexico, February 2009.

29. For an extended discussion of Construmex's business model, see chap. 5 in Sarah Lynn Lopez, "The Remittance House: on the Cultural Landscape of Mexican Migrancy" (master's thesis, University of California, Berkeley, 2006).

30. Construmex employee, interview by phone, Los Angeles, 2005.

31. An architect offering long-distance architectural services for migrants has opened an office in Plaza Mexico, Los Angeles.

32. For information on this program, see SEDESOL (Secretariat of Social Development) and search "Programa de Ahorro y Subsidios para la Vivienda Progresiva (Vivah)," http://www.sedesol.gob.mx.

33. Poverty rates are hard to identify and are defined differently by institutions and government agencies. The US Central Intelligence Agency's statistics of extreme poverty rely on food-based definitions of poverty; more general poverty statistics rely on assets. See CIA, "The World Factbook," http://www.cia.gov/library/publications/the-world-factbook/geos/mx.html.

34. This figure is based on available records. San Miguel's records are kept in the Public Works Department of El Limón's city hall. El Limón is the *cabecera* or county seat for the municipality.

35. Ignacio Robles Pelayo, interview by author, Jalisco, Mexico, December 2008.

36. Salvador Uribe, interview by author, California, March 2010.

37. Several interviews with the Robles family occurred between October 2007 and August 2008.

38. Sergio Robles, interview by author, Jalisco, Mexico, February 2008.

39. Ibid.

40. Sergio Robles, interview by author, Jalisco, Mexico, July 2008.

41. Granting citizenship to unauthorized migrants was a part of a statute called the Immigration Reform and Control Act (IRCA).

42. See Don Mitchell, *Lie of the Land: Migrant Workers and the California Landscape* (Minneapolis: University of Minnesota Press, 1996), for a discussion of harmonious representations of the harsh landscapes in which workers live.

43. For information on the 3×1 program, see SEDESOL, "Programa 3×1 para Migrantes," http://www.sedesol.gob.mx/es/SEDESOL/Programa_3x1_para_Migrantes. For a discussion of the "remittance development model," see chapter 2 below.

44. "Caen las remesas, por culpa de la recession en EU, dice el gobierno mexicano," *La Jornada*, May 20, 2010, http://migracion.jornada.com.mx.

CHAPTER TWO

1. The historical trajectory of 3×1 has been widely published. What is now a nationwide federal 3×1 program is understood to have originated in Zacatecas in the 1980s. However, due to the highly regional nature of remittance development, more historic research needs to be done. For an institutional genealogy of the 3×1 program, see Natasha Iskander, *Creative State: Forty Years of Migration and Development Policy in Morocco and Mexico* (Ithaca, NY: Cornell University Press, 2010).

2. For an overview of migrant-state development initiatives, see Susan Eva Eckstein and Adil Najam, eds., *How Immigrants Impact Their Homelands* (Durham, NC: Duke University Press, 2013).

3. Raúl Delgado-Wise and Luis Eduardo Guarnizo, "Migration and Develop-

ment: Lessons from the Mexican Experience," *Migration Information Source*, February 1, 2007, 5, www.migrationinformation.org/Feature/display.cfm?id=581.

4. Alejandro Portes, "Conclusion: Towards a New World—the Origins and Effects of Transnational Activities," *Ethnic and Racial Studies* 22, no. 2 (March 1999): 463–77.

5. For further discussion of migrants as brokers, see Michael Peter Smith and Matt Bakker, *Citizenship across Borders: The Political Transnationalism of El Migrante* (Ithaca, NY: Cornell University Press, 2008). Also, some individuals who serve on federation boards or as club presidents have achieved economic success in the United States.

6. In Roy Germano, dir., *The Other Side of Immigration*, DVD (Roy Germano Films, 2009).

7. The dominance of men's roles in shaping the built environment through the remittance development model is explored more fully in my next chapter.

8. To visit the current directory of Mexican clubs, go to Instituto de los Mexicanos en el Exterior, "Directorio de Organizaciones y Clubes de Oriundos," www.ime.gob.mx/DirectorioOrganizaciones/. Note that as of December 2013, 157 HTAS were registered in countries other than the United States.

9. Only the states of Baja California, Coahuila, and Tabasco (which had one project in 2012) and the Federal District (DF) are not involved in the program.

10. This information was published online by SEDESOL in 2008 as a part of its yearly review. See sedesol.gob.mx, "3×1 Programa para Migrantes, 2008."

11. In 2010, the federal budget was 557 million pesos, roughly 50 million dollars. H. Cámara de Diputados, "Cuarto Informe Trimestral 2010," Programas de Subsidios del Ramo Administrativo 20, Desarrollo Social (January 2011), 59.

12. See Manuel Orozco, "Remittances, the Rural Sector, and Policy Options in Latin America," Rural Finance Innovation Case Study for Inter-American Dialogue, June 1, 2003, www.migrationinformation.org/feature/display.cfm?ID=128. For a discussion of 3×1's development potential, see Rodolfo García Zamora, "Collective Remittances and the 3×1 Program as a Transnational Social Learning Process," trans. Patricia A. Rosas, background paper presented at the Woodrow Wilson International Center for Scholars, Washington, DC, November 4–5, 2005.

13. Iskander, *Creative State*.

14. Salvador García, conversation with author, Michoacán, Mexico, June 2008.

15. James Scott, *Seeing like a State* (New Haven, CT: Yale University Press, 1998).

16. Gobierno de Jalisco, "Programa 3×1 para Migrantes," Secretaría de Desarrollo Humano, 2007.

17. Basilia Valenzuela, "Los clubes de migrantes oriundos jaliscienses en los Estados Unidos," *Carta Económica Regional* 16, no. 87 (January–March 2004): 3–17.

18. Manuel Gamio's, Paul S. Taylor's, and Stanley West's studies document the goals of migrant groups in the late nineteenth and early twentieth centuries. David Fitzgerald's work examines the role of the Catholic Church in forming HTAS in the mid-twentieth century. Xóchilt Bada provides a brief overview of HTA history. See Manuel Gamio, *Mexican Immigration to the United States: A Study*

of Human Migration and Adjustment (Chicago: University of Chicago Press, 1930), and "Notes Gathered for His Book, Mexican Migration to the United States, and Related Material, 1926-1928," Bancroft Library, University of California, Berkeley; Paul S. Taylor, *Mexican Labor in the United States*, 3 vols. (Berkeley: University of California Press, 1928-34); Stanley West, *The Mexican Aztec Society: A Mexican-American Voluntary Association in Diachronic Perspective* (New York: Arno, 1973); David Fitzgerald, *A Nation of Emigrants: How Mexico Manages Its Migration* (Berkeley: University of California Press, 2009); Xóchilt Bada, "Breve reseña del surgimiento de los clubes de oriundos," *MX sin Fronteras*, no. 34 (October 2006): 10-12.

19. Loose papers in the University of California Bancroft Library's Paul S. Taylor Papers.

20. Ibid.

21. This is not to say that early Mexican HTAS never sent money collectively; they did. However, they appear to have done so in response to major crisis or natural disasters, not on a regular basis.

22. Fitzgerald, *Nation of Emigrants*. See especially chap. 3.

23. Delgado-Wise and Guarnizo, "Migration and Development," 2008.

24. José Ochoa, interview by author, Jalisco, Mexico, September 2007.

25. In a local publication for Los Guajes, *Tagüinchi*, a veteran migrant wrote: "Last month I sent five dollars [to Los Guajes], but I sent it in cash and now I don't know if it arrived. I need to be relieved of my doubts." Migrants want to know whether their money is spent as intended.

26. In 1996 Mexico's Office of Attention to Jaliscienses in the Exterior (OFAJE) was created. It works with Mexico's SEDESOL (which manages federal development programs) and the Office of the Secretary of Human Development (which manages state-level social programs).

27. Gilberto Juárez González, interview by author, Jalisco, Mexico, July 2008.

28. In Jalisco the 3×1 state program has its own committee (separate from the federal government) that decides which projects will be funded.

29. Daniela Geomar, "Sedesol Jalisco impone a migrantes la Cruzada contra el Hambre," *Marcatextos*, May 15, 2013, http://marcatextos.com/jalisco/sedesol -jalisco-impone-a-migrantes-la-cruzada-contra-el-hambre/.

30. Jorge Rosales, interview by author, Oakland, California, March 2009.

31. See Valenzuela, "Los clubes de migrantes," 2004, 28.

32. For information about remittance spending, see Encuesta Nacional de Inclusión Financiera 2012 (INEGI's National household surveys), www3.inegi .org.mx/rnm/index.php/catalog/53.

33. Observed by author at a federation meeting, Dublin, California, February 2009.

34. See SEDESOL for current descriptions of the program, www.sedesol.gob .mx. This language was used in the *Cuarto Informe Trimestral 2008*, translation by the author.

35. Carlos Leal, secretary of COPLADE, interview by author, Jalisco, Mexico, August 2008.

36. Héctor Alarcón, interview by author, Jalisco, Mexico, July 2007.

37. Efraín Jiménez Muñoz, project director of the Zacatecas Federation in 2004, Conference on Borderless Giving, Sanford University. Information about this conference is available at www.federacionzacatecana.org/index.php?section Name=home&subSection=news&story_id=217.

38. *Ultimas Noticias*, September 11, 2009.

39. Manuel Acuña, Semana Jalisco, Federación de Clubes Jaliscienses, 2007, 2; translation by the author.

40. Juan Moreno, Semana Jalisco, Federación de Clubes Jaliscienses, 2007, 3.

41. "I am Jalisco" and "Jalisco-American" are used in the Jalisco Federation of Chicago's promotional materials.

42. Gilberto Juárez González, interview by author, Jalisco, Mexico, July 2008.

43. See Olinka Valdez, Cynthia Pérez, and Bet-birai Nieto, "Sugieren replantear el 3×1; Ya se rebasó," *Imagen Zacatecas*, November 11, 2009.

44. Prominent migrant activists argue that ending the program would threaten the political standing of Jalisco governors. Libier Jimenez, interview by author, Jalisco, Mexico, 2008. Also, an article by Olinka Valdez, "Piden migrantes limitar a los alcaldes en el 3×1," *Imagen de Zacatecas*, November 10, 2009, exposes the tensions migrants have with the municipal presidents in Zacatecas, who, they argue, are taking advantage of the program.

45. Abraham Gabino, interview by author, Jalisco, Mexico, August 2012.

46. In 2012 this was being negotiated by migrant activists—who prefer to remain anonymous—and state-level government officials.

47. This can be contrasted to select aspects of US infrastructural history. In 1896 the United States Postal System proclaimed it a national duty to serve even the most remote homes with "rural free delivery." In 1916 the US federal government passed the Federal Highway Act, which nationalized road building and supported local road development. Although there are inequities in US infrastructure, especially evident on Native American reservations, the inequities in Mexico are far more pervasive.

48. Due to the difficulties of measuring remittances, the Mexican Census and Bank of Mexico have not effectively documented remittances, thus increases in local inequality and in the complexity of personal and familial income are only roughly understood.

49. In Jalisco, the indigenous population is only 0.32 percent of Mexico's total indigenous population.

50. For an argument regarding how this directly influences the distribution of the 3×1 program, see Frances Aparicio and Covadonga Meseguer, "Collective Remittances and the State: The 3×1 Program in Mexican Municipalities," *World Development* 40, no. 1 (January 2012): 206–22.

51. Although Oaxaca's migration is rooted in the mid-twentieth century, repeated international migration is a much more recent phenomenon. See Jeffrey H. Cohen, "The Oaxaca-US Connection and Remittances," *Migration Policy*

Institute, January 2005, http://www.migrationinformation.org/Feature/display .cfm?id=280.

52. It is very difficult to make these claims because the definitions of "truly impoverished" and "in need" are relative to specific localities. Here I am referring to largely indigenous groups without basic services, clean water, or substantial food as "truly impoverished," whereas those who can meet their basic needs but have no insurance or safety net ensuring that they will be able to do so in the future are "in need."

53. See Manuel Orozco and Rebecca Rouse, "Migrant Hometown Associations and Opportunities for Development: A Global Perspective," Migration Policy Institute, February 2007; and Manuel Orozco, "Hometown Associations and Development: Ownership, Correspondence, Sustainability and Replicability," in *New Patterns for Mexico: Observations on Remittances, Philanthropic Giving, and Equitable Development*, ed. Barbara J. Merz, Global Equity Initiative (Cambridge, MA: Harvard University Press, 2005).

54. Roberto Galíndez, interview by author, Illinois, December 2012.

55. President of El Limón, interview by author, Jalisco, Mexico, April 2008.

56. Miguel López Covas, interview by author, Michoacán, Mexico, July 2008.

57. Ing. Cecilia Acero Reyes, SEDESOL, interview by author, Jalisco, Mexico, April 2008.

58. Jaime Almaraz Garibay, director of Fortalecimiento y Desarrollo Social, Secretaría de Desarrollo Humano, interview by author, Jalisco, Mexico, January 2008.

59. SEDESOL primary documents, annual reports of all 3×1 projects for the state of Jalisco, 2002-12.

60. Letters, *La Opinión*, June 13, 2002.

61. Carlos Leal, interview by author, Jalisco, Mexico, August 2008.

62. See Smith and Bakker, *Citizenship across Borders*; and Jonathan Fox and Xochitl Bada, "Migrant Organization and Hometown Impacts in Rural Mexico," *Journal of Agrarian Change* 8, nos. 2-3 (April-July 2008): 435-61.

63. Ananya Roy, *Poverty Capital: The Making of Development* (New York: Routledge, 2010).

64. Sergio Suárez, interview by author, Jalisco, Mexico, August 2012.

CHAPTER THREE

1. See chap. 5 of Susan Buck-Morss's *Dialectics of Seeing* (Cambridge, MA: MIT Press, 1991).

2. While norteños involved in the project and townspeople relayed this exorbitant cost, I was not able to confirm the fee with the two main project sponsors. Additionally, in recognition of the unique circumstances, the band allegedly gave the norteños a $500 discount because, as San Miguel resident Raúl Robles put it, "We are a *pueblito* [little pueblo]."

3. Informal conversation, Jalisco, Mexico, April 2008.

4. Michael Watts and Allan Pred make this argument about the new industrial and capitalist spaces created by places like the Silicon Valley in California. See Allan Pred and Michael Watts, *Reworking Modernity: Capitalisms and Symbolic Discontent* (New Brunswick, NJ: Rutgers University Press, 1992), 7.

5. Fredric Jameson, "Postmodern, or The Cultural Logic of Late Capitalism," *New Left Review*, no. 141 (1984): 53–92.

6. Ibid.

7. Bret Gustafson, "Spectacles of Autonomy and Crisis, or What Bulls and Beauty Queens Have to Do with Regionalism in Eastern Bolivia," *Journal of Latin American Anthropology* 11, no. 2 (2006): 351–79.

8. Julia Pauli, "A House of One's Own! Gender, Migration, and Residence," *American Ethnologist* 35, no. 1 (2008): 171–87.

9. For discussions of tradition and space, see Ananya Roy, "Nostalgias of the Modern," in *The End of Tradition?*, ed. Nezar AlSayyad (London: Routledge, 2004), 63–86.

10. Lagunillas is the only arena in this municipality built with 3×1 funds and migrant remittances completed during the 2007-8 fieldwork year of this study. At that time, three 3×1 rodeos had been built in the region.

11. The fiesta was introduced to Indians by the conquistadores in the 1500s and was supported by both church and state. See Mary Lou LeCompte, "The Hispanic Influence on the History of Rodeo, 1823–1922," *Journal of Sport History* 12, no. 1 (1985): 21–38.

12. Olga Nájera-Ramírez, "Engendering Nationalism: Identity, Discourse, and the Mexican Charro," *Anthropological Quarterly* 67, no. 1 (1994): 3.

13. While the ejido is discussed later in this chapter, for general information see also Wayne Cornelius and David Myhre, *The Transformation of Rural Mexico: Reforming the Ejido Sector* (San Diego: Center for US-Mexican Studies, 1998).

14. See ibid. and Peri Fletcher, *La Casa de Mis Sueños: Dreams of Home in a Transnational Migrant Community* (Boulder, CO: Westview, 1999).

15. Juan Rulfo's story is in his *El llano en llamas* (Mexico City: Fondo de Cultura Económica, 1953).

16. Patricia Pessar and Sarah Mahler argue that the state is an organizing force in which statesmen (who are predominantly male) create networks of alliances based on male horizontality. See Patricia Pessar and Sarah Mahler, "Transnational Migration: Bringing Gender In," *International Migration Review* 37, no. 3 (2003): 812–46.

17. *Charrería* is officially the national sport of Mexico, regulated by the Federación Mexicana de Charrería. It consists of a series of Mexican equestrian events rooted in horsemanship, brought over from Spain during its conquest of the New World. More information is available at http://www.fmcharreria.com.

18. *Jinete* technically means "horse rider" but is also used to mean "bull rider." Also, while no official costume was required to participate, bull riders who could afford to replaced overalls or other everyday clothing with black trousers and sombreros.

19. Antonio Gómez, interview with author, Jalisco, Mexico, March 2008.

20. Yet despite these changes and individuals' desire to bring tractors to farms in Mexico, the 1988 national census found that fewer than half of the country's ejidos were using any kind of modern technology, whether improved seed, fertilizer, or tractors. Only 17 percent of arable ejido land was irrigated in 1988—and more than half of Mexico's farms were ejidos. See Cornelius and Myhre, *Transformation of Rural Mexico*, 8.

21. See chap. 2 of Fletcher, *La Casa*.

22. Benjamín River, interview by author, Jalisco, Mexico, 2007.

23. In 2008 in the municipality, all rodeo remodels initiated by norteños either were managed by norteños or appeared to be defunct.

24. César López, conversation with author, Jalisco, Mexico, 2007.

25. David Harvey argues that the ejido provided the basis of collective security among indigenous groups; the privatization of the ejido is the government, in effect, divesting itself of its responsibilities to maintain that security. See David Harvey, *A Brief History of Neoliberalism* (Oxford: Oxford University Press, 2005), 101.

26. The original conception of the ejido had several flaws. It was not until Lázaro Cárdenas's presidency in the 1930s that ample amounts of rural land were ever redistributed as ejidos. Even then the plan was only incrementally implemented. For decades the sale or lease of ejido land was prohibited, and ejidatarios lost rights to land if they or their family did not directly work it, rendering them stewards rather than owners. An individual's initial land holdings never grew and were continually divided up among future generations. Although illegal sharecropping and renting released some of the pressure created by the *ejidal* system, farmers implicated in this system were increasingly forced to emigrate for work. Thus even before Salinas's policy, ejidos were under stress.

27. The majority of 3×1 projects are not rodeo arenas. In Jalisco, the program was eventually prohibited from being used to build such facilities. Thus clubs and villages built "cultural or social facilities," or "sports projects," with arenas embedded in them to work within program stipulations. This said, in the region under study, at the time of the study, 3×1 money did dramatically change the scale of rodeo building.

28. Employees of 3×1 do not encourage rodeo arena construction. In order to get approval for 3×1 funding, Lagunillas called its project "centro desarrollo comunitario y familiar." This "family and community development center" is a rodeo arena.

29. Although there are twenty-eight localities, only twenty-one have approximately one hundred persons or more.

30. Darío Valdés, interview by author, Jalisco, Mexico, 2007.

31. Mateo Domínguez, interview by author, Jalisco, Mexico, 2007.

32. Ignacio Robles Pelayo, interview by author, Jalisco, Mexico, 2007.

33. Jorge Cortéz, interview by author, Jalisco, Mexico, 2007.

34. Pedro Sánchez, informal conversation with author, Jalisco, Mexico, July 2007.

35. Luin Goldring, "The Gender and Geography of Citizenship in Mexico US Transnational Spaces," *Identities* 7, no. 4 (2001): 514.

36. Felipe Quiñones, interview by author, Jalisco, Mexico, 2007.

37. Jorge Cortéz, interview by author, Jalisco, Mexico, 2007.

38. Fletcher, *La Casa*, 101.

39. Jorge Cortéz, interview by author, Jalisco, Mexico, 2007.

40. Eduardo Ramírez, interview by author, Jalisco, Mexico, 2007.

41. Ibid.

42. Accountant in Obras Públicas, interview by author, Jalisco, Mexico, 2007.

43. This information is based on unofficial interviews I conducted at the Red Cross and La Presidencia, or the municipal office, in Autlán.

44. Eduardo Ramírez, interview by author, Jalisco, Mexico, 2008.

45. "Plan desarrollo urbana, Estado de Jalisco," Universidad de Guadalajara, Centro Universitario de Arte, Arquitectura y Diseño. For more information, see the center's website at www.cuaad.udg.mx. Plans and regional notations are available in the Universidad de Guadalajara library. They are not dated, authored, or cataloged.

46. Between 1980 and 2000, the population of Lagunillas almost halved. See the website of the Instituto Nacional de Estadística y Geografía (INEGI; www.inegi.org.mx) for population data.

47. Women can be *ejidatarias*, but there are not any that I know of in Lagunillas.

48. Felipe Quiñones, interview by author, Jalisco, Mexico, 2007.

49. For further discussion, see chap. 4 of Robert Smith, *Mexican New York: Transnational Lives of New Immigrants* (Berkeley: University of California Press, 2006).

50. In his discussion of eighteenth-century rural Mexico, William Taylor notes that patriarchal forms date from Hispanic times. Many patriarchal characteristics in the eighteenth century—men occupying positions of social status, men having greater freedom of movement, agriculture being the primary economic activity, largely in the hands of men—informed similar social relations in the first half of the twentieth century. For a discussion, see William B. Taylor, *Drinking, Homicide, and Rebellion in Colonial Mexican Villages* (Stanford, CA: Stanford University Press, 1979), 108.

51. Matthew C. Gutmann, "Trafficking in Men: The Anthropology of Masculinity," *Annual Review of Anthropology* 26 (October 1997): 386.

52. See Douglas Massey et al., *Return to Aztlán: The Social Process of International Migration* (Berkeley: University of California Press, 1987).

53. Jeanne Batalova, "Mexican-Born Persons in the US Civilian Labor Force," Migration Policy Institute, Fact Sheet 14, November 2006, www.migrationpolicy.org/pubs/FS14_MexicanWorkers2006.pdf.

54. Ibid.

55. While this was a momentous occasion, many actors involved in the federa-

tion at that time argued that she was the "foot soldier" for another, more powerful, male activist who could no longer be elected to hold that position.

56. See chap. 7, Mary Ryan, *Mysteries of Sex: Tracing Women and Men through American History* (Chapel Hill: University of North Carolina Press, 2006).

57. See Victor Espinosa, *El dilema del retorno: Migración, género y pertenencia en un contexto transnacional* (Mexico City: Colegio de Michoacán, 1998), and Leigh Binford and Maria D'Aubeterre, eds., *Conflictos migratorios transnacionales y respuestas comunitarias* (Mexico City: Instituto de Ciencias Sociales y Humanidades, 2000).

58. In Lagunillas the remittance rodeo was spearheaded by a migrant who enjoys increased status and power in the United States. The president of the Los Angeles HTA eventually came to own the factory he had cleaned; his economic success allowed him to contribute substantial funds for the rodeo. See Goldring, "Gender and Geography," for a discussion of male-dominated HTA projects.

59. Matthew C. Gutmann argues that the ranchero identity as a type of rural Mexican masculinity was initially conceived of and written about by Americans. See his *The Meanings of Macho: Being a Man in Mexico City* (Berkeley: University of California Press, 1996).

60. Quotation from a video of the 2007–8 rodeo inauguration event produced by Club Lagunillas; this video is not available publicly.

61. Michael S. Kimmel, "The Cult of Masculinity: American Social Character and the Legacy of the Cowboy," in *Beyond Patriarchy: Essays by Men on Pleasure, Power and Change*, ed. Michael Kaufman (Oxford: Oxford University Press, 1987), 239.

62. William Cronon, *Nature's Metropolis: Chicago and the Great West* (New York: W. W. Norton, 1991), 219–20.

63. Pina Hernández, interview by author, Jalisco, Mexico, 2007.

64. See Doreen Massey, *Space, Place, and Gender* (Minneapolis: University of Minnesota Press, 1994).

65. Quotation from the Club Lagunillas video of the 2007–8 rodeo inauguration.

66. Darío Valdés, interview by author, Jalisco, Mexico, 2007.

67. Héctor Alarcón, interview by author, Jalisco, Mexico, March 2008.

CHAPTER FOUR

The epigraph to chapter 4 is from Carlos Monsiváis, "Dreaming of Utopia," *NACLA Report on the Americas* 29 (1995): 39–41, quoted in Amelia Malagamba-Ansótegui, *Caras Vemos, Corazones No Sabemos / Faces Seen, Hearts Unknown: The Human Landscape of Mexican Migration*, exh. cat. (Notre Dame, IN: Snite Museum, University of Notre Dame, 2006), 10.

1. *Hijos ausentes* is a term commonly used for emigrants. People also shorten it and simply say *hijos*.

2. See David Scott Fitzgerald, "Immigrant Impacts in Mexico: A Tale of Dissimilation," in *How Immigrants Impact Their Homelands*, ed. Susan Eva Eckstein and Adil Najam (Durham, NC: Duke University Press, 2013), 115.

3. Anthropologist Robert Kemper defines *compadrazgo* as a system of ritualized personal relations established between two sets of individuals: the child and his or her godparents, and the parents and godparents. Compadrazgo is usually associated with life-cycle rites within the Catholic Church, such as baptism, First Communion, and marriage, but its ties are also performed on other occasions such as emergency loans and graduations. For rural communities, migration to both Mexican and US cities has affected the moments when, and ways in which, compadrazgo is performed. For a discussion of rural versus urban compadrazgo, see Robert Kemper, "Compadrazgo in Urban Mexico," *Anthropological Quarterly* 55, no. 1 (January 1982): 17-30.

4. Roger Rouse, "Questions of Identity: Personhood and Collectivity in Transnational Migration to the United States," *Critique of Anthropology* 15, no. 4 (1995): 371.

5. See Sharin Zukin, *The Cultures of Cities* (Oxford: Blackwell, 1995), and Pierre Bourdieu, *Distinctions: A Social Critique of the Judgment of Taste*, trans. Richard Nice (Cambridge, MA: Harvard University Press, 1984).

6. For an extended discussion of how culture is produced in place, see Don Mitchell, *Cultural Geography: A Critical Introduction* (Malden, MA: Blackwell, 2000).

7. Mary Louise Pratt also refers to transnational spaces born of intertwined economies as sites of multivocality. See Mary Louise Pratt, *Imperial Eyes: Travel Writing and Transculturation* (London: Routledge, 1992).

8. For theories of place and culture, see Akhil Gupta and James Ferguson, "Beyond 'Culture': Space, Identity, and the Politics of Difference," *Cultural Anthropology* 7, no. 1 (February 1992): 6-23.

9. For information regarding the historical development of plazas in the American Southwest, see Chris Wilson, "Center Plaza, Plaza, Square: Three Traditions of Place Making," in *The Plazas of New Mexico*, ed. Chris Wilson and Stefanos Polyzoides (San Antonio, TX: Trinity University Press, 2011).

10. Richard Kagan, *Urban Images of the Hispanic World, 1493-1793* (New Haven, CT: Yale University Press, 2000), 34.

11. Daniel D. Arreola, "Plaza Towns of South Texas," *Geographical Review* 82, no. 1 (January 1992): 67.

12. In rural Jalisco these traditions are dying out. For example, 2007 was the last year the serenata was practiced in the pueblo Pegueros. Around 2002 was the last year it was practiced in the larger town of Tepatitlán.

13. According to village inhabitants, during the first half of the twentieth century when the government was offering campesinos ejido land and roles as ejidatarios, the priest of San Juan warned that an alliance with the government would damn them.

14. Fernando Santiago, priest of San Juan, personal photograph album, my transcription and translation, Jalisco, Mexico, 2007.

15. Francisco Moto, an albañil or vernacular builder who lives in San Juan, estimates that out of two hundred households approximately eighty contribute labor, materials, food, or money to public works projects. Since the inhabitants cannot rely on outside labor or funding, Moto has a hard time understanding why more families do not contribute to the building process.

16. Ramón Murillo, interview by author, Jalisco, Mexico, June 2008.

17. Ibid.

18. Miguel Ortiz, informal conversation with author, California, August 2008.

19. Ibid.

20. According to San Juan's website, the population was 654 in 1990; by 2005 it had fallen to 503. A fifth of the current population is sixty or older.

21. Raquel Maldonado, interview by author, Jalisco, Mexico, June 2008.

22. Vicente Rubio, interview by author, Jalisco, Mexico, June 2008.

23. Javier and Ruby Villaseñor, interview by author, California, June 2007.

24. Ramón Murillo, interview by author, Jalisco, Mexico, June 2008.

25. Paco Velázquez, informal conversation, Jalisco, Mexico, June 2008.

26. Ramón Murillo, interview by author, Jalisco, Mexico, June 2008.

27. Ibid.

28. Mónica Maldonado, interview by author, Jalisco, Mexico, June 2008.

29. These rules were printed and posted in the main civic office in the village. Murillo, interview by author, June 2008.

30. David Henkin's study of antebellum New York points to the introduction of signs and public posters as a marker of the encroachment of modernity. See David Henkin, *City Reading: Written Words and Public Spaces in Antebellum New York* (New York: Columbia University Press, 1999).

31. Ricardo Negrete, interview by author, Jalisco, Mexico, June 2008.

32. Gupta and Ferguson's notion of place-making in "Beyond 'Culture'" draws on the structures of feeling that bring space, time, and memory into the production of location.

33. Juan Zamora, interview by author, Jalisco, Mexico, June 2008.

34. My observation of an HTA club meeting, Los Angeles, August 2008.

35. Vicente Rubio, informal conversation, California, August 2008.

36. Ramón Murillo, interview by author, Jalisco, Mexico, June 2008.

37. Juan Zamora, interview by author, Jalisco, Mexico, June 2008.

38. These trends have mostly been discussed by journalists. Annie Murphy, "Mexico's Drug War Is Changing Childhood," NPR, November 27, 2012, http://www.npr.org/2012/11/27/166027034/mexicos-drug-war-is-changing-childhood.

39. Peggy Levitt's study of social remittances brings attention to the transmission of cultural behaviors and attitudes including gangs. See Levitt, "Social Remittances: Migration Driven Local-Level Forms of Cultural Diffusion," *International Migration Review* 32, no. 4 (1998).

40. Miguel López Covas, interview by author, Michoacán, Mexico, August 2008.

41. AbouMaliq Simone, *For the City Yet to Come: Changing African Life in Four Cities* (Durham, NC: Duke University Press) 2004.

42. Informal conversation, field notes, Guanajuato, Mexico, June 2004.

43. The cost of the event, one hundred pesos, is equal to what many inhabitants earn per day in San Juan for manual labor. I went to the dance with a young man, his fiancé, and her sister. As is customary, he paid the four hundred pesos for our tickets and the two hundred pesos to buy us four beers. The total (600 pesos) amounted to the maximum he could earn for six days of work.

44. Verónica Rubio, informal conversation, Jalisco, Mexico, June 2008.

45. Juan Zamora, interview by author, California, November 2011.

46. Félix Maldonado, conversation with author, Jalisco, Mexico, June 2008.

47. Rodolfo González wrote an unpublished, untitled article for the community of La Ciénega in the municipality of El Limón about the building of the cultural center, dated 2007.

48. Rubén Parra, interview by author, Jalisco, Mexico, September 2007.

49. Vicente Rubio, informal conversation, California, August 2008.

50. Ramón Murillo, interview by author, Jalisco, Mexico, June 2008.

51. This figure is an estimate given by the leaders of the HTA.

52. This drop in membership could also be caused by the downturn in the economy, which affected many migrants' incomes.

53. Several inhabitants of San Juan voiced this opinion. In part the municipality considers that it has exhausted its obligations to San Juan through the center, because while the project accounted for only 5 percent of the Public Works Department's annual budget, municipal officials who worked on the project say that it consumed at least 50 percent of their time and increased their work hours. Public works engineer Hugo Galindo was supposed to be dedicating 95 percent of his budget and time to other projects throughout the municipal region, which includes not only San Juan but also the pueblos of San Miguel, El Palomar, La Ciénega, and the cabecera El Limón. Other pressing projects such as road construction, water leaks, and school remodeling have been deprioritized.

54. This stipend is money allocated by the federal government's public agency Desarrollo Integral de la Familia (DIF). It is the closest program to a social welfare program for the elderly in this community.

55. Ramón Murillo, interview by author, Jalisco, Mexico, June 2008.

56. Vicente Rubio, informal conversation, Los Angeles, August 2008.

57. Rouse, "Questions of Identity," 368.

58. Juan Zamora, interview by author, Jalisco, Mexico, June 2008.

CHAPTER FIVE

1. Armando Juárez, interview by author, Jalisco, Mexico, June 2008.

2. The amount of money Juárez is receiving is above the monthly average for

Americans. I did not see specific records. This total might include his wife's social security checks as well.

3. Lupe Martínez, interview by author, Jalisco, Mexico, June 2008.

4. The migrants who face particularly difficult choices in retirement are those who have been remitting for several decades. According to a Pew study, while men aged twenty years and younger have the highest propensity to remit, one-fourth of those involved in the study remit even after twenty to thirty years in the United States. Roberto Suro, "A Survey of Remittance Senders and Receivers," in *Beyond Small Change: Making Migrant Remittances Count*, ed. Donald F. Terry and Steven R. Wilson (Washington, DC: Inter-American Development Bank, 2005), 25.

5. Academics have focused on migrant health as it relates to old age and on migrant "generations" but not on how aging influences identity and space.

6. Some returned migrants do receive pensions and social security checks in Mexico.

7. Gretchen Livingston, "Hispanics, Health Insurance and Health Care Access," Pew Research Hispanic Trends Project, September 25, 2009, http://www.pew hispanic.org/2009/09/25/hispanics-health-insurance-and-health-care-access/. Also note that in 2013 more than half of the 11.1 million unauthorized migrants in the United States were from Mexico, but this number is always changing.

8. "Mexico: Agriculture, Remittances, Social Security," *Migration News* 10, no. 1 (2003), http://migration.ucdavis.edu/mn/more.php?id=23_0_2_0.

9. In the early 2000s, 56 percent of white males received pensions. Roger Waldinger and Renee Reichi, "Second-Generation Mexicans: Getting Ahead or Falling Behind?," Migration Policy Institute, March 1, 2006.

10. Throughout rural Jalisco, government-sponsored programs and funds to support the elderly are incremental and unreliable.

11. For one of the first ethnographic accounts of the compadrazgo system, see George Foster, *Tzintzuntzan: Mexican Peasants in a Changing World* (Boston: Little, Brown, 1967).

12. Manuel Gamio, *Mexican Immigration to the United States: A Study of Human Migration and Adjustment* (Chicago: University of Chicago Press, 1930), 147.

13. Roger Magazine and Martha Areli Ramírez Sánchez, "Continuity and Change in San Pedro Tlalcuapan, Mexico: Childhood, Social Reproduction, and Transnational Migration," in *Generations and Globalization: Youth, Age, and Family in the New World Economy*, ed. Jennifer Cole and Deborah Durham (Bloomington: Indiana University Press, 2007), 52–73. Also see that book's introduction.

14. While the term *traslado* means "transfer," in the context of migrant burials it is used to represent the movement of cadavers.

15. Efraín Jiménez Muñoz, "Borderless Giving," presentation at the Global Philanthropy Forum, Fourth Annual Conference on Borderless Giving, Stanford University, CA, March 2005.

16. Françoise Lestage, "Apuntes relativos a la repatriación de los cuerpos de los mexicanos fallecidos en Estados Unidos," *Migraciones Internacionales* 4, no. 4 (2008): 209–20.

17. Customs agents, interview by author, Jalisco, Mexico, March 2008.

18. Carolina Díaz, phone interview by author, California, August 2008.

19. Armando Juárez, interview by author, Jalisco, Mexico, March 2008.

20. Here I am discussing closure for family members in Mexico, but it should be noted that one of the more difficult moments for undocumented migrants in the United States is losing a mother or father in Mexico and not being able to return for the funeral service.

21. Fernando Gomez, interview by author, Jalisco, Mexico, July 2008.

22. During previous research, in 2004, I visited a small pueblo in Guanajuato that had no personal telephones and only one public telephone.

23. Rita Álvarez in *El Tagünichi*, January 1998. This magazine is available only by subscription.

24. "Mexico lindo y querido" was written by Chucho Monge. For a discussion of how this song reflects the culture of death in Mexico, see Adrián Félix, "Posthumous Transnationalism: Postmortem Repatriation from the United States to México," *Latin American Research Review* 46, no. 3 (2011): 157–79.

25. Several interviewees in the towns of Quila, Los Guajes, and Autlán de Navarro affirm the importance of attending not only the funeral service but also the procession from the familial home to the cemetery.

26. Félix, "Posthumous Transnationalism," 174.

27. See Stanley West, *The Mexican Aztec Society: A Mexican-American Voluntary Association in Diachronic Perspective* (New York: Arno, 1973); Gamio, *Mexican Immigration*; Paul S. Taylor, *Mexican Labor in the United States*, 3 vols. (Berkeley: University of California Press, 1928–34).

28. Taylor, *Mexican Labor*, 63.

29. West, *Mexican Aztec Society*, 140.

30. Taylor, *Mexican Labor*, 140.

31. According to Garibay, his program does not have an official name, and it was not officially presented as a part of 3×1 Estatal, indicating that it was still in the experimental phase. Garibay himself was born in the United States and had served as the president of a social club in California for many years. It is because of this experience that he received his current position with the secretariat. His unique position as both an immigrant in Mexico and a government official gives him a role as a voice for the emigrant community at large.

32. Jaime Almaraz Garibay, director of Fortalecimiento y Desarrollo Social, Secretaría de Desarrollo Humano, interview by author, Jalisco, Mexico, January 2008.

33. Félix, "Posthumous Transnationalism."

34. Roberto Galíndez, interview by author, Illinois, December 2012.

35. HTA members, interviews by author, California, 2007–8.

36. Rebeca Bishop, interview by author, November 2011.

37. José Luis Treviño, interview by author, Chicago, October 2011.

38. Carolina Díaz, interview by author, Los Angeles, August 2008.

39. Daniel Gutiérrez, interview by author, April 2008.

40. On the flags, see Bruce Finley, "Immigrants' Final Trip Home," *Denver Post*, March 28, 2008. Also, often Mexican entrepreneurs are at the forefront of transnational businesses. Funeraria Latina is owned not only by a family from Nayarit (Jalisco's neighboring state) but also by a family of migrants who come from a long line of funeral directors still working in Mexico.

41. Concepción Rodríguez, interview by author, Chicago, November 2012.

42. Five different funeral-home directors in the south of Jalisco repeated this estimate. However, it is hard to compare the costs of Mexican and US funerals, since the standards and desired amenities are different.

43. Migrants' experiences in the United States contribute to the expansion, renovation, and rearticulation of cemeteries in rural Mexico. In Sylvia Stevens's documentary film *Oaxacalifornia* (1995), a migrant expresses his desire to organize the cemetery of his hometown, applying skills for maintaining orderly spaces that he has gained as a gardener in the United States.

44. Lupe Martínez, interview by author, June 2008.

45. Key to this transformation is the implementation of the grid. For a discussion of the history of the gridded cemetery as a rational space in early-nineteenth-century America, see chap. 6 in Dell Upton, *Another City: Urban Life and Urban Spaces in the New American Republic* (New Haven, CT: Yale University Press, 2008).

46. Arturo Salazar, interview by author, Jalisco, Mexico, July 2007.

47. Raquel Maldonado, interview by author, Jalisco, Mexico, June 2008.

48. According to a funeral director in El Grullo, the body is now kept on view longer as the family waits for norteños to arrive.

49. Salvador Luis, interview by author, Jalisco, Mexico, July 2008.

50. Ibid.

51. Ibid.

52. See chap. 3 in Octavio Paz, *The Labyrinth of Solitude: Life and Thought in Mexico*, trans. Lysander Kemp (New York: Grove, 1985; orig. Spanish version 1961).

53. *El Tagüinchi*, August 2002, 11.

54. Sandra Nichols, "Technology Transfer through Mexican Migration," *Grassroots Development Journal* 25, no. 1 (2004): 27–34, http://www.iaf.gov/index.aspx?page=864.

55. Village residents, informal conversation with author, Jalisco, Mexico, December 2007.

56. *El Tagüinchi*, October 1997, 6.

57. See Jonathan Fox and Xochitl Bada, "Migrant Organization and Hometown Impacts in Rural Mexico," *Journal of Agrarian Change* 8, nos. 2–3 (April-July 2008): 435–61.

58. When Benedict Anderson famously coined the phrase "imagined community," he was referring to the national scale. Benedict Anderson, *Imagined Communities: Reflections on the Origin and Spread of Nationalism* (London: Verso, 1983).

59. Ramón Camacho, interview by author, Jalisco, Mexico, March 2008.

60. Ibid.

61. Donations are often noted in the magazine's front pages; otherwise they are given stand-alone announcements.

62. Back cover of *El Tagüinchi*, April 2002; translation mine.

63. Back cover of *El Tagüinchi*, February 2004.

64. During my fieldwork I was able to visit eight asilos, all of which followed a courtyard plan.

65. *El Tagüinchi*, August 2002, 11.

66. Ramón Camacho, interview by author, Jalisco, Mexico, March 2008.

67. For context, the annual public works budget of Juchitlán for the head town and all of its surrounding localities was 2,148,000 pesos in 2005–6. State budget office at the municipality of Tapatlán, June 2008.

68. Jorge Muñoz, interview by author, Jalisco, Mexico, March 2008.

69. Also, poor design decisions are evident in the building's garden, which is not illustrated in the architect's original plans. The unplanned garden space adjacent to the building's west wing is large and was expensive to build. Ornate iron benches and lampposts are stationed adjacent to fixed planters. However, poured-in-place concrete was used to make the patio floors, planters, and an over-six-foot wall that isolates the space from both the inhabitants' rooms and the town street.

70. The only other institutions in Los Guajes are buildings that have the support of either the government or the Catholic Church. The government has funded the Casa de Salud (which allows Guajeños to receive medical vaccinations but does not house a doctor) and a school that uses television-based learning in lieu of teachers, who are too expensive to support.

71. The only asilo in the cabecera of Juchitlán opened in 1982 to treat the local inhabitants with disabilities, several of whom have nobody to look after them because all their children are in the United States.

72. Silvia Macías, interview by author, Jalisco, Mexico, January 2008.

73. The director waits every year to find out if the annual funding will come through. So far, the municipality allots two thousand pesos a month to the asilo, and the rest comes from donations. Fortune would have it that a US movie producer, Ned Tanen, has an assistant who is from Juchitlán. Tanen came to visit the town and has been giving three hundred dollars a month to the asilo since 1998.

74. Arturo Salazar, interview by author, Jalisco, Mexico, August 2007.

75. Benicia Fontana, interview by author, Jalisco, Mexico, January 2007.

76. "El abuelo y la distancia," *El Tagüinchi*, February 2004, 10.

77. Gustavo Chávez, interview by author, Jalisco, Mexico, January 2008.

78. Birdy Velásquez, interview by author, Jalisco, Mexico, September 2007.

79. Ramón Camacho, interview by author, Jalisco, Mexico, January 2008.

80. Between 2004 and 2012, nine asilo projects are recorded in the federal 3×1 program documents in Jalisco. This does not include non-HTA asilos built with migrant funds nor 3×1 Estatal asilos. Moreover, more may have been built in the federal program using a different name.

81. I attended the 3×1 conference in Degollado, Jalisco, in 2007.

82. Salvador García, interview by author, California, May 2007.

83. The Mexican government attempts to assist migrant retirees primarily through indirect channels. In terms of migrant health, the government supports aging migrants through the Instituto de los Mexicanos en el Exterior (IME) by educating the diaspora about how to take advantage of US health services that are already available to them but underused. The state is also promoting a "totalization" social security agreement with the United States, which would allow workers with employment histories in both Mexico and the United States to qualify for benefits in the social security system based on the sum of their work in both countries. The Mexican government has also advocated on behalf of migrants by pressuring the United States to allow workers to obtain credit for working even if they are employed under false social security numbers. These measures, however, do not solve the problems created by the challenged compadrazgo system. See Laureen Laglagaron, "Protection through Integration: The Mexican Government's Efforts to Aid Migrants in the United States," National Center on Immigrant Integration Policy, Migration Policy Institute, January 2010, www.migrationpolicy.org/pubs/IME-Jan2010.pdf. Also see "Mexico: Agriculture, Remittances, Social Security," *Migration News* 10, no. 1 (January 2003), http://migration.ucdavis.edu/mn/more.php?id=23_0_2_0.

CHAPTER SIX

1. According to the Instituto de los Mexicanos en el Exterior, after Los Angeles, the second largest population of Jaliscienses with *matrículas consulares de alta seguridad* (MICAS) live in Chicago. Available at http://www.ime.gob.mx/index .php?option=com_content&view=article&id=19&Itemid=507&lang=es.

2. This claim, often made anecdotally, refers to the estimated three million Latinos across the Midwest, which is just under the population of Monterrey at four million.

3. Notable exceptions include Gabriela Arredondo, *Mexican Chicago: Race, Indentity and the Nation, 1916–1939* (Champaign: University of Illinois Press, 2008); Patricia Zamundio Grave, *Rancheros en Chicago: Vida y conciencia en una historia de migrantes* (Mexico City: Miguel Angel Porrua, 2009); and Marcia Farr, *Rancheros in Chicagoacán: Language and Identity in a Transnational Community* (Austin: University of Texas Press, 2006).

4. Nicholas de Genova, "Race, Space, and the Reinvention of Latin America in Chicago," *Latin American Perspectives* 25, no. 5 (issue 102; September 1998): 89.

5. See the Report Rendered to the Honorable Federal Board of Investigation by the Comité Mexicano de Bienestar Social of Brawley, California, February 1935. Bancroft Library, Paul S. Taylor Papers. Box 14:38. Also chap. 7 in Don Mitchell, *Lie of the Land: Migrant Workers and the California Landscape* (Minneapolis: University of Minnesota Press, 1996).

6. For information regarding Chinese associations and their headquarters, see

Yong Chen, *Chinese San Francisco, 1850–1943: A Trans-Pacific Community* (Redwood City, CA: Sanford University Press, 2002).

7. Data on how many Mexican states have opened offices in the United States is not publicly available. The Instituto de los Mexicanos en el Exterior and the Mexican consulate do not post this information on their websites.

8. Roberto Galíndez, interview by author, Illinois, December 2012. Also see migration information at the Migration Policy Institute's website, http://www .migrationinformation.org/datahub/acscensus.cfm#.

9. Alfonso R. Joule, interview by author, Chicago, 2011.

10. Ibid.

11. Pina Hernández, interview by author, Los Angeles, 2012.

12. José Luis Gutiérrez, interview by author, Chicago, October 2011.

13. Untitled organization documents obtained from the Federación de Clubes Michoacanos en Illinois (May 2012).

14. Ibid.

15. José Luis Gutiérrez, interview by author, October 2011.

16. Claudia Lucero, interview by author, November 2011.

17. José Luis Gutiérrez, interview by author, October 2011.

18. William Sites and Rebecca Vonderlack-Navarro, "Tipping the Scale: State Rescaling and the Strange Odyssey of Chicago's Mexican Hometown Associations," in *Remaking Urban Citizenship: Organizations, Institutions, and the Right to the City,* ed. Michael P. Smith and Michael McQuarrie (New Brunswick, NJ: Transaction, 2012).

19. Sergio Suárez, interview by author, Chicago, October 2011.

20. Alicia Calderón, "Promete Arana 2 casas Jalisco," *Mural* (Guadalajara), August 22, 2000, 3.

21. Lucero Amador, "Controversia por Casa Jalisco: Dirigentes locales niegan que se esté trabajando en ella; contradicen version del gobernador," *La Opinión,* May 24, 2002.

22. "Fedejal: Un camino de superación constante," *Ultimas Noticias,* April 15, 2011. "Jalisco without borders" is also a slogan used on Fedejal promotional pamphlets.

23. Francisco de Anda, "Ve Emilio Paz en Mexico," *Mural Web,* February 23, 2011.

24. José Luis Treviño, interview by author, Chicago, October 2011.

25. Sergio Suárez, interview by author, Jalisco, Mexico, August 2012.

26. José Luis Treviño, interview by author, Chicago, October 2011.

27. Informal conversation with participant, Chicago, May 2011.

28. José Luis Treviño, interview by author, Chicago, October 2011.

29. Gilberto Juárez González, interview by author, Jalisco, Mexico, July 2008.

30. Richard Mines and Sandra Nichols, "The Mexican *Mercado Paisano*: A Framework to Study Its Development Potential in Migrant-Dependent Communities," December 2005, http://www.geocommunities.org.

31. Author notes from public general assembly, Casa Jalisco, Chicago, October 2012.

32. Judith de la Mora, interview by author, Chicago, October 2012.

33. Fedejal, "Participacion de eventos de Fedejal durante el 2011," unpublished report.

34. José Luis Treviño, interview by author, Chicago, October 2011.

35. Sergio Suárez, interview by author, Chicago, October 2011.

36. Gilberto Juárez González, interview by author, Jalisco, Mexico, July 2008.

37. I do not have access to Fedejal or Jaltrade financial records. These figures are drawn from interviews with both government officials and migrant activists.

38. Judith de la Mora, interview by author, Chicago, October 2012.

39. Michael P. Smith and Matt Bakker make the argument that migrants are transnationalized through cross-border politics; here we see a similar process occurring with US state officials. See Michael Peter Smith and Matt Bakker, *Citizenship across Borders: The Political Transnationalism of El Migrante* (Ithaca, NY: Cornell University Press, 2008).

40. Claudia Lucero, interview by author, Chicago, November 2011.

41. Sergio Suárez, interview by author, Chicago, October 2011.

42. Charrería had been practiced throughout the Southwest long before it reached the Midwest. In Los Angeles, a large formal Mexican sports arena known as Pico Rivera was built in 1978. Informal arenas predate this, but their history remains unwritten.

43. For an extensive treatise on the history, meaning, and practice of the charrería, see Kathleen Mullen Sands, *Charrería Mexicana: An Equestrian Folk Tradition* (Tucson: University of Arizona Press, 1993).

44. Mary Daniels, "Tony's Mexican Rodeo: All the Stops Are Pulled," *Chicago Tribune*, September 10, 1971, B5.

45. Mexican charros first performed in Chicago at the Chicago World's Fair. Sands, *Charrería Mexicana*, 75.

46. Constanza Montana, "Mexican-Style Rodeo Finds a Home in City," *Chicago Tribune*, August 28, 1989, 1.

47. Camerino Gonzáles, interview by author, Chicago, November 2012.

48. Camerino Gonzáles and Adolfo Peña remember an African American by the name of Mr. Latin as the first in Illinois to rent bulls to Mexicans for sport.

49. Doña Peña, informal conversation with author, Chicago, November 2012.

50. For a detailed description of the lienzo grounds and their symbolic and social importance, see chapt. 7 in Sands, *Charrería Mexicana*.

51. The owner of ranch La Esperanza in Rochelle, another once-small family farm converted into a lienzo complex amid the cornfields of Illinois, rents stables to migrants from all over Mexico for only $100 a month, compared with the $300 monthly fees common throughout the Midwest.

52. Nicholas Flores, interview by author, Chicago, October 2012.

53. Informal conversation with author, Chicago, October 2012.

54. Michael Conzen, "How Cities Internalize Their Former Urban Fringes: A Cross-Cultural Comparison," *Urban Morphology* 13, no. 1 (2009): 29–54.

55. Camerino Gonzáles, interview by author, Chicago, November 2012.

56. See its website at www.decharros.com/federacion/index.htm.

57. Migrant women and charro daughters also extend Mexico's *escaramuza* tradition north. Teams of bare-back side saddle riders perform at the beginning of events. See chapter 6, Sands, *Charrería Mexicana*.

58. Camerino Gonzáles, interview by author, Chicago, November 2012.

59. Raúl Muñoz, interview by author, Chicago, October 2011.

60. Sands, *Charrería Mexicana*, 227.

61. Camerino Gonzáles, interview by author, Chicago, November 2012.

62. Agustín Durán, "Diversión para los Angelinos, ayuda para los jaliscienses," *La Opinión*, June 2, 2005.

63. Ibid.

64. Pedro Salazar, interview by author, Chicago, November 2012.

65. Miguel Muñoz, interview by author, Chicago, October 2012.

66. Ibid.

67. These figures were corroborated in four interviews with event promoters. However, since the jaripeo is not officially registered and there is no public record of most sites, there may be other locations.

68. Efraín Espinoza, interview by author, Chicago, October 2012.

69. Miguel Muñoz, interview by author, Chicago, October 2012.

70. Efraín Espinoza, interview by author, Chicago, October 2012.

71. Pedro Salazar, interview by author, Chicago, October 2012.

72. Rábano de Apango, interview by author, Chicago, September 2012.

73. Miguel Muñoz, interview by author, Chicago, October 2012.

74. Ibid.

75. Pedro Salazar, interview by author, Chicago, October 2012.

76. Ibid.

77. Professionals in the American spectator sport of bull riding make annual salaries, whereas a jinite makes an average of $200 to $300 per ride in Chicago. Some promoters pay them up to $500 per ride. Only famous PBR riders actually make $500,000 a year; nonetheless, the comparison makes a dramatic point about vastly different earning potentials.

78. Gonzalo Rios, interview by author, Chicago, September 2012.

79. Ibid.

80. Constanza Montana, "Mexican-style Rodeo Finds a Home in City," *Chicago Tribune*, August 28, 1989, 1.

81. Gonzalo Rios, interview by author, Chicago, September 2012.

82. For ongoing coverage of these debates, visit Charro USA at http://charrousa .com/. Also Patricia Leigh Brown, "Rough Events at Mexican Rodeos in U.S. Criticized," *New York Times*, June 12, 2008.

83. Concepción Rodríguez, interview by author, Chicago, November 2012.

84. While traslados have continued in Chicago since the 1970s, they have greatly increased more recently; they are a relatively new phenomenon within the context of migration between Mexico and the United States, dating to the nineteenth century.

85. The death registers at the oldest Mexican Catholic church in Chicago, Our Lady of Guadalupe, were not begun until the late 1980s.

86. This is the average of deaths per year from 1978 to 2011.

87. Death registers, St. Agnes of Bohemia, 1968–87, 1987–2008, 2008–12. Burial permit book, St. Procopius, 1960–80, 1980–2012. Courtesy of the Archdiocese of Chicago.

88. Death register, St. Agnes of Bohemia, 1968–87, 1987–2008, 2008–12.

89. Rebeca Bishop, interview by author, November 2011.

90. Manuel Martínez, interview by author, October 2012.

91. Concepción Rodríguez, interview by author, Chicago, November 2012.

92. *Red de Prevención y Apoyo: Manual para el voluntario*, Consulado General de México en Chicago, August 2010.

93. Casimir Pulaski, phone interview by author, Chicago, October 2012.

94. The cemetery will then open and close the grave site for free, charging the family only for the "vault box." Families benefiting from this service are required to buy the cheapest available coffin and have the most basic service. Dalia Rocotello, answered questionnaire for Catholic Charities, October 2012.

95. Padre Alvaro Nova, phone interview by author, Chicago, October 2012.

96. Aldo Marin, phone interview by author, Chicago, November 2012.

97. Concepción Rodríguez, interview by author, Chicago, November 2012.

98. Phyllis Burns, interview by author, Chicago, October 2012.

99. Ibid.

100. See Nezar AlSayyad, ed., *Hybrid Urbanism: On the Identity Discourse and the Built Environment* (Westport, CT: Praeger, 2001).

CONCLUSION

1. In several interviews with acquaintances of García, I was not able to find out more specific information about his work history. Also, the name of the restaurant Hacienda Tecalitlan did not have an accent, whereas the town of Tecalitlán does.

2. Sergio Suárez, interview by author, October 2011.

3. Ibid.

4. Ibid.

5. I use the term *worlding* following AbdouMaliq Simone's description of urban migrants in African cities connecting distant places and operating at large scales. See Simone, "On the Worlding of African Cities," *African Studies Review* 44, no. 2 (2001): 15–41. Also see Ananya Roy, "Urbanism, Worlding Practices and the Theory of Planning," *Planning Theory* 10, no. 6 (February 2011): 6–14.

6. "remittance, n.," *OED Online*.

7. "remit, v.," *OED Online*.

8. Sergio Suárez, interview by author, Jalisco, Mexico, August 2012.

9. Luis Frausto, interview by author, Jalisco, Mexico, December 2007.

10. Sergio Suárez, interview by author, Jalisco, Mexico, August 2012. Also see

Xóchilt Bada, "Participatory Planning across Borders: Mexican Migrant Civic Engagement in Community Development," *Latin Americanist* 55, no. 4 (December 2011): 9–33.

11. While some of these findings regarding the 3×1 program may soon be written into project guidelines, my field observations in 2007 and 2008 and again in 2012 revealed that they had not been resolved on the ground.

12. Ananya Roy, "Commentary: Placing Planning in the World—Transnationalism as a Practice and Critique," *Journal of Planning Education and Research* 31, no. 4 (April 2011): 406–15.

13. José Refugio de la Torre Curiel, informal conversation, June 2008, Jalisco, Mexico.

14. The absolute population of rural Mexico (counted as populations of less than 2,500) began to decline in 2005, whereas the proportional rural population has been declining throughout the twentieth century. For information on the age, gender, and fertility rates of rural populations, see László J. Kuslcsár and Katherine J. Curtis, eds., *The International Handbook of Rural Demography* (New York: Springer, 2011).

15. Some HTAs have invested in businesses through the government's 3×1 program, which also supports what they call "productive projects," or projects that generate local income in Mexico. These projects, however, have not yet made as large an impact on the environment as private enterprises.

Index

Page numbers followed by *n* plus a number indicate endnotes. Page numbers followed by *f* indicate figures.

Printed in Great Britain
by Amazon